Student Quick Tips

Use this Student Quick Tips guide for a quick and easy start with McGraw-Hill Connect. You'll get valuable tips on registering, doing assignments, and accessing resources, as well as information about the support center hours.

Getting Started

D0211891

TIP: To get started in Connect, you will need the following:

- Your instructor's Connect Web Address

> Sample of Connect Web Address:
>
> http://www.mcgrawhillconnect.com/class/instructorname_section_name

- Connect Access Code

TIP: If you do not have an access code or have not yet secured your tuition funds, you can click "Free Trial" during registration. This trial will provide temporary Connect access (typically three weeks) and will remind you to purchase online access before the end of your trial.

Registration and Sign In

1. Go to the Connect Web Address provided by your instructor
2. Click on **Register Now**
3. Enter your email address

TIP: If you already have a McGraw-Hill account, you will be asked for your password and will not be required to create a new account.

4. Enter a registration code or choose **Buy Online** to purchase access online

(Continued: **Registration and Sign In**)

5. Follow the on-screen directions

TIP: Please choose your Security Question and Answer carefully. We will ask you for this information if you forget your password.

6. When registration is complete, click on **Go to Connect Now**

7. You are now ready to use **Connect**

Trouble Logging In?

- Ensure you are using the same email address you used during registration

- If you have forgotten your password, click on the "Forgot Password?" link at your Instructor's Connect Course Web Address

- When logged into Connect, you can update your account information (e.g. email address, password, and security question/answer) by clicking on the *"My Account"* link located at the top-right corner

Home (Assignments)

TIP: If you are unable to begin an assignment, verify the following:

- The assignment is available (start and due dates)

- That you have not exceeded the maximum number of attempts

- That you have not achieved a score of 100%

- If your assignment contains questions that require manual grading, you will not be able to begin your next attempt until your instructor has graded those questions

TIP: Based on the assignment policy settings established by your Instructor, you may encounter the following limitations when working on your assignment(s):

- Ability to Print Assignment

- Timed assignments – once you begin a "*timed assignment*," the timer will not stop by design

TIP: "*Save & Exit*" vs. "*Submit*" button

- If you are unable to complete your assignment in one sitting, utilize the "*Save & Exit*" button to save your work and complete it at a later time

- Once you have completed your assignment, utilize the "*Submit*" button in order for your assignment to be graded

Library

TIP: The *Library* section of your Connect account provides shortcuts to various resources.

- If you purchased ConnectPlus, you will see an *eBook* link, which can also be accessed from the section information widget of the *Home* tab

- *Recorded Lectures* can be accessed if your instructor is using *Tegrity Campus* to capture lectures. You may also access recorded lectures when taking an assignment by clicking on the projector icon in the navigation bar

- Many McGraw-Hill textbooks offer additional resources such as narrated slides and additional problems, which are accessible through the *Student Resources* link

Reports

TIP: Once you submit your assignment, you can view your available results in the *Reports* tab.

- If you see a dash (-) as your score, your instructor has either delayed or restricted your ability to see the assignment feedback

- Your instructor has the ability to limit the amount of information (e.g. questions, answers, scores) you can view for each submitted assignment

Need More Help?

CONTACT US ONLINE

Visit us at:

www.mcgrawhillconnect.com/support

Browse our support materials including tutorial videos and our searchable Connect knowledge base. If you cannot find an answer to your question, click on "Contact Us" button to send us an email.

GIVE US A CALL

Call us at:

1-800-331-5094

Our live support is available:

Mon-Thurs: 8 am – 11 pm CT
Friday: 8 am – 6 pm CT
Sunday: 6 pm   11 pm CT

—

Welcome to
Gregg College Keyboarding & Document Processing
11th Edition

Your complete learning/teaching *system*
Your guide to success

Textbook

Word Manual

GDP (Gregg Document Processing)
Web-Based Software

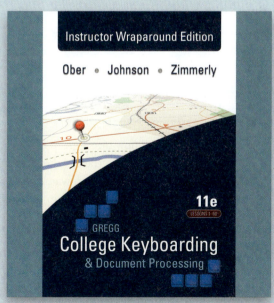

Instructor Wraparound Edition

Online GDP Software
New! Online functionality
Same program; *now* Web-based

Students complete each part of the lesson from inside the **GDP software**. Students can tell at a glance if an exercise has not yet been started, is in progress, or has been completed.

This online software now offers greater accessibility for use at home, in class, and in labs—perfect for distance learning! Its easy-to-use interface makes this system simple for both you and your students . . . so that you spend more time teaching the skills you want, not learning the program. The GDP software also now allows for automatic keystroking and format scoring.

With GDP's new online functionality, updates are now seamless.

MAP+
The best just got better!

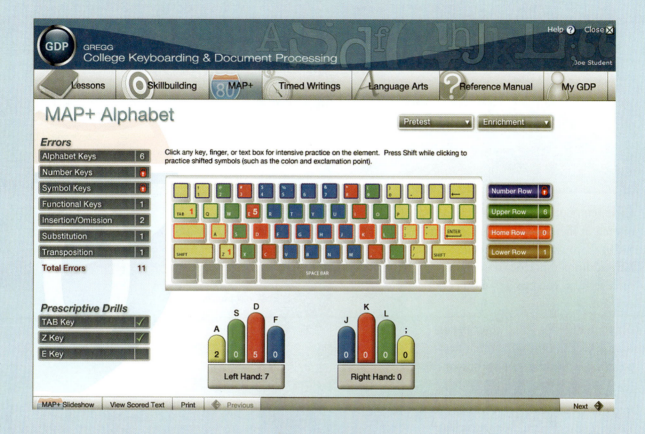

MAP+ (Misstroke Analysis and Prescription) is a *diagnostic tool* within GDP/11 that analyzes each student's pretest misstrokes and prescribes individualized remediation drills based on a powerful new scoring algorithm. MAP+ includes these features:

- **New! Unlimited drill lines**—*Now begin with Lesson 1.*

- **Interactive**—Features a streamlined interactive screen, which allows students to click anywhere for intensive practice on that key or kind of reach.

- **Continuous new drills**—Generate three *new* drill lines every time the student clicks a key or specific reach.

- **New! Deeper content**—Allows students to take a pretest and practice either alphabetic copy, numbers, or numbers and symbols.

- **Integrated**—Is a required part of each unit, although students can access MAP+ at any time from the lesson menu.

New! Enrichment Pages
More drill lines for faster touch-typing skills

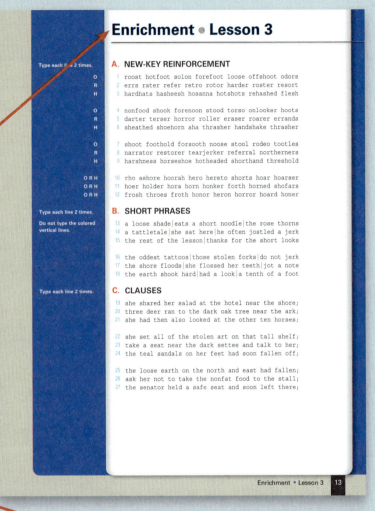

Enrichment pages appear at the end of each of the new-key lessons (Lessons 1–20). If you want your students to have additional practice on each of these lessons, you can assign them as desired.

Using the GDP system, you can customize GDP to include Enrichment pages as part of the lesson requirements.

With **MAP+**, students also have unlimited new practice drills—*beginning with Lesson 1*. Every time they access MAP+ for a specific lesson, new drill lines appear that contain only those words students can type up to that point.

Individualized Skillbuilding
In every lesson

Warmups at the start of each lesson comprise 3 lines. Line 1 is an alphabetic sentence to review all reaches; Line 2 practices a particular type of reach; Line 3 contains easy words to help build speed.

Skillbuilding (building straight-copy speed and accuracy) is built into *every lesson*—15′–20′ of *individualized* skill-building routines.

Each student always practices on the type of drill that is appropriate for him or her and for which the **individualized** goals are challenging—but attainable.

The **timed writings** in every even-numbered lesson are controlled for difficulty, contain all letters of the alphabet, and are the exact length needed to achieve that lesson's speed goal.

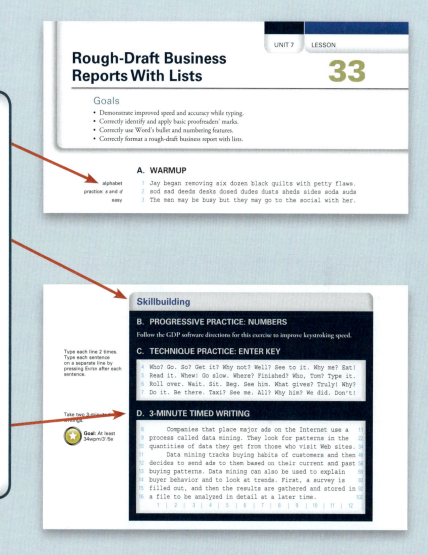

UNIT 7   LESSON

Rough-Draft Business Reports With Lists

33

Goals
- Demonstrate improved speed and accuracy while typing.
- Correctly identify and apply basic proofreaders' marks.
- Correctly use Word's bullet and numbering features.
- Correctly format a rough-draft business report with lists.

A. WARMUP

alphabet 1 Jay began removing six dozen black quilts with petty flaws.
practice: s and d 2 sod sad deeds desks dosed dudes dusts sheds sides soda suds
easy 3 The men may be busy but they may go to the social with her.

Skillbuilding

B. PROGRESSIVE PRACTICE: NUMBERS
Follow the GDP software directions for this exercise to improve keystroking speed.

C. TECHNIQUE PRACTICE: ENTER KEY

Type each line 2 times. Type each sentence on a separate line by pressing ENTER after each sentence.

4 Who? Go. So? Get it? Why not? Well? See to it. Why me? Eat!
5 Read it. Whew! Go slow. Where? Finished? Who, Tom? Type it.
6 Roll over. Wait. Sit. Beg. See him. What gives? Truly! Why?
7 Do it. Be there. Taxi? See me. All? Why him? We did. Don't!

D. 3-MINUTE TIMED WRITING

Take two 3-minute writings.

Goal: At least 34wpm/3′/5e

8   Companies that place major ads on the Internet use a   11
9 process called data mining. They look for patterns in the   22
10 quantities of data they get from those who visit Web sites. 34
11   Data mining tracks buying habits of customers and then 46
12 decides to send ads to them based on their current and past 58
13 buying patterns. Data mining can also be used to explain   69
14 buyer behavior and to look at trends. First, a survey is   80
15 filled out, and then the results are gathered and stored in 92
16 a file to be analyzed in detail at a later time.   102
   1 | 2 | 3 | 4 | 5 | 6 | 7 | 8 | 9 | 10 | 11 | 12

Language Arts
A critical document processing skill

Language arts (punctuation rules, usage, proofreading, composing, and spelling) are systematically covered. Short, easy-to-grasp exercises are incorporated throughout Lessons 21–120 with increasing difficulty.

The rules are presented, practiced, and then illustrated in the documents that students type in that lesson—for immediate reinforcement.

Study the rules at the right.

RULE
, independent clause

The underline calls attention to a point in the sentence where a comma might mistakenly be inserted.

Language Arts

D. COMMAS AND SENTENCES

Use a comma between independent clauses joined by a coordinate conjunction (unless both clauses are short).

Ellen left her job with IBM, and she and her sister went to Paris.
But: Ellen left her job with IBM and went to Paris with her sister.
But: John drove and I navigated.

Note: An independent clause is one that can stand alone as a complete sentence. The most common coordinate conjunctions are *and, but, or,* and *nor.*

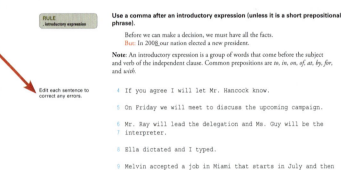

RULE
, introductory expression

Use a comma after an introductory expression (unless it is a short prepositional phrase).

Before we can make a decision, we must have all the facts.
But: In 2008 our nation elected a new president.

Note: An introductory expression is a group of words that come before the subject and verb of the independent clause. Common prepositions are *to, in, on, of, at, by, for,* and *with.*

Edit each sentence to correct any errors.

4 If you agree I will let Mr. Hancock know.

5 On Friday we will meet to discuss the upcoming campaign.

6 Mr. Ray will lead the delegation and Ms. Guy will be the
7 interpreter.

8 Ella dictated and I typed.

9 Melvin accepted a job in Miami that starts in July and then
10 left for a two-week vacation.

11 Now that it is light outside we can begin moving the
12 furniture.

13 It was a well-deserved victory and it didn't come any too
14 soon.

Correspondence
27-8
Business Letter in Block Style

, introductory expression

, independent clause

October 10, 20-- | Mr. Nick Limpett | Marketing Manager | Secure Investments Inc. | 398 East Wacker Drive | Chicago, IL 60601 | Dear Mr. Limpett:
¶ Are you searching for a suitable conference site for your next corporate meeting? If so, the Paradise Valley Resort in Scottsdale, Arizona, offers you every amenity imaginable.
¶ Our luxury resort accommodations and stunning Sonoran Desert views are minutes away from the largest mall in the Southwest and hundreds of shops, galleries, and Scottsdale eateries. We are conveniently located only 12 miles from Phoenix Sky Harbor International Airport. Paradise Valley Resort has 40,000 square feet of flexible meeting space, including stunning outdoor venues. Our in-house audiovisual staff will make sure that your event is flawless.
¶ I've enclosed several brochures for your convenience. Let me know if I can be of service in any way. Your success is our success, and I hope to hear from you soon.
Sincerely yours, | Ms. Julie Mays | Corporate Event Specialist | urs | Enclosures

New! Expanded Ten-Key Practice

Students learn to touch-type the entire ten-key pad—a frequent job requirement. After Lesson 20, a new **Ten-Key Numeric Keypad** supplementary lesson teaches the touch typing of both the number keys *and the arithmetic operators* (+ - * and /)—for a total of 55 new lines of drills.

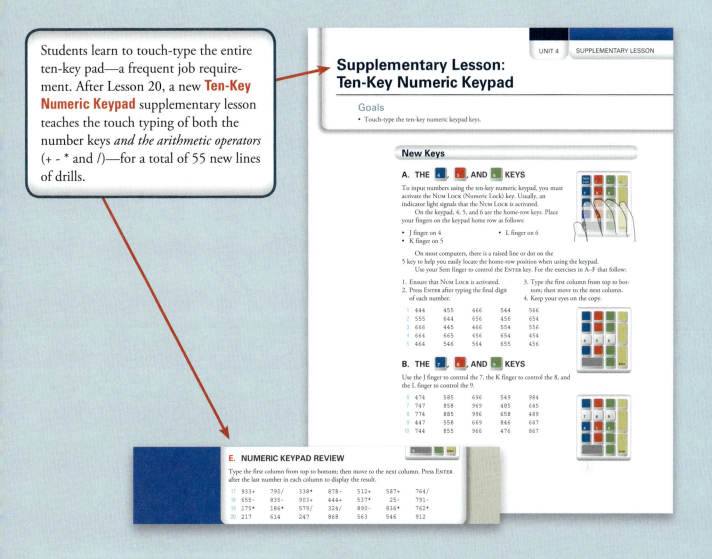

Word Processing Commands
Introduced on a *need-to-know* basis

Word processing commands are introduced when they are needed to format a particular job (in this lesson, students need to learn the Italic and Underline commands).

Students are referred to the corresponding lesson in the *Word Manual*, which contains step-by-step directions, with screen shots and practice exercises so that students don't get lost.

When students finish the practice exercises in the *Word Manual*, they are referred back to the text.

Formatting

E.   WORD PROCESSING: ITALIC AND UNDERLINE

Study Lesson 30 in your Word Manual. Complete all of the shaded steps while at your computer. Then format the documents that follow.

Document Processing

GO TO Word Manual

Correspondence
30-17
Memo

Underline the text to be emphasized.

Italicize the book title.

MEMO TO: All Executive Assistants | **FROM:** Robbie Holt, Staff Development Coordinator | **DATE:** March 25, 20-- | **SUBJECT:** Standardizing Document Formats
¶ Last month we received our final shipment of new laser printers. The installation of these printers in your offices marked the final phaseout of all ink-jet printers.
¶ Because all of us can now use a variety of standardized fonts in our correspondence, please note the following change: From now on, all titles in tables, correspondence, and reports should be set in Calibri 14. This new formatting change will help us to standardize our communications.
¶ The latest edition of the book *Quick Reference for the Automated Office* has two pages of helpful information on laser printers. I have attached my comments. Please read these pages carefully, and we will discuss them at our next meeting.
urs | Attachment

Correspondence Review   30
LESSON

Italic and Underline

To italicize or underline text as you type:

I
Italic button

1. From the **Home** tab, **Font** group, click the **Italic** or **Underline** button.

   Or: Press **CTRL + I** (italic) or **CTRL + U** (underline).

U
Underline button

2. Type the text you want italicized or underlined; then click the **Italic** or **Underline** button again to turn off italic or underline.

plain text

italic text

underlined text

To italicize or underline existing text:

1. Select the text to be italicized or underlined; or for a single word, simply click inside the word.
2. Click the **Italic** or **Underline** button.

   Or: Press **CTRL + I** or **CTRL + U**.

   Italic and **Underline** are toggle buttons. Click the button once to activate the feature and again to deactivate it. To undo this formatting, select the text and then click the desired button.

PRACTICE

1. Type the first line—underline "not" and italicize the book title, *To Kill a Mockingbird*; press **ENTER** 1 time, and type the second sentence exactly as shown:

   ```
   I will not have time to read To Kill a Mockingbird
   before Friday.
   I will have time to read This Old House.
   ```

REFER TO Word Manual

L. 21: Choose a Command, From the Quick Access Toolbar

Use **Quick Print** to immediately print a copy of the entire document on your default printer: from the **Microsoft Office** button, click the list arrow to the right of the **Print** button, and click **Quick Print**. See Lesson 21 for steps to add Quick Print to the toolbar.

3. Click the desired print options from the **Print** window.

Click **Current** page to print just the page containing the insertion point.

Click **Pages**, and type the page range if you want to print only certain pages (for example, typing "2-4" would cause pages 2 through 4 of a document to print).

To print only a part of a document, select the desired text. Click the **Microsoft Office** button, point to the **Print** button, and click **Print** or press **CTRL + P**. Under **Page range**, click **Selection**.

PRACTICE (continued)

1. Print 2 copies of *practice-24*.
2. Save changes to *practice-24*, and return to GDP.

Check with your instructor before printing anything!

GO TO Textbook

GDP Instructor Help
Right where you need it!

The ***Instructor Wraparound Edition (IWE)*** offers lesson plans and reduced-size student pages (shown in the red border above) to enhance classroom instruction. In addition to a mini-methods section at the front of the *IWE*, the side and bottom panels on each lesson page contain:

- Suggested times for each lesson part

- Miniature copies of the solutions for the documents students type in that lesson

- Solutions to language arts activities

- Marginal teaching notes—right where they are needed

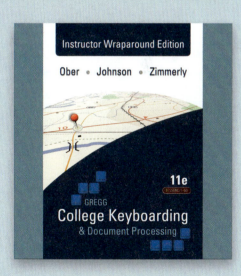

No More Grading Papers!
New! GDP now scores both keystroking and *formatting* errors

Instructors decide whether to have GDP automatically assign a grade to each document—based on parameters they choose—or to assign a grade manually.

GDP goes green.
Documents don't need to be printed because they are stored and graded electronically.

New! The customizable **GPS (Grade Posting System)** gradebook allows complete flexibility in setting up grades—with an easy-to-use, intuitive interface. Students can check their current average at any point in the school term, and instructors can save the gradebook in a comma-delimited format for uploading to Excel or to learning management systems (LMS) such as Blackboard or Angel.

Contents

PART 1
The Alphabet, Number, and Symbol Keys

PART 2
Basic Business Documents

PART 3
Correspondence, Reports, and Employment Documents

SKILLBUILDING

Preface

Gregg College Keyboarding & Document Processing is a multicomponent instructional program designed to give the student and the instructor a high degree of flexibility and a high degree of success in meeting their respective goals. The textbook is offered in several volumes: *Lessons 1–20, Lessons 1–60, Lessons 61–120,* and *Lessons 1–120.* The GDP software is a Web-delivered, PC-compatible program providing complete lesson-by-lesson instruction for each of the 120 text lessons. The document processing *Word Manual,* used in conjunction with the textbook for Lessons 21–120, teaches the document processing skills needed to create efficient business documents using Microsoft Word.

The Kit Format

For student and instructor convenience, the core components of this instructional system—the textbook, the *Word Manual,* and the Gregg College Keyboarding & Document Processing (GDP) software—are available in a variety of kit formats.

Kit 1: Lessons 1–60 This kit, designed for the first keyboarding course, provides the Lessons 1–60 textbook, the *Word Manual,* and an access card to the GDP software. Since this kit is designed for the beginning student, its major objectives are to develop touch control of the keyboard and proper keyboarding techniques, to build basic speed and accuracy, and to provide practice in applying those basic skills to the formatting of e-mails, reports, letters, memos, tables, and other kinds of personal and business communications.

Kit 2: Lessons 61–120 This kit, designed for the second course, provides the Lessons 61–120 textbook, the *Word Manual,* and an access card to the GDP software. This course continues the development of basic keyboarding skills and emphasizes the formatting of various kinds of business correspondence, reports, tables, electronic forms, and desktop publishing projects from arranged, unarranged, handwritten, and rough-draft sources.

Kit 3: Lessons 1–120 This kit, designed for both the first and second course, provides the Lessons 1–120 textbook, the *Word Manual,* and an access card to the GDP software.

Kit 4: Lessons 1–20 This kit, designed for shorter keyboarding courses, provides the Lessons 1–20 text and an access card to the GDP software.

Supporting Materials

Gregg College Keyboarding & Document Processing offers the following instructional materials:

- The special *Instructor Wraparound Edition (IWE)* offers lesson plans and reduced-size student pages to enhance classroom instruction. Distance-learning tips, instructional methodology, adult learner strategies, and special needs features also are included in this wraparound edition. New to this edition are miniature solutions for each document the students type; they are shown in the margins of the IWE.
- The *Tests and Solutions Manual* provides solution keys for all of the formatting in Lessons 25–120 in addition to objective tests and alternative document processing tests for each part.

What's New in the 11th Edition Text?

New-Key Introduction (Lessons 1–20)

- A new Enrichment page has been added to each of the first 20 lessons—for additional practice and faster development of touch-typing skills.
- MAP+ (Misstroke Analysis and Prescription) can now be used beginning with Lesson 1, thus providing unlimited new practice drills for each of the new-key lessons.
- A new supplementary lesson, Ten-Key Numeric Keypad, follows Lesson 20; it teaches the touch typing of both the number keys and arithmetic operators (+, -, /, and *), with 55 new drill lines.
- Only 3 new keys are introduced in each lesson (instead of 4)—to provide more intensive practice on each new key; all keys are still introduced in Lessons 1–20.
- The order in which new keys are introduced has been refined to balance the workload between each hand and to take into consideration how frequently keys are used. For example, in previous editions, the hyphen key was introduced early (in Lesson 6) because students used it for manual word division. With Word's automatic hyphenation feature, students don't use this key as much anymore, and the hyphen is now introduced in Lesson 11.

Skillbuilding

- MAP+ now provides an analysis and prescription of the number and symbol keys (previously, only alphabetic reaches were included). Because of this, (a) Diagnostic Practice: Symbols and Punctuation and (b) Diagnostic Practice: Numbers have been removed.
- Every Warmup exercise has been revised. Line 1 of each Warmup is now an alphabetic sentence to review all reaches, Line 2 practices a particular type of reach, and Line 3 contains easy words to build speed.

Document Processing

- Formatting correspondence (new Unit 6) is now introduced before formatting reports (new Unit 7).
- The formatting of bulleted/numbered lists in Lesson 33 and table column headings in Lesson 38 has been simplified.
- More e-mail messages are included with added coverage of formatting, such as bulleted lists, tables, and attachments.
- Eleven new Word commands are introduced: Zoom (L. 24), Widow/Orphan Control (L. 32), Table—Align Bottom (L. 38), AutoCorrect—Hyperlink (L. 49), Bookmarks and Hyperlinks (L. 89), Cover Page—Insert (L. 90), Table—Tab (L. 92), Page Color (L. 107), Mail Merge (L. 113–115), Style Set—Word 2007 (Appendix A), and PDF Format (Appendix C).
- The electronic resume in Lesson 52 (which is not being used much anymore) has been replaced by job-interviewing documents.
- The Web project in Unit 23 has been changed from creating a company home page to (a) creating an online resume and (b) introducing Mail Merge.
- Each lesson of the *Instructor's Wraparound Edition* now displays a miniature solution for each document students type in that lesson.

Introduction to the Student

Starting a Lesson

Each lesson begins with the goals for that lesson. Read the goals carefully so that you understand the purpose of your practice. In the example at the right (from Lesson 26), the goals for the lesson are to type at least 30 wpm (words per minute) on a 3-minute timed writing with no more than 5 uncorrected errors and to correctly format a business letter in block style with standard punctuation.

Building Straight-Copy Skill

Warmups. Each lesson begins with a Warmup that reinforces learned alphabet, number, and/or symbol keys; practices specific reaches; and builds speed.

Skillbuilding. The Skillbuilding portion of each lesson includes a variety of drills to individualize your keyboarding speed and accuracy development. Instructions for completing the drills are always provided beside each activity.

Additional Skillbuilding drills are included in the back of the textbook and on the GDP correlated software. These drills are intended to help you meet your individual goals.

Measuring Straight-Copy Skill

Straight-copy skill is measured in wpm. All timed writings are the exact length needed to meet the speed goal for the lesson. If you finish a timed writing before time is up, you have automatically reached your speed goal for the lesson.

Counting Errors. Specific criteria are used for counting errors. The GDP software counts an error when

1. Any stroke is incorrect.
2. Any punctuation after a word is incorrect or omitted. The word before the punctuation is counted as incorrect.
3. The spacing after a word or after its punctuation is incorrect. The word is counted as incorrect.
4. A letter or word is omitted or repeated.
5. A direction about spacing, indenting, and so on, is not followed.
6. Words are transposed.

(**Note:** Only one error is counted for each word, no matter how many errors it may contain. The GDP correlated software automatically proofreads your copy and marks any errors for you.)

Determining Speed. To compute your typing speed in wpm, the GDP software counts every 5 strokes, including spaces, as 1 "word." Horizontal word scales below an activity divide lines into 5-stroke words. Vertical word scales to the right of an activity show the number of words in each line cumulatively totaled.

For example, the illustration that follows is for a 2-minute timed writing. If you complete line 30, you have typed 11 words. If you complete line 31, you have typed 22 words. Use the bottom word scale to determine the word count of a partial line. Add that number to the cumulative total for the last complete line. The GDP correlated software automatically computes your wpm speed for you.

Goals

- Type at least 30wpm/3'/5e by touch.
- Correctly format a business letter in block style with standard punctuation.

Take two 2-minute
timed writings.

Goal: At least
19wpm/2'/5e

```
30        Zachary just paid for six seats and quit because he    11
31   could not get the views he required near the middle of the   22
32   field. In August he thinks he may go to the ticket office    34
33   to purchase tickets.                                         38
      1  |  2  |  3  |  4  |  5  |  6  |  7  |  8  |  9  |  10  |  11  |  12
```

Correcting Errors

You will make numerous errors while you are learning the keyboard; do not be overly concerned about them. Errors will decrease as you become familiar with the keyboard. Error-correction settings in the GDP software determine whether you can correct errors in timed writings and drills. Consult your instructor for error-correction guidelines.

To correct an error, press BACKSPACE (shown as ← on some keyboards) to delete the incorrect character(s). Then type the correct character(s).

If you notice an error on a different line, use the up, down, left, or right arrows to move the insertion point immediately to the left or right of the error. Press BACKSPACE to delete a character to the left of the insertion point or DELETE to delete a character to the right of the insertion point.

Typing Technique

Correct position at the keyboard enables you to type with greater speed and accuracy and with less fatigue. When typing for a long period, rest your eyes occasionally by looking away from the screen. Change position, walk around, or stretch when your muscles feel tired. Making such movements and adjustments may help prevent your body from becoming too tired. In addition, long-term bodily damage, such as carpal tunnel syndrome, can be prevented.

Follow these ergonomic principles when typing:

Workstation

1. Position your chair so that your upper and lower legs form a greater-than-90-degree angle and your lower back is supported, with your knees slightly lower than your hips.
2. Position your text on either side of the monitor as close to the monitor vertically and horizontally as possible.
3. Position the mouse on a pad next to and at the same height as your keyboard.
4. Tilt the top of the monitor slightly away from you and slightly farther than an arm's length from you.

Position at the Keyboard

5. Center your body in front of the keyboard.
6. Sit slightly reclined, with your lower back touching the back of the chair and your feet flat on the floor.
7. Keep your elbows close to your body in a relaxed position.
8. Curve your fingers naturally over the home-row position, with the back of your hands at the same angle as the keyboard.
9. Move the mouse with your whole arm—not just your wrist.

Keystroking

10. Operate all keys by touch, using the correct fingers.
11. Keep your eyes on the copy most of the time while typing.

12. Keep your forearms at a slight downward slant and raise your hands slightly when typing so that your wrists do not touch the keyboard.
13. Make quick, light strokes, returning your fingers immediately to the home-row position or moving to the next position after each stroke.

29"–30"

Tension-Reducing Exercises

A variety of government and health sources recommend the following exercises for computer users. Perform one exercise from each group, hold each position for three seconds, and repeat each exercise three times.

Neck

1. Look forward and slowly tilt your head as far to the left as possible. Then slowly tilt your head as far to the right as possible.
2. Slowly tilt your head forward until your chin rests on your chest. Then slowly tilt your head as far back as possible.

Shoulders

3. Roll your shoulders forward in a large circle. Then roll your shoulders backward in a large circle.
4. Extend both arms out to your side. Then slowly stretch them toward your back and squeeze your shoulder blades together. Finally, slowly bring your arms forward and touch the tops of your hands together in front of you.

Back

5. Place both hands behind your head, and slowly stretch your upper body backward. Then slowly bend all the way forward, stretching your arms toward the floor.
6. While seated, grab your left knee with both hands and slowly pull your leg in toward your body. Then repeat with your right knee.

Eyes

7. Close your eyes tightly. Then open them as wide as you can, blinking rapidly.
8. Follow the 20/20/20 rule: every 20 minutes, stare at an object 20 feet away for 20 seconds.

Reference Manual

COMPUTER SYSTEM
keyboard, R-2B
parts of, R-2A

CORRESPONDENCE
application letter, R-12B
attachment notation, R-4D, R-7C
blind copy notation, R-5B
block style, R-3A
body, R-3A
company name, R-5B
complimentary closing, R-3A
copy notation, R-3C, R-5B
date line, R-3A
delivery notation, R-3C, R-4A, R-5B
e-mail, R-5C–D
enclosure notation, R-3B, R-5B
envelope formatting, R-6A
executive stationery, R-4A
half-page stationery, R-4B
indented displays, R-3A
inside address, R-3A
international address, R-3D, R-5A
letter folding, R-6B
letterhead, R-3A
lists, R-3B–C, R-5B, R-12C–D
memo, R-4D, R-7C, R-9C
modified-block style, R-3B, R-3D
multiline lists, R-3B, R-5B, R-12C–D
multipage, R-5A–B, R-8A–D, R-13C
on-arrival notation, R-5A
open punctuation, R-4C
page number, R-5A–B, R-8A–D,
    R-10A–D, R-13C
personal-business, R-3D, R-12B
postscript notation, R-5B
quotation, long, R-3A
reference initials, R-3A, R-4D, R-5B
return address, R-3D, R-12B
salutation, R-3A
simplified style, R-3C
single-line lists, R-3C, R-12C–D
standard punctuation, R-3A
subject line, R-3C, R-4D, R-5A,
    R-7C
tables in, R-4D, R-5A, R-13C–D
window envelope, folding for, R-6B
window envelope, formatted for,
    R-4C
writer's identification, R-3A

EMPLOYMENT DOCUMENTS
application letter, R-12B
resume, R-12A

FORMS
R-14A

LANGUAGE ARTS
abbreviations, R-22
adjectives and adverbs, R-20
agreement, R-19
apostrophes, R-17
capitalization, R-21
colons, R-18
commas, R-15 to R-16
grammar, R-19 to R-20
hyphens, R-17
italics (or underline), R-18
mechanics, R-21 to R-22
number expression, R-21 to R-22
periods, R-18
pronouns, R-20
punctuation, R-15 to R-18
quotation marks, R-18
semicolons, R-16
sentences, R-19
underline (or italics), R-18
word usage, R-20

PROOFREADERS' MARKS
R-14C

REPORTS
academic style, R-8C–D
agenda, meeting, R-11A
APA style, R-10A–B
author/page citations, R-10C
author/year citations, R-10A
bibliography, R-9B
business, R-8A–B, R-9A
byline, R-8A, R-10A
citations, R-9D, R-10A–D
date, R-8A
endnotes, R-8C–D, R-9C
footnotes, R-8A–B, R-9A
hanging indent, R-10D
header, R-10A–B, R-10D
headings, R-9D, R-10C
headings, main, R-10A
headings, paragraph, R-8A, R-8C,
    R-9A
headings, side, R-8A–C, R-9A
indented display, R-8B, R-8D
itinerary, R-11C
left-bound, R-9A
legal document, R-11D
line numbers, R-11D
lists, R-8A, R-8C, R-9A, R-9C,
    R-11A, R-12A, R-12C–D
margins, R-9D
memo report, R-9C
minutes of a meeting, R-11B
MLA style, R-10C–D
multiline lists, R-8A, R-8C, R-11A,
    R-12A, R-12C–D

multipage academic, R-8C–D
multipage business, R-8A–B
outline, R-7A
page number, R-8B, R-8D, R-10A–B
paragraph heading, R-8A, R-9C
quotation, long, R-8B, R-8D
references page, APA style, R-10B
resume, R-12A
side heading, R-8A, R-9C
single-line lists, R-9A, R-9C, R-11A,
    R-12A, R-12C–D
spacing, R-9D
special features, R-9D
subheadings, R-10A
subject line, 2-line, R-9C
subtitle, R-8A
table of contents page, R-7D
tables in, R-8B
title, R-7A–B, R-8A–C, R-10A,
    R-10C
title, 2-line, R-8C, R-9A, R-10A,
    R-10C
title page, R-7B
transmittal memo, R-7C
works-cited page, MLA style, R-10D

TABLES
2-line column heading, R-13B
body, R-13A
bottom-aligned, R-13A–B
boxed, R-5A, R-8B, R-13A
braced column headings, R-13A
capitalization, columns, R-13D
column headings, R-4D, R-5A, R-8B,
    R-13A–D
dollar signs, R-8B, R-13A–B, R-13D
heading block, R-5, R-8B, R-13A–D
in correspondence, R-4D, R-5A,
    R-13C
in reports, R-8B
note, R-8B, R-13A
number, R-8B, R-13C
numbers in, R-4D, R-8B, R-13A–C
open, R-13B
percent signs, R-13B, R-13D
ruled, R-4D, R-13C
source, R-8B
special features, R-13D
subtitle, R-8B, R-13A–B, R-13D
table number, R-8B, R-13C
tables, R-4D, R-5A, R-8B, R-13A–C
title, R-5A, R-8B, R-13A–D
total line, R-13A, R-13C–D
vertical placement, R-13D

U.S. POSTAL SERVICE STATE ABBREVIATIONS
R-14B

Reference Manual

A. MAJOR PARTS OF A COMPUTER SYSTEM

Printer

Display screen

Monitor

CD/DVD drive

Disk drive

Mouse

Keyboard

B. THE COMPUTER KEYBOARD

ESCAPE key

Function keys

BACKSPACE key

Navigation keys

TAB key

CAPS LOCK key

SHIFT key

NUM LOCK key

Alternate keys

Windows keys

Control keys

ENTER key

Arrow keys

Ten-Key numeric keypad

Reference Manual

A. BUSINESS LETTER IN BLOCK STYLE

(with standard punctuation and indented display)

Date line ↓5X
September 5, 20— ↓4X

Inside address Ms. Joan R. Hunter
Bolwater Associates
One Parklands Drive
Darien, CT 06820 ↓2X

Salutation Dear Ms. Hunter: **Standard punctuation** ↓2X

Body You will soon receive the signed contract to have your organization conduct a one-day workshop for our employees on eliminating repetitive-motion injuries in the workplace. As we agreed, this workshop will apply to both our office and factory workers and you will conduct separate sessions for each group. ↓2X

We revised Paragraph 4-b shown below to require the instructor of this workshop to be a full-time employee of Bolwater Associates: ↓2X

→indent 0.5" Paragraph 4-b of the Bolwater Associates agreement is hereby ←indent 0.5"
amended as follows: The instructor of the one-day workshop on
Indented display eliminating repetitive-motion injuries at the workplace must be a
full-time employee of Bolwater Associates. ↓2X

If this revision is satisfactory, please sign and return one copy of the contract for our files. We look forward to this opportunity to enhance the health of our employees. I know that all of us will enjoy this workshop. ↓2X

Complimentary closing Sincerely, ↓4X **Standard punctuation**

Signature *Jeffrey Olszewski*

Writer's identification Jeffrey Olszewski
Vice President for Operations

Reference initials

B. BUSINESS LETTER IN MODIFIED-BLOCK STYLE

(with multiline list and enclosure notation)

left tab: 3.25" (centerpoint)

→ tab 3.25" (centerpoint) ↓5X
May 15, 20— ↓4X

Mr. Ichiro Xie
Bolwater Associates
One Parklands Drive
Darien, CT 06820 ↓2X

Dear Mr. Xie: ↓2X

I am returning a signed contract to have your organization conduct a one-day workshop for our employees on eliminating repetitive-motion injuries in the workplace. We have made the following changes to the contract: ↓2X

Multiline list 1. We revised Paragraph 4-b to require the instructor of this workshop to be a full-time employee of Bolwater Associates.
2. We made changes to Paragraph 10-c to require our prior approval of the agenda for the workshop. ↓2X

If these revisions are satisfactory, please sign and return one copy of the contract for our files. We look forward to this opportunity to enhance the health of our employees. I know that all of us will enjoy this workshop. ↓2X

→ tab 3.25" (centerpoint) Sincerely, ↓4X

Jeffrey Olszewski

Jeffrey Olszewski
Vice President for Operations ↓2X

Enclosure notation pec
Enclosure

C. BUSINESS LETTER IN SIMPLIFIED STYLE

(with subject line, single-line list; enclosure, delivery, and copy notations)

↓5X
October 5, 20— ↓4X

Mr. Dale P. Griffin
Bolwater Associates
One Parklands Drive
Darien, CT 06820 ↓3X

Subject line WORKSHOP CONTRACT ↓3X

I am returning the signed contract, Mr. Griffin, to have your organization conduct a one-day workshop for our employees on eliminating repetitive-motion injuries in the workplace. We have amended the following sections of the contract: ↓2X

Single-line list • Paragraph 4-b
• Table 3
• Attachment 2 ↓2X

If these revisions are satisfactory, please sign and return one copy of the contract for our files. We look forward to this opportunity to enhance the health of our employees. I know that all of us will enjoy this workshop. ↓4X

Rogena Kyles

ROGENA KYLES, DIRECTOR ↓2X

Enclosure notation iww
Delivery notation Enclosure
Copy notation By e-mail
c: Legal Department

D. PERSONAL-BUSINESS LETTER IN MODIFIED-BLOCK STYLE

(with international address and return address)

left tab: 3.25" (centerpoint)

→ tab 3.25" (centerpoint) ↓5X
July 15, 20— ↓4X

Mr. Luis Fernandez
Vice President
Arvon Industries, Inc.
International address 21 St. Claire Avenue East
Toronto, ON M4T IL9
CANADA ↓2X

Dear Mr. Fernandez: ↓2X

As a former employee and present stockholder of Arvon Industries, I wish to protest the planned sale of the Consumer Products Division. ↓2X

According to published reports, consumer products accounted for 19 percent of last year's corporate profits, and they are expected to account for even more this year. In addition, Dun & Bradstreet predicts that consumer products nationwide will outpace the general economy for the next five years. ↓2X

I am concerned about the effect that this planned sale might have on overall corporate profits, on our cash dividends for investors, and on the economy of Melbourne, where the two consumer-products plants are located. Please ask your board of directors to reconsider this matter. ↓2X

→ tab 3.25" (centerpoint) Sincerely, ↓4X

Jeanine Ford

Return address Jeanine Ford
901 East Benson, Apt. 3
Fort Lauderdale, FL 33301
U.S.A.

Reference Manual

A. BUSINESS LETTER ON EXECUTIVE STATIONERY

(7.25" × 10.5"; 1" side margins; with delivery notation)

↓5X
July 18, 20--
↓4X

Mr. Rodney Eastwood
BBL Resources
523 Northern Ridge
Fayetteville, PA 17222
↓2X

Dear Rodney:
↓2X

I see no reason why we should continue to consider the locality around Geraldton for our new plant. Even though the desirability of this site from an economic view is undeniable, there is not sufficient housing readily available for our workers.
↓2X

In trying to control urban growth, the city has been turning down the building permits for much new housing or placing so many restrictions on foreign investment as to make it too expensive.

Please continue to seek out other areas of exploration where we might form a joint partnership.
↓2X

Sincerely,
↓4X

Jennifer Gwatkin

Jennifer Gwatkin, Director
↓2X

mme
By fax

<mark>Delivery notation</mark>

B. BUSINESS LETTER ON HALF-PAGE STATIONERY

(5.5" × 8.5"; 0.75" side margins)

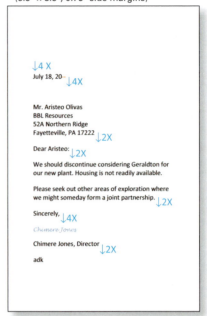

↓4 X
July 18, 20--
↓4X

Mr. Aristeo Olivas
BBL Resources
52A Northern Ridge
Fayetteville, PA 17222
↓2X

Dear Aristeo:
↓2X

We should discontinue considering Geraldton for our new plant. Housing is not readily available.

Please seek out other areas of exploration where we might someday form a joint partnership.
↓2X

Sincerely,
↓4X

Chimere Jones

Chimere Jones, Director
↓2X

adk

C. BUSINESS LETTER FORMATTED FOR A WINDOW ENVELOPE

(with open punctuation)

↓5X
July 18, 20--
↓3X

Ms. Reinalda Guerrero
BBL Resources
52A Northern Ridge
Fayetteville, PA 17222
↓3X

Dear Ms. Guerrero   <mark>Open punctuation</mark>
↓2X

I see no reason why we should even continue to consider the locality around Geraldton for our new plant. Even though the desirability of this site from an economic view is undeniable, there is insufficient housing readily available for our workers.
↓2X

In trying to control urban growth, the city has been turning down the building permits for new housing or placing so many restrictions on foreign investment as to make it too expensive.

Please continue to seek out other areas of exploration where we might form a joint partnership.
↓2X

Sincerely   <mark>Open punctuation</mark>
↓4X

Augustus Mays

Augustus Mays
Vice President for Operations
↓2X

woc

D. MEMO

(with ruled table, left- and right-aligned columns, and attachment notation)

↓5X →tab
MEMO TO: Nancy Price, Executive Vice President
↓2X

FROM: Arlyn J. Bunch, Operations *ajb*

DATE: July 18, 20--

SUBJECT: New Plant Site
↓2X

As you can see from the attached letter, I've informed BBL Resources that I see no reason why we should continue to consider the locality around Geraldton for our new plant. Even though the desirability of this site from an economic standpoint is undeniable, there is insufficient housing available. In fact, as of June 25, the number of appropriate single-family houses listed for sale within a 25-mile radius of Geraldton was as follows:
↓2X

<mark>Ruled table</mark>

Agent	Units
Belle Real Estate	123
Castleton Homes	11
Red Carpet	9
Geraldton Homes	5

↓1X

In addition, in trying to control urban growth, Geraldton has been either turning down building permits for new housing or placing excessive restrictions on them. Because of this deficiency of housing for our employees, we have no choice but to look elsewhere.
↓2X

woc
<mark>Attachment notation</mark> Attachment

Reference Manual

A. MULTIPAGE BUSINESS LETTER

(page 1; with on-arrival notation, international address, subject line, and boxed table)

↓5X
May 13, 20-- ↓2X

On-arrival notation CONFIDENTIAL ↓2X

Mr. Lester Thompson
Associate Director
British Mutual Broadcasting
International address 24 Portland Place
London WIN 4BB
ENGLAND ↓2X

Dear Mr. Thompson: ↓2X

Subject line Subject: International Study Tour ↓2X

I have been invited by the Federal Communications Commission to participate in a study of television news programming in six European countries. The enclosed report explains the purpose of the study in detail. ↓2X

I have been assigned to lead a study group through six European countries to gather firsthand information on this topic. In addition to me, our group will consist of the following members: ↓2X

Boxed table

14 pt INTERNATIONAL STUDY TOUR GROUP ↓1X		
Name	**Organization**	**Location**
Mrs. Katherine Grant	WPQR-TV	Los Angeles, CA
Dr. Manuél Cruz	Miami Herald	Miami, FL
Mr. Richard Logan	Cable News Network	Atlanta, GA
Ms. Barbara Brooks	Associated Press	Chicago, IL

12 pt↓

↓1X
Our initial plans are for the team to spend at least one full day in each of these countries. That, of course, could change. Many different events have been planned. I will be organizing and facilitating meeting with the news programming

B. MULTIPAGE BUSINESS LETTER

(page 2; with page number; multiline list; company name; and enclosure, delivery, copy, postscript, and blind copy notations)

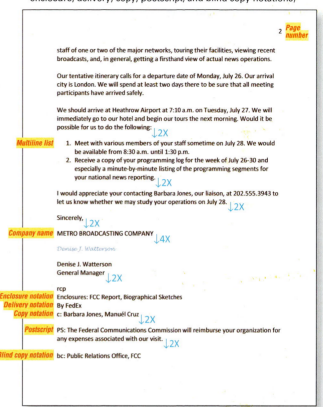

2 **Page number**

staff of one or two of the major networks, touring their facilities, viewing recent broadcasts, and, in general, getting a firsthand view of actual news operations.

Our tentative itinerary calls for a departure date of Monday, July 26. Our arrival city is London. We will spend at least two days there to be sure that all meeting participants have arrived safely.

We should arrive at Heathrow Airport at 7:10 a.m. on Tuesday, July 27. We will immediately go to our hotel and begin our tours the next morning. Would it be possible for us to do the following: ↓2X

Multiline list
1. Meet with various members of your staff sometime on July 28. We would be available from 8:30 a.m. until 1:30 p.m.
2. Receive a copy of your programming log for the week of July 26-30 and especially a minute-by-minute listing of the programming segments for your national news reporting. ↓2X

I would appreciate your contacting Barbara Jones, our liaison, at 202.555.3943 to let us know whether we may study your operations on July 28. ↓2X

Sincerely, ↓2X

Company name METRO BROADCASTING COMPANY ↓4X

Denise J. Watterson

Denise J. Watterson
General Manager ↓2X

rcp
Enclosure notation Enclosures: FCC Report, Biographical Sketches
Delivery notation By FedEx
Copy notation c: Barbara Jones, Manuél Cruz ↓2X

Postscript PS: The Federal Communications Commission will reimburse your organization for any expenses associated with our visit. ↓2X

Blind copy notation bc: Public Relations Office, FCC

C. E-MAIL MESSAGE IN MICROSOFT OUTLOOK

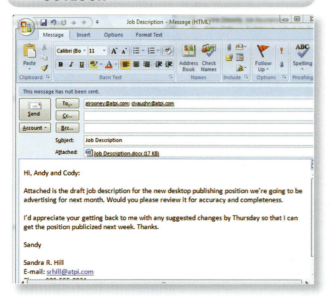

D. E-MAIL MESSAGE IN MSN HOTMAIL

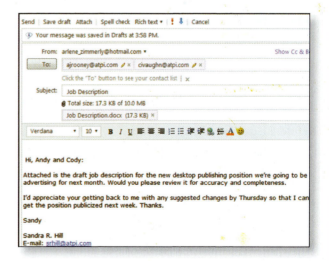

Reference Manual

A. FORMATTING ENVELOPES

A standard large (No. 10) envelope is 9.5 by 4.125 inches. A standard small (No. 6¾) envelope is 6.5 by 3.625 inches.

A window envelope requires no formatting, since the letter is formatted and folded so that the inside address is visible through the window.

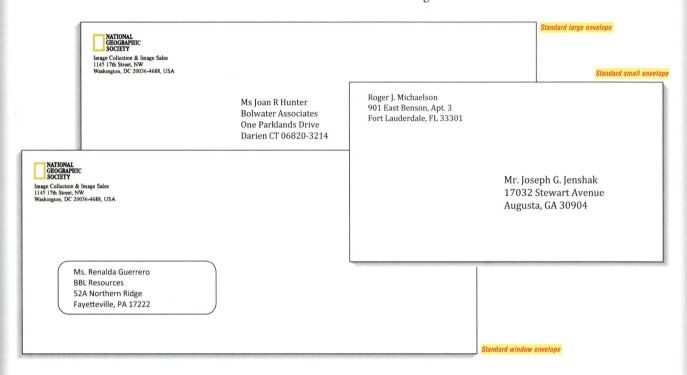

Standard large envelope

NATIONAL GEOGRAPHIC SOCIETY
Image Collection & Image Sales
1145 17th Street, NW
Washington, DC 20036-4688, USA

Ms Joan R Hunter
Bolwater Associates
One Parklands Drive
Darien CT 06820-3214

Standard small envelope

Roger J. Michaelson
901 East Benson, Apt. 3
Fort Lauderdale, FL 33301

Mr. Joseph G. Jenshak
17032 Stewart Avenue
Augusta, GA 30904

NATIONAL GEOGRAPHIC SOCIETY
Image Collection & Image Sales
1145 17th Street, NW
Washington, DC 20036-4688, USA

Ms. Renalda Guerrero
BBL Resources
52A Northern Ridge
Fayetteville, PA 17222

Standard window envelope

B. FOLDING LETTERS

To fold a letter for a large envelope:

1. Place the letter *face up,* and fold up the bottom third.
2. Fold the top third down to 0.5 inch from the bottom edge.
3. Insert the last crease into the envelope first, with the flap facing up.

To fold a letter for a small envelope:

1. Place the letter *face up,* and fold up the bottom half to 0.5 inch from the top.
2. Fold the right third over to the left.
3. Fold the left third over to 0.5 inch from the right edge.
4. Insert the last crease into the envelope first, with the flap facing up.

To fold a letter for a window envelope:

1. Place the letter *face down* with the letterhead at the top, and fold the bottom third of the letter up.
2. Fold the top third down so that the address shows.
3. Insert the letter into the envelope so that the address shows through the window.

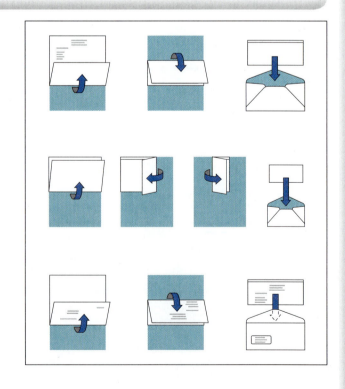

Reference Manual

A. OUTLINE

(with 2-line title)

```
right tab: 0.3"
left tabs: 0.4", 0.7"
```

↓5X

2-line title 14 pt **AN ANALYSIS OF THE SCOPE AND EFFECTIVENESS**
OF ONLINE ADVERTISING ↓2X

12 pt ↓ **The Status of Point-and-Click Selling** ↓2X

Jonathan R. Evans ↓2X

January 19, 20-- ↓2X

→ tab 0.3"   I.   INTRODUCTION ↓2X
→ tab 0.4"   II. SCOPE AND TRENDS IN INTERNET ADVERTISING
                  A. Internet Advertising
                  B. Major Online Advertisers
→ tab 0.7"   C. Positioning and Pricing
                  D. Types of Advertising ↓2X
             III. ADVERTISING EFFECTIVENESS
                  A. The Banner Debate
                  B. Increasing Advertising Effectiveness
                  C. Measuring ROI

             IV. CONCLUSION

B. TITLE PAGE

(with 2-line title)

center page ↓

2-line title 14 pt **AN ANALYSIS OF THE SCOPE AND EFFECTIVENESS**
OF ONLINE ADVERTISING ↓2X

12 pt ↓ **The Status of Point-and-Click Selling** ↓12X

Submitted to ↓2X

Luis Torres
General Manager
ViaWorld, International ↓12X

Prepared by ↓2X
Jonathan R. Evans
Assistant Marketing Manager
ViaWorld, International ↓2X

January 19, 20--

C. TRANSMITTAL MEMO

(with 2-line subject line and attachment notation)

↓5X →tab
MEMO TO: Luis Torres, General Manager ↓2X

FROM: Jonathan R. Evans, Assistant Marketing Manager jre

DATE: January 19, 20--

2-line subject line **SUBJECT:** An Analysis of the Scope and Effectiveness of Current Online
→tab Advertising in Today's Marketplace ↓2X

Here is the final report analyzing the scope and effectiveness of Internet advertising that you requested on January 5. ↓2X

The report predicts that the total value of the business-to-business e-commerce market will continue to increase by geometric proportions. New technologies aimed at increasing Internet ad interactivity and the adoption of standards for advertising response measurement and tracking will contribute to this increase. Unfortunately, as discussed in this report, the use of "rich media" and interactivity in Web advertising will create its own set of problems.

I enjoyed working on this assignment, Luis, and learned quite a bit from my analysis of the situation. Please let me know if you have any questions about the report. ↓2X

plw
Attachment notation Attachment

D. TABLE OF CONTENTS

```
left tab: 0.5"
right dot-leader tab: 6.5"
```

↓5X
14 pt **CONTENTS** ↓2X

12 pt ↓ INTRODUCTION .... →tab 6.5" 1 ↓2X

SCOPE AND TRENDS IN ONLINE ADVERTISING .... 3 ↓2X

→tab 0.5" Internet Advertising Spending .... →tab 6.5" 4
Major Online Advertisers 5
Positioning and Pricing 7
Types of Advertising .... 8 ↓2X

ADVERTISING EFFECTIVENESS 9

The Banner Debate 9
Increasing Advertising Effectiveness 11
Measuring ROI 12

CONCLUSION 13

APPENDIX

Sample Internet Advertising 15
Proposed WEFA Standards 18

BIBLIOGRAPHY 19
```
```

Reference Manual

A. MULTIPAGE BUSINESS REPORT

(page 1; with side and paragraph headings, multiline list, footnote references, and footnotes)

2-line title · ↓5X · 14 pt **AN ANALYSIS OF THE SCOPE AND EFFECTIVENESS OF ONLINE ADVERTISING** ↓2X

Subtitle · 12 pt ↓ **The Status of Point-and-Click Selling** ↓2X

Byline · Jonathan R. Evans ↓2X

Date · January 19, 20— ↓2X

Online advertising uses the Internet for the sole purpose of delivering marketing messages to customers. Some examples of online advertising are ads on search engine results pages, banner ads, interactive media ads, and online classified advertising. One major benefit of online advertising is the immediate publishing of content that is not limited by geography or time. Interactive advertising presents fresh challenges for advertisers.[1] ↓2X · Footnote reference

Side heading · **GROWTH FACTORS** ↓2X

Online business has grown in tandem with the expanding number of Internet users. That trend will only increase as time goes on. ↓2X

Paragraph heading · **Uncertainty**. The uncertainties surrounding advertising on the Internet remain one of the major impediments to the expansion. ↓2X

Reasons for Not Advertising Online. A recent survey found two main reasons cited for not advertising online:[2] ↓2X

Multiline list
1. The difficulty of determining return on investment, especially in terms of repeat business and first-time shoppers.
2. The lack of reliable tracking and measurement data.

Footnotes
[1] Shannon Newsome, "Effective Online Advertising," *E-Mail Marketing Daily*, August 12, 2010, p. R6.
[2] "eWebStats: Online Trends in the United States," *eWebStats Home page*, August 11, 2010, <http://www.ewebstats.com/trends/ad>, accessed on September 7, 2010.

B. MULTIPAGE BUSINESS REPORT

(last page; with page number, indented display, side heading, boxed table with table number and note, and footnote)

3 · Page number

who argue that banners have a strong potential for advertising effectiveness point out that it is not the banner format itself that presents a problem to advertising effectiveness, but rather the quality of the banner and the attention to its placement. According to Steven Mocha, president of Web Ads International: ↓2X

→indent 0.5″ A banner ad notifies visitors of the product or service and presents ←indent 0.5″ reasons why the consumer should choose the product in question. If the reasons are not compelling, then the banner ad has failed to achieve its purpose. If the banner ad is unattractive and obtrusive, it will alienate the consumer. When written and designed well, the banner ad is extremely effective in garnering business.[4] ↓2X

Indented display

Thus, while some analysts continue to argue that the banner advertisement is passé, there is little evidence of its abandonment. Instead, ad agencies are focusing on increasing the banner's effectiveness. ↓2X

SCOPE AND TRENDS IN ONLINE ADVERTISING ↓2X

Starting from zero in 1994, analysts agree that the volume of Internet advertising spending has risen rapidly. However, as indicated in Table 3, analysts provide a wide range of the exact amount of such advertising. ↓2X

Table number title · 14 pt · 12 pt ↓

Table 3. INTERNET ADVERTISING Current Year Estimates	
Source	Estimate
Internet Advertising Conference	$3.92 billion
Forecaster	3.30 billion
IPC International	3.20 billion
Brown Media	980 million
Note: This information is subject to change.	

↓1X

Table note · ↓1X
The differences in estimates of total Web advertising spending is generally attributed to the different methodologies used by the research agencies to gather the data. Further research is pending and will be reported next month.

[4] Steven Mocha, "Banner Ads That Really Work," *The Online Advertising Journal*, June 17, 2010, p. D1.

C. MULTIPAGE ACADEMIC REPORT

(page 1; with 2-line title, endnote references, and multiline list)

2-line title · ↓5SS · 14 pt **AN ANALYSIS OF THE SCOPE AND EFFECTIVENESS** ↓1DS

OF ONLINE ADVERTISING ↓1DS

12 pt ↓ **The Status of Point-and-Click Selling** ↓1DS

Jonathan R. Evans ↓1DS

January 19, 20— ↓1DS

One major benefit of online advertising is the immediate publishing of content that is not limited by geography or time. ↓1DS

GROWTH FACTORS ↓1DS

Online business has grown in tandem with the expanding number of Internet users, which is growing exponentially each year.[i] ↓1DS · Endnote reference

Reasons for Not Advertising Online. A recent survey conducted by TAIR found two main reasons cited for not advertising online:[ii]

Multiline list
1. The difficulty of determining return on investment, especially in terms of repeat business and first-time shoppers.
2. The lack of reliable tracking and measurement data.

Obviously, there are many other reasons in addition to these two for not advertising online. However, with the growing number of Internet users, these

D. MULTIPAGE ACADEMIC REPORT

(last page; with page number, indented display, and endnotes)

14 · Page number

advertising effectiveness, but rather the quality of the banner and the attention to the banner placement. According to Mike Windsor, president of Ogilvy Interactive: ↓1DS

→indent 0.5″ It's more a case of bad banner ads, just like there are bad TV ads. The ←indent 0.5″ space itself has huge potential. As important as using the space within the banner creatively is to aim it effectively. Unlike broadcast media, the Web offers advertisers the opportunity to reach a specific audience based on data gathered about who is surfing at a site and what their interests are.[vii] ↓2SS

Indented display

From an advertiser's perspective, most effective Internet ads do more than just deliver information to the consumer and grab the consumer's attention— they also gather information about consumers (e.g., through "cookies" and other methodologies). From the consumer's perspective, this type of interactivity may represent an intrusion and an invasion of privacy.

Endnotes
[i] Shannon Newsome, "Effective Online Advertising," *E-Mail Marketing Daily*, July 12, 2010, p. R6.
[ii] "eWebStats: Online Trends in the United States," *eWebStats Home page*, August 11, 2010, <http://www.ewebstats.com/trends/ad>, accessed on September 7, 2010.
[iii] Barbara Fisher, "Net Ratings Index Predicts Rise in Web Ads," *Advertising Today*, July 19, 2010, p. 10.
[iv] Ron Heisman, "Internet Banner Ads Growth Trends," *Internet Associates Conference Home page*, November 13, 2010, <http://www.iac.net/conference>, accessed on December 8, 2010.
[v] Alexis Dirkson, "Point-and-Click Bargains for Internet Ad Surfers," *Internet Age*, March 8, 2010, p. 12.
[vi] Andrew Romero, "Gathering Statistics to Grow Your Internet Business," *The Wall Street Journal*, March 2, 2010, p. C20.
[vii] Lisa Gunderson, "Banner Banter" *The London Financial Times*, June 17, 2010, p. D1.

Reference Manual

A. LEFT-BOUND BUSINESS REPORT

(page 1; with 2-line title, single-line list, and footnotes)

left margin: 1.5"
right margin: *default* 1"

2-line title ↓5X
14 pt **AN ANALYSIS OF THE SCOPE AND EFFECTIVENESS**
OF ONLINE ADVERTISING ↓2X

12 pt ↓ **The Status of Point-and-Click Selling** ↓2X

Jonathan R. Evans ↓2X

January 19, 20— ↓2X

Online advertising uses the Internet for the sole purpose of delivering marketing messages to customers. Some examples of online advertising are as follows: ads on search engine results pages, banner ads, interactive media ads, and e-mail marketing. One major benefit of online advertising is the immediate publishing of content that is not limited by geography or time. Interactive advertising presents new challenges for advertisers.[1] ↓2X

GROWTH FACTORS ↓2X

Online business has grown in tandem with the expanding number of Internet users. That trend will only increase as time goes on. ↓2X

Uncertainty. The uncertainties surrounding advertising on the Internet remain one of the major impediments to the expansion. All of the Internet advertising industry is today in a state of flux. ↓2X

Reasons for Not Advertising Online. A recent survey found two main reasons cited for not advertising online:[2] ↓2X

Single-line list
1. The difficulty of determining return on investment.
2. The lack of reliable tracking and measurement data.

Footnotes
[1] Shannon Newsome, "Effective Online Advertising," *E-Mail Marketing Daily,* July 12, 2010, p. R6.
[2] "eWebStats: Online Trends in the United States," *eWebStats Home page,* August 11, 2010, <http://www.ewebstats.com/trends/ad>, accessed on September 7, 2010.

B. BIBLIOGRAPHY

(for business or academic style using either endnotes or footnotes)

hanging indent ↓
12 pt ↓   14 pt **BIBLIOGRAPHY** ↓2X   ↓5X

Book—one author Adams, Ana B., *Internet Advertising,* Brunswick Press, Boston, 2009. ↓2X

Annual report AdNet Incorporated, *2010 Annual Report,* BCI, Inc., San Francisco, 2010.

Newspaper article An, Sang Jin, "Banner Ad Frenzy," *The Wall Street Journal,* July 12, 2010, p. R6.

Book—two authors Arlens, Rachel, and Seymour Schell, *E-Vertising,* New England Publishing, → hanging indent Cambridge, Mass., 2009.

Book—organization as author Directory of Internet Business Services, International Corporate Libraries Assoc., New York, 2009.

WWW page "eWebStats: Online Trends in the United States," *eWebStats Home page,* August 11, 2010, <http://www.ewebstats.com/trends/ad>, accessed on September 7, 2010.

Journal article— paged continuously Ingram, Fred, "Hiring Trends in Online Advertising," *Personnel Quarterly,* Vol. 30, September 2009, pp. 104-116.

Journal article— paged each issue Johnson, Jennifer, "WebRatings Index Shows 8% Rise in Web Ads," *Advertising Today,* July 19, 2010, p. 18.

Online database "Motivational Advertising Techniques," *Advertising Encyclopedia,* N.D., <http://www.adtech.com/motivational_advertising_techniques.html>, accessed on January 7, 2010.

Government document National Institute of Psychology, *Who Clicks? An Analysis of Internet Advertising,* TNIP Publication No. ADM 82-1195, U.S. Government Printing Office, Washington, 2009.

E-mail Williams, Dennis V., "Reaction to Analysis of Internet Ads," e-mail message, August 18, 2010.

C. MEMO REPORT

(page 1, with 2-line subject line, endnote references, and single-line list)

↓5X →tab
MEMO TO: Luis Torres, General Manager ↓2X

FROM: Jonathan R. Evans, Assistant Marketing Manager *jre*

DATE: January 19, 20—

2-line subject line **SUBJECT:** An Analysis of the Scope and Effectiveness of Current Online →tab Advertising in Today's Marketplace ↓2X

Online advertising uses the Internet and World Wide Web for the sole purpose of delivering marketing messages to customers. Some examples of online advertising are ads on search engine results pages, banner ads, interactive media ads, social network site advertising, online classified advertising, advertising networks, and e-mail marketing, including e-mail spam. ↓2X

One major benefit of online advertising is the immediate publishing of information and content that is not limited by geography or time. To that end, the emerging area of interactive advertising presents fresh challenges for advertisers.[i] **Endnote reference** Such challenges are opportunities for growth. ↓2X

GROWTH FACTORS ↓2X

Online business has grown in tandem with the expanding number of Internet users. That trend will only increase as time goes on. ↓2X

Uncertainty. The uncertainties surrounding advertising on the Internet remain one of the major impediments to the expansion. All of the Internet advertising industry is today in a state of flux.

Reasons for Not Advertising Online. A recent survey found two main reasons cited for not advertising online:[ii] ↓2X

Single-line list
1. The difficulty of determining return on investment.
2. The lack of reliable tracking and measurement data.

D. FORMATTING REPORTS

Margins, Spacing, and Indents. Begin the first page of each section (for example, the table of contents, first page of the body, and bibliography pages) 2 inches from the top of the page. Begin other pages 1 inch from the top. Use 1-inch default side and bottom margins for all pages. For a left-bound report, add 0.5 inch to the left margin. Single-space business reports. Double-space academic reports and indent paragraphs.

Titles and Headings. Center the title in 14-pt. font. Single-space multiline titles in a single-spaced report, and double-space multiline titles in a double-spaced report. Insert 1 blank line before and after all parts of a heading block (may include the title, subtitle, author, and/or date), and format all lines in bold. Format side headings in bold, at the left margin, with 1 blank line before and after them. Format paragraph headings at the left margin for single-spaced reports and indented for double-spaced reports in bold, followed by a period in bold and one space.

Citations. Format citations using Word's footnote (or endnote) feature.

Margins, Spacing, Headings, and Citations for APA- or MLA-Style Reports. See page R-10.

Reference Manual

A. REPORT IN APA STYLE

(page 3; with header, 2-line title, byline, main heading, subheading, and citations)

top, bottom, and side margins: *default* (1")
double-space throughout

Online Advertising 3 `Header`

`2-line title` An Analysis of the Scope and Effectiveness

of Online Advertising

`Byline` Jonathan R. Evans

→ tab Online advertising uses the Internet for the sole purpose of delivering

marketing messages to customers. Some examples of online advertising are ads

on search engine results pages, banner ads, interactive media ads, online

classifieds, advertising networks, and e-mail marketing (Gunderson, 2011, p. D1). `Citation`

One major benefit of online advertising is the immediate publishing of

content that is not limited by geography or time. To that end, interactive

advertising presents fresh challenges for advertisers (Newsome, 2010).

`Main heading` Growth Factors

Online business has grown in tandem with the expanding number of

Internet users. That trend will only increase as time goes on (Arlens & Schell).

`Subheading` *Uncertainty* ← `Italic`

The uncertainties surrounding Internet advertising are impeding its

expansion. A recent survey found two main reasons cited for not advertising

online. The first is the difficulty of determining return on investment, especially in

terms of repeat business and first-time shoppers. The second is the lack of reliable

tracking and measurement data ("eWebStats," 2010).

B. REFERENCES IN APA STYLE

(page 14; with header)

top, bottom, and side margins: *default* (1")
double-space throughout

Online Advertising 14 `Header`

hanging indent ↓ References

`Book—one author` Adams, A. B. (2009). *Internet advertising and the upcoming electronic upheaval.*

→ hanging indent Boston: Brunswick Press.

`Annual report` AdNet Incoporated. (2010). *2010 annual report.* San Francisco: BCI, Inc.

`Newspaper article` An, S. J. (2010, July 12). Banner ad frenzy. *The Wall Street Journal*, p. R6.

`Book—two authors` Arlens, R., & Seymour, S. (2010). *E-vertising.* Cambridge, MA: New England

Publishing.

`Book—organization as author` *Directory of business and financial services.* (2009). New York: International

Corporate Libraries Association.

`WWW page` eWebStats: Advertising revenues and trends. (n.d.). New York: eMarketer.

Retrieved August 11, 2010, from

http://www.emarketer.com/ewebstats/2507manu.ad

`Journal article—paged continuously` Ingram, F. (2009). Trends in online advertising. *Personnel Quarterly, 20,* 804-816.

`Journal article—paged each issue` Johnson, J. (2010, July 19). WebRatings Index shows 4% rise in Web ads.

Advertising Today, 39, 18.

`Online database` Motivational advertising techniques. (2010, January). *Advertising Encyclopedia.*

Retrieved January 7, 2010, from http://www.adtech.com/ads.html

`Government document` National Institute of Psychology (2009). *Who clicks? An analysis of Internet*

advertising (TNIP Publication No. ADM 82-1195). Washington, DC.

C. REPORT IN MLA STYLE

(page 1; with header, heading, 2-line title, and citations)

top, bottom, and side margins: *default* (1")
double-space throughout

Evans 1 `Header`

`Heading` Jonathan R. Evans

Professor Inman

Management 302

19 January 20--

`2-line title` An Analysis of the Scope and Effectiveness

of Online Advertising

→ tab Online advertising uses the Internet for the sole purpose of delivering

marketing messages to customers. Some examples of online advertising are ads

on search engine results pages, banner ads, interactive media ads, social network

site advertising, online classifieds, and e-mail marketing (Gunderson D1). `Citation`

One major benefit of online advertising is the immediate publishing of

information and content that is not limited by geography or time. To that end,

interactive advertising presents fresh challenges for advertisers (Newsome 59).

Online business has grown in tandem with the expanding number of

Internet users. That trend will only increase as time goes on (Arlens & Schell 376-

379). The uncertainties surrounding Internet advertising remain one of the major

impediments to the expansion. A recent survey found two main reasons cited for

not advertising online. The first is the difficulty of determining return on

investment. The second is the lack of reliable tracking and measurement data.

D. WORKS CITED IN MLA STYLE

(page 14; with header and hanging indent)

top, bottom, and side margins: *default* (1")
double-space throughout

Evans 14 `Header`

hanging indent ↓ Works Cited

`Book—one author` Adams, Ana. B. *Internet Advertising and the Upcoming Electronic Upheaval.*

→ hanging indent Boston: Brunswick Press, 2009.

`Annual report` AdNet Incoporated. *2010 Annual Report.* San Francisco: BCI, Inc., 2010.

`Newspaper article` An, Sang Jin. "Banner Ad Frenzy." *The Wall Street Journal*, 12 July 2010: R6.

`Book—two authors` Arlens, Rachel, and Seymour Schell. *E-vertising.* Cambridge, MA: New England

Publishing, 2009.

`Book—organization as author` Corporate Libraries Association. *Directory of Business and Financial Services.* New

York: Corporate Libraries Association, 2009.

`WWW page` "eWebStats: Advertising Revenues and Trends." 11 Aug. 2009. 7 Jan. 2010

<http://www.emarketer.com/ewebstats/ad>.

`Journal article—paged continuously` Ingram, Frank. "Trends in Online Advertising." *Personnel Quarterly* 20 (2010):

804-816.

`Journal article—paged each issue` Johnson, June. "WRI shows 4% rise in Web ads." *WebAds Today* 19 July 2010: 18.

`Online database` *Motivational Advertising Techniques.* 2010. Advertising Encyclopedia. 7 Jan. 2010

<http://www.adtech.com/ads.html>.

`Government document` National Institute of Psychology. *Who clicks?* TNIP Publication No. ADM 82-1195.

Washington, DC. GPO: 2010.

`E-mail` Williams, Dan V. "Reaction to Internet Ads." E-mail to the author. 18 Aug. 2010.

Reference Manual

A. MEETING AGENDA

↓5X

14 pt MILES HARDWARE EXECUTIVE COMMITTEE ↓2X

12 pt ↓ Meeting Agenda ↓2X

June 7, 20— ↓2X

Numbered list: default format

1. Call to order
2. Approval of minutes of May 5 meeting
3. Progress report on building addition and parking lot restrictions (Norman Hodges and Anthony Pascarelli)
4. May 15 draft of Five-Year Plan
5. Review of National Hardware Association annual convention
6. Employee grievance filed by Ellen Burrows (John Landstrom)
7. New expense-report forms (Anne Richards)
8. Announcements
9. Adjournment

B. MINUTES OF A MEETING

↓5X

14 pt RESOURCE COMMITTEE ↓2X

12 pt ↓ Minutes of the Meeting ↓2X

March 13, 20— ↓1X

ATTENDANCE	The Resource Committee met on March 13, 20—, at the Airport Sheraton in Portland, Oregon, with all members present. Michael Davis, chairperson, called the meeting to order at 2:30 p.m. ↓1X
APPROVAL OF MINUTES	The minutes of the January 27 meeting were read and approved as presented.
OLD BUSINESS	The members of the committee reviewed the sales brochure on electronic copyboards and agreed to purchase one for the conference room. Cynthia Giovanni will secure quotations from at least two suppliers.
NEW BUSINESS	The committee reviewed a request from the Purchasing Department for three new computers. After extensive discussion regarding the appropriate use of the computers and software to be purchased, the committee approved the request.
ADJOURNMENT	The meeting was adjourned at 4:45 p.m. The next meeting is scheduled for April 13 in Suite B. ↓2X Respectfully submitted, ↓4X *D. S. Madsen* D. S. Madsen, Secretary

(Note: Table shown with "View Gridlines" active.)

C. ITINERARY

↓5X

14 pt PORTLAND SALES MEETING ↓2X

12 pt ↓ Itinerary for Dorothy Turner ↓2X

March 12-15, 20— ↓1X

THURSDAY, MARCH 12	↓1X
5:10 p.m.-7:06 p.m.	Flight from Detroit to Portland; Northwest 83 (800-555-1212); e-ticket; Seat 8D; nonstop. ↓2X Jack Weatherford (Home: 503-555-8029; Office: 503-555-7631) will meet your flight on Thursday, provide transportation during your visit, and return you to the airport on Saturday morning. Airport Sheraton (503-555-4032) King-sized bed, nonsmoking room; late arrival guaranteed; Reservation No. 30ZM6-02. ↓1X
FRIDAY, MARCH 13	
9 a.m.-5:30 p.m.	Portland Sales Meeting 1931 Executive Way, Suite 10 Portland, OR 97211 (503-555-7631)
SATURDAY, MARCH 14	
7:30 a.m.-2:47 p.m.	Flight from Portland to Detroit; Northwest 360; e-ticket; Seat 9a; nonstop.

(Note: Table shown with "View Gridlines" active.)

D. LEGAL DOCUMENT

(with line numbers)

left tabs: 1", 3.25"
right tab: 6.5"

line numbers (court documents only)

```
 1   STATE OF NEVADA                    → tab 6.5"  IN DISTRICT COURT  ↓2X
 2
 3   COUNTY OF CLARK                    NORTHEAST JUDICIAL DISTRICT  ↓2X
 4
 5   JOHN C. SMITH      → tab 3.25")       NO.  1 space, 20 underscores
 6   209 East Clark Avenue            ) tab 6.5"
 7   Las Vegas, NV 89155-1603         )
 8                                    )
 9   → tab 1"  Plaintiff,  → tab 3.25")
10                                    )
11           vs.                      )      → tab 6.5"  SUMMONS
12                                    )
13   FAITH GEORGIA                    )
14                                    )
15           Defendant.               )
16                                                      ↓2X
17   THE STATE OF NEVADA TO THE ABOVE-NAMED DEFENDANT:  ↓2X
18
19   → tab 1"  You are hereby summoned and required to appear and defend
20   against the Complaint in this action, which is hereby served upon you by serving
21   upon the undersigned an Answer or other proper response within twenty (20)
22   days after the service of the Summons and Complaint upon you, exclusive of the
23   day of service.  ↓2X
24
25           If you fail to do so, judgment by default will be taken against you for
26   the relief demanded in the Complaint.
27
28           SIGNED this _____ day of July, 20—.  ↓2X
29
30                                    underscores to the right margin
31   1 space;
32   5 underscores;  → tab 3.25"  Jim Roe  → tab 6.5" Attorney at Law
33   1 space                             229 South Civic Way
34                                       Laughlin, NV 89029-2648
35                                       Telephone: 702-555-1205
                                         Attorney for Plaintiff
```

Reference Manual

A. RESUME

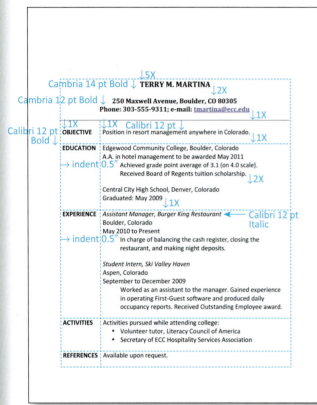

Cambria 14 pt Bold ↓ **TERRY M. MARTINA** ↓5X ↓2X
Cambria 12 pt Bold ↓ **250 Maxwell Avenue, Boulder, CO 80305**
Phone: 303-555-9311; e-mail: tmartina@ecc.edu ↓1X

Calibri 12 pt Bold ↓ ↓1X ↓1X Calibri 12 pt ↓
OBJECTIVE Position in resort management anywhere in Colorado. ↓1X

EDUCATION Edgewood Community College, Boulder, Colorado
A.A. in hotel management to be awarded May 2011
→ indent 0.5" Achieved grade point average of 3.1 (on 4.0 scale).
Received Board of Regents tuition scholarship. ↓2X

Central City High School, Denver, Colorado
Graduated: May 2009 ↓1X

EXPERIENCE *Assistant Manager, Burger King Restaurant* ← Calibri 12 pt Italic
Boulder, Colorado
May 2010 to Present
→ indent 0.5" In charge of balancing the cash register, closing the
restaurant, and making night deposits.

Student Intern, Ski Valley Haven
Aspen, Colorado
September to December 2009
Worked as an assistant to the manager. Gained experience
in operating First-Guest software and produced daily
occupancy reports. Received Outstanding Employee award.

ACTIVITIES Activities pursued while attending college:
• Volunteer tutor, Literacy Council of America
• Secretary of ECC Hospitality Services Association

REFERENCES Available upon request.

(Note: Table shown with "View Gridlines" active.)

B. APPLICATION LETTER IN BLOCK STYLE

(with return address)

↓5X
March 1, 20-- ↓4X

Mr. Lou Mansfield, Director
Human Resources Department
Rocky Resorts International
P.O. Box 1412
Denver, CO 80214 ↓2X

Dear Mr. Mansfield: ↓2X

Please consider me an applicant for the position of concierge for Suite Retreat, as
advertised in last Sunday's *Denver Times.* ↓2X

I will receive my A.A. degree in hotel management from Edgewood Community
College in May and will be available for full-time employment immediately. In
addition to my extensive coursework in hospitality services and business, I've had
experience in working for a ski lodge similar to Suite Retreats in Aspen. As a
lifelong resident of Colorado and an avid skier, I would be able to provide your
guests with any information they request.

After you've reviewed my enclosed resume, I would appreciate having an
opportunity to discuss with you why I believe I have the right qualifications and
personality to serve as your concierge. I can be reached at 303-555-9311. ↓2X

Sincerely, ↓4X

Terry M. Martina

Return address Terry M. Martina
250 Maxwell Avenue, Apt. 8
Boulder, CO 80305 ↓2X

Enclosure

C. FORMATTING LISTS

Numbers or bullets are used in documents to call attention to items in a list and to increase readability. If the sequence of the list items is important, use numbers rather than bullets.

• Insert 1 blank line before and after the list.
• Use Word's default format for all lists in either single- or double-spaced documents, including lists in documents such as a meeting agenda. Any carryover lines will be indented automatically.
• Use the same line spacing (single or double) between lines in the list as is used in the rest of the document.

The three bulleted and numbered lists shown at the right are all formatted correctly.

D. EXAMPLES OF DIFFERENT TYPES OF LISTS

According to the Internet Advertising Bureau, the following are the most common types of advertising on the Internet:

• Banner ads that feature some type of appropriate animation to attract the viewer's attention and interest.
• Sponsorship, in which an advertiser sponsors a content-based Web site.
• Interstitials, ads that flash up while a page downloads.

There is now considerable controversy about the effectiveness of banner advertising. As previously noted, a central goal of banner advertisements is to

*****

According to the Internet Advertising Bureau, the following are the most common types of advertising on the Internet, shown in order of popularity:

1. Banner ads
2. Sponsorship
3. Interstitials

There is now considerable controversy about the effectiveness of banner advertising. As previously noted, a central goal of banner advertisements is to

*****

According to the Internet Advertising Bureau, the following are the most

common types of advertising on the Internet:

• Banner ads that feature some type of appropriate animation to attract the

viewer's attention and interest.

• Sponsorship, in which an advertiser sponsors a Web site.

• Interstitials, ads that flash up while a page downloads.

There is now considerable controversy about the effectiveness of banner

advertising. As previously noted, a central goal of banner advertisements is to

Reference Manual

A. BOXED TABLE

(with subtitle; bottom-aligned and braced column headings; left- and right-aligned columns; total line and table note)

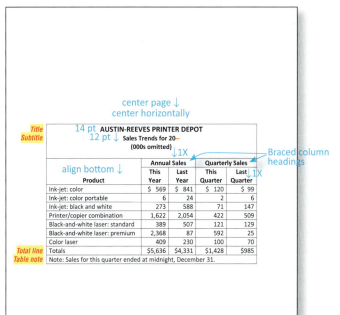

B. OPEN TABLE

(with 2-line title; 2-line centered, bottom-aligned column headings; left- and right-aligned columns; column entries with dollar and percent signs)

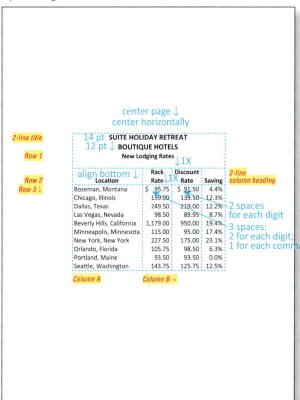

(Note: Table shown with "View Gridlines" active.)

C. RULED TABLE

(with table number, title, centered column headings, and total line)

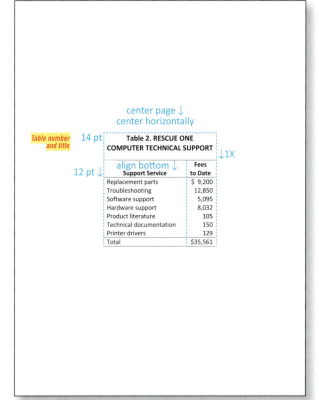

(Note: Table shown with "View Gridlines" active.)

D. FORMATTING TABLES

The three basic styles of tables are boxed, open, and ruled. Tables have vertical columns (Column A), horizontal rows (Row 1), and intersecting cells (Cell A1). Center a table vertically that appears alone on the page. Insert 1 blank line before and after a table that appears within a document. Automatically adjust column widths and horizontally center all tables.

Heading Block. Merge any cells in Row 1, and type the heading block. Center and bold throughout. Type the title in all-caps, 14-pt. font, and the subtitle in upper- and lowercase, 12-pt. font. If a table has a number, type *Table* in upper- and lowercase. Follow the table number with a period and 1 space. Insert 1 blank line below the heading block.

Column Headings. Center column headings. Type in upper- and lowercase and bold. Bottom-align all column headings if a row includes a 2-line column heading. Merge desired cells for braced headings.

Column Entries. Left-align text columns, and right-align number columns. Capitalize only the first word and proper nouns in column entries.

Column Entry Dollar and Percent Signs. Insert the dollar sign only before the amount in the first entry and before a total amount entry. Align the dollar sign with the longest amount in the column, inserting spaces after the dollar sign as needed (allowing for 2 spaces for each digit and 1 space for each comma). Repeat the percent sign for each number in each column entry (unless the column heading identifies the data as percentages).

Table Note and Total Line. For a note line, merge the cells of the last row and use "Note" followed by a colon. For a total line, add a top and bottom border, use "Total" or "Totals" as appropriate, and add a percent or dollar sign if needed.

A. FORMATTING BUSINESS FORMS

Many business forms can be created and filled in by using templates that are provided within commercial word processing software. Template forms can be used "as is" or they can be edited. Templates can also be used to create customized forms for any business.

When a template is opened, the form is displayed on screen. The user can then fill in the necessary information, including personalized company information. Data are entered into cells or fields, and you can move quickly from field to field with a single keystroke—usually by pressing Tab or Enter.

B. U.S. POSTAL SERVICE ABBREVIATIONS

(for States, Territories, and Canadian Provinces)

States and Territories

Alabama	AL
Alaska	AK
Arizona	AZ
Arkansas	AR
California	CA
Colorado	CO
Connecticut	CT
Delaware	DE
District of Columbia	DC
Florida	FL
Georgia	GA
Guam	GU
Hawaii	HI
Idaho	ID
Illinois	IL
Indiana	IN
Iowa	IA
Kansas	KS
Kentucky	KY
Louisiana	LA
Maine	ME
Maryland	MD
Massachusetts	MA
Michigan	MI
Minnesota	MN
Mississippi	MS
Missouri	MO
Montana	MT
Nebraska	NE
Nevada	NV
New Hampshire	NH
New Jersey	NJ
New Mexico	NM
New York	NY
North Carolina	NC
North Dakota	ND
Ohio	OH
Oklahoma	OK
Oregon	OR
Pennsylvania	PA
Puerto Rico	PR
Rhode Island	RI
South Carolina	SC
South Dakota	SD
Tennessee	TN
Texas	TX
Utah	UT
Vermont	VT
Virgin Islands	VI
Virginia	VA
Washington	WA
West Virginia	WV
Wisconsin	WI
Wyoming	WY

Canadian Provinces

Alberta	AB
British Columbia	BC
Labrador	LB
Manitoba	MB
New Brunswick	NB
Newfoundland	NF
Northwest Territories	NT
Nova Scotia	NS
Ontario	ON
Prince Edward Island	PE
Quebec	PQ
Saskatchewan	SK
Yukon Territory	YT

C. PROOFREADERS' MARKS

Proofreaders' Marks	Draft	Final Copy
Omit space	data base	database
Insert	if hes going	if he's not going,
Capitalize	Maple street	Maple Street
Delete	a final draft	a draft
Insert space	allready to	all ready to
Change word	and if you	and when you
Use lowercase letter	our President	our president
Paragraph	... to use it. We can	... to use it. We can
Don't delete	a true story	a true story
Spell out	the only 1	the only one
Transpose	they all see	they see all

Proofreaders' Marks	Draft	Final Copy
SS Single-space	first line / second line	first line / second line
ds Double-space	first line / second line	first line / second line
Move right	Please send	Please send
Move left	May I	May I
Bold	Column Heading	**Column Heading**
ital Italic	Time magazine	*Time* magazine
u/l Underline	Time magazine	Time magazine readers
Move as shown	readers will see	will see

Language Arts For Business

(50 "must-know" rules)

PUNCTUATION

Commas

RULE 1
, direct address
(L. 21)

Use commas before and after a name used in direct address.

> Thank you, John, for responding to my e-mail so quickly.
> Ladies and gentlemen, the program has been canceled.

RULE 2
, independent clause
(L. 27)

Use a comma between independent clauses joined by a coordinate conjunction (unless both clauses are short).

> Ellen left her job with IBM, and she and her sister went to Paris.
> But: Ellen left her job with IB<u>M</u> and went to Paris with her sister.
> But: John drov<u>e</u> and I navigated.

Note: An independent clause is one that can stand alone as a complete sentence. The most common coordinate conjunctions are *and*, *but*, *or*, and *nor*.

 The underline calls attention to a point in the sentence where a comma might mistakenly be inserted.

RULE 3
, introductory expression
(L. 27)

Use a comma after an introductory expression (unless it is a short prepositional phrase).

> Before we can make a decision, we must have all the facts.
> But: In 2004 our nation elected a new president.

Note: An introductory expression is a group of words that come before the subject and verb of the independent clause. Common prepositions are *to*, *in*, *on*, *of*, *at*, *by*, *for*, and *with*.

RULE 4
, direct quotation
(L. 41)

Use a comma before and after a direct quotation.

> James said, "I shall return," and then left.

RULE 5
, date
(L. 51)

Use a comma before and after the year in a complete date.

> We will arrive on June 2, 2006, for the conference.
> But: We will arrive on June 2 for the conference.

RULE 6
, place
(L. 51)

Use a comma before and after a state or country that follows a city (but not before a ZIP Code).

> Joan moved to Vancouver, British Columbia, in May.
> Send the package to Douglasville, GA 30135, by Express Mail.
> But: Send the package to Georgia by Express Mail.

Reference Manual

RULE 7
, series
(L. 61)

Use a comma between each item in a series of three or more.

We need to order paper, toner, and font cartridges_for the printer.

They saved their work, exited their program, and turned off their computers_when they finished.

Note: Do not use a comma after the last item in a series.

RULE 8
, transitional expression
(L. 61)

Use a comma before and after a transitional expression or independent comment.

It is critical, therefore, that we finish the project on time.

Our present projections, you must admit, are inadequate.

But: You must admi_t_our present projections are inadequate.

Note: Examples of transitional expressions and independent comments are *in addition to, therefore, however, on the other hand, as a matter of fact,* and *unfortunately.*

RULE 9
, nonessential expression
(L. 71)

Use a comma before and after a nonessential expression.

Andre, who was there, can verify the statement.

But: Anyone_who was ther_e can verify the statement.

Van's first book, *Crisis of Management*, was not discussed.

Van's boo_k Crisis of Management_was not discussed.

Note: A nonessential expression is a group of words that may be omitted without changing the basic meaning of the sentence. Always examine the noun or pronoun that comes before the expression to determine whether the noun needs the expression to complete its meaning. If it does, the expression is *essential* and does *not* take a comma.

RULE 10
, adjacent adjectives
(L. 71)

Use a comma between two adjacent adjectives that modify the same noun.

We need an intelligent, enthusiasti_c individual for this job.

But: Please order a ne_w bulletin board for our mai_n conference room.

Note: Do not use a comma after the second adjective. Also, do not use a comma if the first adjective modifies the combined idea of the second adjective and the noun (for example, *bulletin board* and *conference room* in the second example above).

Semicolons

RULE 11
; no conjunction
(L. 97)

Use a semicolon to separate two closely related independent clauses that are not joined by a conjunction (such as *and, but, or,* or *nor*).

Management favored the vote; stockholders did not.

But: Management favored the vote‚ but stockholders did not.

RULE 12
; series
(L. 97)

Use a semicolon to separate three or more items in a series if any of the items already contain commas.

Staff meetings were held on Thursday, May 7; Monday, June 7; and Friday, June 12.

Note: Be sure to insert the semicolon *between* (not within) the items in a series.

Reference Manual

Hyphens

RULE 13
- number
(L. 57)

Hyphenate compound numbers between twenty-one and ninety-nine and fractions that are expressed as words.

> Twenty-nine recommendations were approved by at least three-fourths of the members.

RULE 14
- compound adjective
(L. 67)

Hyphenate compound adjectives that come before a noun (unless the first word is an adverb ending in -ly).

> We reviewed an up-to-date report on Wednesday.
> But: The report was up to date.
> But: We reviewed the highly rated report.

Note: A compound adjective is two or more words that function as a unit to describe a noun.

Apostrophes

RULE 15
' singular noun
(L. 37)

Use 's to form the possessive of singular nouns.

> The hurricane's force caused major damage to North Carolina's coastline.

RULE 16
' plural noun
(L. 37)

Use only an apostrophe to form the possessive of plural nouns that end in s.

> The investors' goals were outlined in the stockholders' report.
> But: The investors outlined their goals in the report to the stockholders.
> But: The women's and children's clothing was on sale.

RULE 17
' pronoun
(L. 37)

Use 's to form the possessive of indefinite pronouns (such as someone's or anybody's); do not use an apostrophe with personal pronouns (such as hers, his, its, ours, theirs, and yours).

> She could select anybody's paper for a sample.
> It's time to put the file back into its cabinet.

Colons

RULE 18
: explanatory material
(L. 91)

Use a colon to introduce explanatory material that follows an independent clause.

> The computer satisfies three criteria: speed, cost, and power.
> But: The computer satisfies the three criteria of speed, cost, and power.
> Remember this: only one coupon is allowed per customer.

Note: An independent clause can stand alone as a complete sentence. Do not capitalize the word following the colon.

Periods

RULE 19
. polite request
(L. 91)

Use a period to end a sentence that is a polite request.

> Will you please call me if I can be of further assistance.

Note: Consider a sentence a polite request if you expect the reader to respond by doing as you ask rather than by giving a yes-or-no answer.

Quotation Marks

RULE 20
" direct quotation
(L. 41)

Use quotation marks around a direct quotation.

> Harrison responded by saying, "Their decision does not affect us."
> But: Harrison responded by saying that their decision does not affect us.

RULE 21
" title
(L. 41)

Use quotation marks around the title of a newspaper or magazine article, chapter in a book, report, and similar terms.

> The most helpful article I found was "Multimedia for All."

Italics (or Underline)

RULE 22
title or title
(L. 41)

Italicize (or underline) the titles of books, magazines, newspapers, and other complete published works.

> Grisham's *The Brethren* was reviewed in a recent *USA Today* article.

Reference Manual

GRAMMAR

Sentences

RULE 23
fragment
(L. 21)

Avoid sentence fragments.

Not: She had always wanted to be a financial manager. But had not had the needed education.

But: She had always wanted to be a financial manager but had not had the needed education.

Note: A fragment is a part of a sentence that is incorrectly punctuated as a complete sentence. In the first example above, "but had not had the needed education" is not a complete sentence because it does not contain a subject.

RULE 24
run-on
(L. 21)

Avoid run-on sentences.

Not: Mohamed is a competent worker he has even passed the MOS exam.

Not: Mohamed is a competent worker, he has even passed the MOS exam.

But: Mohamed is a competent worker; he has even passed the MOS exam.

Or: Mohamed is a competent worker. He has even passed the MOS exam.

Note: A run-on sentence is two independent clauses that run together without any punctuation between them or with only a comma between them.

Agreement

RULE 25
agreement singular
agreement plural
(L. 67)

Use singular verbs and pronouns with singular subjects; use plural verbs and pronouns with plural subjects.

I was happy with my performance.

Janet and Phoenix were happy with their performance.

Among the items discussed were our raises and benefits.

RULE 26
agreement pronoun
(L. 81)

Some pronouns (*anybody, each, either, everybody, everyone, much, neither, no one, nobody,* and *one*) are always singular and take a singular verb. Other pronouns (*all, any, more, most, none,* and *some*) may be singular or plural, depending on the noun to which they refer.

Each of the employees has finished his or her task.

Much remains to be done.

Most of the pie was eaten, but most of the cookies were left.

RULE 27
agreement intervening words
(L. 81)

Disregard any intervening words that come between the subject and verb when establishing agreement.

That box, containing the books and pencils, has not been found.

Alex, accompanied by Tricia and Roxy, is attending the conference and taking his computer.

RULE 28
agreement nearer noun
(L. 101)

If two subjects are joined by *or, either/or, neither/nor,* or *not only/but also,* make the verb agree with the subject nearer to the verb.

Neither the coach nor the players are at home.

Not only the coach but also the referee is at home.

But: Both the coach and the referee are at home.

Pronouns

RULE 29
nominative pronoun
(L. 107)

Use nominative pronouns (such as *I, he, she, we, they,* and *who*) as subjects of a sentence or clause.

> The programmer and <u>he</u> are reviewing the code.
> Barb is a person <u>who</u> can do the job.

RULE 30
objective pronoun
(L. 107)

Use objective pronouns (such as *me, him, her, us, them,* and *whom*) as objects of a verb, preposition, or infinitive.

> The code was reviewed by the programmer and <u>him</u>.
> Barb is the type of person <u>whom</u> we can trust.

Adjectives and Adverbs

RULE 31
adjective/adverb
(L. 101)

Use comparative adjectives and adverbs (*-er, more,* and *less*) when referring to two nouns or pronouns; use superlative adjectives and adverbs (*-est, most,* and *least*) when referring to more than two.

> The <u>shorter</u> of the <u>two</u> training sessions is the <u>more</u> helpful one.
> The <u>longest</u> of the <u>three</u> training sessions is the <u>least</u> helpful one.

Word Usage

RULE 32
accept/except
(L. 117)

***Accept* means "to agree to"; *except* means "to leave out."**

> All employees <u>except</u> the maintenance staff should <u>accept</u> the agreement.

RULE 33
affect/effect
(L. 117)

***Affect* is most often used as a verb meaning "to influence"; *effect* is most often used as a noun meaning "result."**

> The ruling will <u>affect</u> our domestic operations but will have no <u>effect</u> on our Asian operations.

RULE 34
farther/further
(L. 117)

***Farther* refers to distance; *further* refers to extent or degree.**

> The <u>farther</u> we drove, the <u>further</u> agitated he became.

RULE 35
personal/personnel
(L. 117)

***Personal* means "private"; *personnel* means "employees."**

> All <u>personnel</u> agreed not to use e-mail for <u>personal</u> business.

RULE 36
principal/principle
(L. 117)

***Principal* means "primary"; *principle* means "rule."**

> The <u>principle</u> of fairness is our <u>principal</u> means of dealing with customers.

Reference Manual

MECHANICS

Capitalization

RULE 37
≡ sentence
(L. 31)

Capitalize the first word of a sentence.

> Please prepare a summary of your activities.

RULE 38
≡ proper noun
(L. 31)

Capitalize proper nouns and adjectives derived from proper nouns.

> Judy Hendrix drove to Albuquerque in her new Pontiac convertible.

Note: A proper noun is the official name of a particular person, place, or thing.

RULE 39
≡ time
(L. 31)

Capitalize the names of the days of the week, months, holidays, and religious days (but do not capitalize the names of the seasons).

> On Thursday, November 25, we will celebrate Thanksgiving, the most popular holiday in the fall.

RULE 40
≡ noun #
(L. 77)

Capitalize nouns followed by a number or letter (except for the nouns *line, note, page, paragraph,* and *size*).

> Please read Chapter 5, which begins on page 94.

RULE 41
≡ compass point
(L. 77)

Capitalize compass points (such as *north, south,* or *northeast*) only when they designate definite regions.

> From Montana we drove south to reach the Southwest.

RULE 42
≡ organization
(L. 111)

Capitalize common organizational terms (such as *advertising department* and *finance committee*) only when they are the actual names of the units in the writer's own organization and when they are preceded by the word *the*.

> The report from the Advertising Department is due today.
> But: Our advertising department will submit its report today.

RULE 43
≡ course
(L. 111)

Capitalize the names of specific course titles but not the names of subjects or areas of study.

> I have enrolled in Accounting 201 and will also take a marketing course.

Number Expression

RULE 44
general
(L. 47)

In general, spell out numbers zero through ten, and use figures for numbers above ten.

> We rented two movies for tonight.
> The decision was reached after 27 precincts sent in their results.

<table>
<tr><td>

RULE 45
figure
(L. 47)

</td><td>

Use figures for

- **Dates. (Use *st, d,* or *th* only if the day comes before the month.)**

    The tax report is due on April 15 (not *April 15th*).
    We will drive to the camp on the 23d (or *23rd* or *23ʳᵈ*) of May.

- **All numbers if two or more *related* numbers both above and below ten are used in the same sentence.**

    Mr. Carter sent in 7 receipts, and Ms. Cantrell sent in 22.
    But: The 13 accountants owned three computers each.

- **Measurements (time, money, distance, weight, and percent).**

    The $500 statue we delivered at 7 a.m. weighed 6 pounds.

- **Mixed numbers.**

    Our sales are up 9½ (or *9.5*) percent over last year.

</td></tr>
</table>

RULE 45 — # figure (L. 47)

Use figures for

- **Dates. (Use *st, d,* or *th* only if the day comes before the month.)**
    The tax report is due on April 15 (not *April 15th*).
    We will drive to the camp on the 23d (or *23rd* or *23rd*) of May.
- **All numbers if two or more *related* numbers both above and below ten are used in the same sentence.**
    Mr. Carter sent in 7 receipts, and Ms. Cantrell sent in 22.
    But: The 13 accountants owned three computers each.
- **Measurements (time, money, distance, weight, and percent).**
    The $500 statue we delivered at 7 a.m. weighed 6 pounds.
- **Mixed numbers.**
    Our sales are up 9½ (or *9.5*) percent over last year.

RULE 46 — # word (L. 57)

Spell out

- **A number used as the first word of a sentence.**
    Seventy-five people attended the conference in San Diego.
- **The shorter of two adjacent numbers.**
    We have ordered 3 two-pound cakes and one 5-pound cake for the reception.
- **The words *million* and *billion* in round numbers (do not use decimals with round numbers).**
    Not: A $5.00 ticket can win $28,000,000 in this month's lottery.
    But: A $5 ticket can win $28 million in this month's lottery.
- **Fractions.**
    Almost one-half of the audience responded to the question.

Abbreviations

RULE 47 — abbreviate none (L. 67)

In general business writing, do not abbreviate common words (such as *dept.* or *pkg.*), compass points, units of measure, or the names of months, days of the week, cities, or states (except in addresses).

Almost one-half of the audience indicated they were at least 5 <u>feet</u> 8 inches tall.

Note: Do not insert a comma between the parts of a single measurement.

RULE 48 — abbreviate measure (L. 87)

In technical writing, on forms, and in tables, abbreviate units of measure when they occur frequently. Do not use periods.

14 oz	5 ft 10 in	50 mph	2 yrs 10 mo

RULE 49 — abbreviate lowercase (L. 87)

In most lowercase abbreviations made up of single initials, use a period after each initial but no internal spaces.

a.m.	p.m.	i.e.	e.g.	e.o.m.

Exceptions: mph   mpg   wpm

RULE 50 — abbreviate ≡ (L. 87)

In most all-capital abbreviations made up of single initials, do not use periods or internal spaces.

OSHA	PBS	NBEA	WWW	VCR	MBA		

Exceptions: U.S.A.   A.A.   B.S.   Ph.D.   P.O.   B.C.   A.D.

PART 1

The Alphabet, Number, and Symbol Keys

Keyboarding in Arts, Audio, Video Technology, and Communication Services

Occupations in this cluster deal with organizing and communicating information to the public in various forms and media.

This cluster includes jobs in radio and television broadcasting, journalism, motion pictures, the recording industry, the performing arts, multimedia publishing, and the entertainment services. Book editors, computer artists, technical writers, radio announcers, news correspondents, camera operators, and home page designers are just a few jobs within this cluster.

Qualifications and Skills

Strong oral and written communication skills and technical skills are necessary for anyone in communications and media. Without a doubt, competent keyboarding skill is extremely advantageous.

Working in the media requires creativity, talent, and accurate use of language. In journalism, being observant, thinking clearly, and seeing the significance of events are all of utmost importance. Announcers must have exceptional voices, excellent speaking skills, and a unique style. The ability to work under pressure is important in all areas of media.

Goals

Keyboarding

- Type by touch the letter, number, and symbol keys.
- Demonstrate proper typing technique.
- Use the correct spacing with punctuation.
- Type at least 28 words per minute on a 2-minute timed writing with no more than 5 errors.

Objective Test

- Answer questions with acceptable accuracy on an objective test.

Keyboarding: The Alphabet

LESSON 1

Home-Row Keys: A S D F J K L ;
Space Bar Enter Backspace

LESSON 2

New Keys: E N T

LESSON 3

New Keys: O R H

LESSON 4

New Keys: I Left Shift .

LESSON 5

New Keys: B U C

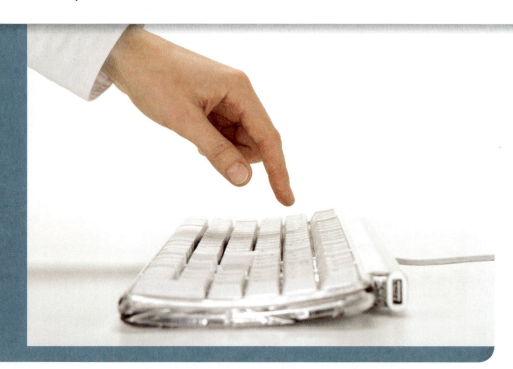

Home-Row Keys

1

Goals

- Touch-type the home-row keys—A S D F J K L ;.
- Touch-type the SPACE BAR, ENTER, and BACKSPACE keys.
- Type at least 10wpm/1′/3e; that is, type at least 10 words per minute (wpm) on a 1-minute timed writing while making no more than 3 uncorrected errors.

New Keys

A. HOME-ROW POSITION

The A S D F J K L and ; keys are called the *home-row keys.*

1. Place the fingers of your left hand lightly over the A, S, D, and F keys and the fingers of your right hand lightly over the J, K, L, and ; keys, as shown in the illustration below.
2. Feel the raised markers on the F and J keys; they will help you keep your

fingers on the home-row keys. You are now in home-row position. Each finger is named for the home-row key it controls. Thus, your left little finger is known as the A finger, and your right little finger is known as the Sem finger (short for *semicolon*).

B. THE [SPACE BAR] AND [ENTER] KEYS

The SPACE BAR is located beneath the letter keys and is used to space between words and after punctuation marks. Tap the SPACE BAR with a downward and inward (toward your body) motion of the right thumb.

The ENTER key moves the insertion point to the beginning of a new line. Reach to the ENTER key with the Sem finger (the little finger of your right hand), keeping your J finger at home. Quickly return the Sem finger to home-row position after tapping ENTER.

C. PRACTICE THE HOME-ROW KEYS

Type each line 1 time, pressing the SPACE BAR where you see a space and pressing the ENTER key at the end of each line (indicated by ↵). Tap ENTER 2 times (indicated by ↵ ↵) to insert a blank line between each set of drill lines.

```
1  asdf jkl; asdf jkl; asdf jkl; ↵
2  asdf jkl; asdf jkl; asdf jkl; ↵↵

3  asdf jkl; asdf jkl; asdf jkl; ↵
4  asdf jkl; asdf jkl; asdf jkl; ↵
```

> **!** Say the name of each key to yourself as you type it.

D. THE F AND J KEYS

```
5  fff fff jjj jjj fff jjj fjf fjf jfj jfj fff fj jf
6  fff fff jjj jjj fff jjj fjf fjf jfj jfj fff fj jf
```

E. THE D AND K KEYS

```
7  ddd ddd kkk kkk ddd kkk dkd dkd kdk kdk ddd dk kd
8  ddd ddd kkk kkk ddd kkk dkd dkd kdk kdk ddd dk kd
```

> **!** Rest your other fingers *lightly* over the keys while you're typing.

F. THE S AND L KEYS

```
9   sss lll sss lll sss lll sls sls lsl lsl sss sl ls
10  sss lll sss lll sss lll sls sls lsl lsl sss sl ls
```

G. THE A AND ; KEYS

```
11  aaa ;;; aaa ;;; aaa ;;; a;a a;a ;a; ;a; aaa a; ;a
12  aaa ;;; aaa ;;; aaa ;;; a;a a;a ;a; ;a; aaa a; ;a
```

Use the Sem finger.

H. THE ← KEY

The BACKSPACE key deletes the last character you typed. Reach to the BACKSPACE key with the Sem finger (the little finger of your right hand), keeping your J finger at home. Quickly return the Sem finger to home-row position after tapping BACKSPACE.

Looking at your keyboard and keeping your J finger at home, reach for and quickly press the BACKSPACE key and immediately return your little finger to the Sem key. Do this several times—until you can make the reach without looking at your fingers.

In the drill line below, follow these directions:

1. Type the group of letters as shown.
2. When you reach the BACKSPACE sign (←), backspace 1 time to delete the last keystroke typed.
3. Then type the next letter. For example, you will type *as*, press BACKSPACE 1 time, and then type *d*, thus changing *as* to *ad*.

13 as←d; dadk←s; sas←d; laf←d; jal←k; sal←d; lasd←s;

Space 1 time after a semicolon (but not before).

Skillbuilding

I. WORD BUILDING

```
14  a ad ads; l la las lass; f fa fad; s sa sal sala;
15  d da dad; f fa fal fall; l la lad; j ja jas jass;

16  s sa sad; f fl fla flak; a as ask; s sa sas sass;
17  a ad add; a al alf alfa; j ja jak; a al ala alas;
```

J. 1-MINUTE TIMED WRITING

Take two 1-minute timed writings. Try to complete the passage each time. If you finish, press ENTER 2 times and start over again. The number scale below line 18 shows the number of words credited for typing a partial line. The software will automatically score your timed writings for speed and accuracy.

```
18  ask a sad lad; a fall fad; add a jak salad; a lad
        1 | 2 | 3 | 4 | 5 | 6 | 7 | 8 | 9 | 10
```

Goal: At least 10wpm/1'/3e

See "Introduction to the Student" at the front of your text for guidance on how speed and accuracy are measured.

Enrichment • Lesson 1

Type each line 2 times.

A. NEW-KEY REINFORCEMENT

1 a dads jass la daff ad add dak lad lads daks adds
2 ads fad lall lass fads alas alfa fala sad alfalfa

3 sal falda all fall sala as falls salad salsa flak
4 asks flask sass dad flasks skald dada jak ask lad

5 alas ask salads dads dak sala fad falda flask sal
6 alfalfa add fads all salad flak lass flask ads as

B. SHORT PHRASES

Type each phrase on a separate line; that is, press ENTER 1 time at the end of each line. Type each line 2 times; then press ENTER 2 times to insert a blank line between each line. Do not space after a semicolon if it is the last character on the line; instead, immediately after typing the semicolon, press ENTER.

7 a lad;
8 a lass;
9 a fall;

10 ask dad;
11 add all;
12 as a fad;

13 a fall ad;
14 dad falls;
15 jak salad;

16 add a lad;
17 ask a lass;
18 all flasks;

19 fall salads;
20 a lad asks dad;
21 a sad lass falls;

C. PARAGRAPH TYPING

First, type the following paragraph 1 time. Do not press ENTER at the end of each line; instead, let Word wrap end your lines for you. After you type the three lines 1 time, press ENTER 2 times and then type the three-line paragraph again.

22 fall salad; add a jak ad; alfalfa salad; ask a
23 sad lad; a lad asks dad; a lass asks dad; a sad
24 lad falls; a sad lad asks a dad; as a lass falls;

New Keys

Goals

- Touch-type the E, N, and T keys.
- Type at least 11wpm/1'/3e.

Fingers are named for home-row keys. For example, the middle finger of the left hand is the D finger.

Tap the SPACE BAR with a downward and inward motion of your right thumb.

A. WARMUP

```
1  aa ss dd ff jj kk ll ;; fj dk sl a; asdf jkl; a;s
2  ask dad; a flask; a salsa salad; as sad as a lass
3  add salsa; fall fads; alas a sad lass; a dad; jak
```

New Keys

B. NEW-KEY PROCEDURE

Follow this procedure when learning a new key:

1. Place your fingers on the home-row keys.
2. Look in the left margin of your lesson to see which finger controls the new key.
3. While looking at your keyboard and without actually typing, move the correct finger to the new key and back to home-row position. Do this several times—until you can make the reach without looking at your fingers.
4. Now, with your fingers still on the home-row keys, type the drill lines while keeping your eyes on the copy.
5. If you forget the location of a key, stop typing and repeat step 3.
6. You will make numerous errors while you are learning the keyboard; do not be overly concerned about them. Errors will decrease as you become more familiar with the keyboard.

Keep the A finger at home as you reach for E.

Use the D finger.

C. THE E KEY

4 ddd ded ded ede ede eee alae dead eels fed jelled
5 eke lead see fed fee safe eel ease seal deal dead
6 deed feed jell keel lead seal elks fade leek seek
7 a fake deal; feed a flea; lease a desk; sell ale;

Keep the Sem finger at home as you reach for N.

Use the J finger.

D. THE N KEY

8 jjj jnj jnj njn njn nnn and sadness ends deafness
9 knee kennel sneak an fan dens fen lens sedan lend
10 dean sane lane sank keen lens seen fend lank send
11 lend a needle; send jeans and sandals; needs land

Keep the A finger at home as you reach for T.

Use the F finger.

E. THE T KEY

12 fff ftf ftf tft tft ttt ate jet aft felt ant east
13 latte tat test at fat jest let ate late east daft
14 deft feet lent state taste tenet sets detest lets
15 a fast jet left at ten; staked a tent; tall tales

Skillbuilding

F. MINIMUM-CHANGE PRACTICE

Only one letter changes in each word.

16 lent sent send tend tent test nest lest fest jest
17 lake take tale tall tell fell felt feet feat seat
18 seed teed tend send sand land lend fend feed feel

19 lens tens fens fans tans tens dens dent lent sent
20 sank tank talk tale kale dale date late lane lank
21 jets lets less lass last fast fest feet feat seat

G. NEW-KEY REVIEW

E
N
T

22 easel deafen deed defeat defend delete dense ease
23 annals fanned kennel tenant tan and dean den fend
24 at attend attest detest estate fatten jest jetted

E
N
T

25 deaden dented detest eases eaten eel effete elate
26 keen land lend neat sent need net sedan seen send
27 tests kettle latent tent latest nettle tee settee

E
N
T

28 eke jested else ended estate fee lessee feed fete
29 tanned ant sense eaten knee sneak stand tend tent
30 settle state talent tan taste tenant tenet tsetse

H. CLAUSES

31 a tense staff deleted data; test a fast delta jet
32 a tenant dented a sedan; a sad tale ended at ten;
33 fasten a tan anklet; a lad ate a steak at a feast
34 a tall dean sat at a sedate settee; take an asset

I. 1-MINUTE TIMED WRITING

Take two 1-minute timed writings. Let word wrap end each line. Press ENTER only at the end of line 36.

 Goal: At least 11wpm/1'/3e

35 a tenant leased a fast jet and landed at a sedate   10
36 lake;   11

   1 | 2 | 3 | 4 | 5 | 6 | 7 | 8 | 9 | 10

Enrichment • Lesson 2

Type each line 2 times.

E
N
T

E
N
T

E
N
T

E N T
E N T
E N T

A. NEW-KEY REINFORCEMENT

1 fleet steel assets deafen lessee deed elate kneel
2 annals fanned nene anneal needle fennel leaden an
3 tats detest latest jet tsetse stats attest settle

4 detest lessen see leek skeet elands estate fallen
5 flan keen lean send knee sank land keen lane fend
6 aft let eta net alt fat sat ant ate set jet tanks

7 sleek leaden leaded needle easel knell sleets eke
8 and ant den end fan fen ken nee nets ten tan sane
9 settee state kettle tattle taste task kaftan test

10 nest detent tens sanest knelt neat teens dent net
11 tensed ante tanned talent sent nest latent fanjet
12 anklet tenant tend eaten attend assent ten fasten

Type each line 2 times.

Do not type the colored vertical lines that separate each phrase.

B. SHORT PHRASES

13 jet lease|sent fast|tan sedan|sent less|ten seats
14 dense lad|ten deeds|sent east|ten tasks|least tan
15 jet fleet|let feast|neat deal|neat feat|least sad

16 let stall|net leads|let stand|stale ale|let sneak
17 sent left|net deals|ten dates|sent data|ten lakes
18 ten desks|neat seat|ten deals|ate steak|let taste

Type each line 2 times.

C. CLAUSES

19 a teen ate at least ten dates and sat at a stand;
20 fasten a faded saddle and sandal at a sad estate;
21 a tall tan fanjet landed at a flat delta and sat;

22 all lasses tasted a lean steak and felt less sad;
23 a tenant sent kale salads and ate fat leeks fast;
24 a dad skated at a lake and leaned left at a tent;

25 take a seat at a settee and taste tea and salads;
26 a tall tenant leased a sedate teal sedan and sat;
27 at least a lad tasted steak and ale and ate fast;

New Keys

Goals

- Touch-type the O, R, and H keys.
- Type at least 12wpm/1′/3e.

A. WARMUP

<table>
<tr><td>learned keys</td><td>1</td><td>take a jet and taste a flat steak at a tall tent;</td></tr>
<tr><td>concentration</td><td>2</td><td>skedaddle attendant senseless flatlands steadfast</td></tr>
<tr><td>easy</td><td>3</td><td>an ant lent an elf a snake; an elk let an ant eat</td></tr>
</table>

New Keys

Keep the J finger at home as you reach for O.

Use the L finger.

B. THE [O] KEY

4 lll lol lol olo olo ooo do eons foe jot kook lots
5 no too so to not ton eon foe jot lot no dodo dojo
6 took soon solo onto oleo tool look foot fool soon
7 a felon loaded a lot of loose loot on an old lot;

Keep the A finger at home as you reach for R.

Use the F finger.

C. THE [R] KEY

8 fff frf frf rfr rfr rrr are drat erased fro okras
9 enroll ore errs tree rear ardor drear raked radar
10 erred rotor retro error rare rater rear errs dare
11 a red deer ran free for an area near a rear door;

Keep the Sem finger at home as you reach for H.

Use the J finger.

D. THE [H] KEY

12 jjj jhj jhj hjh hjh hhh ah adhere heh offhand shh
13 ankh oh rho she the ha he oh hah haha harsh heath
14 shah hallah the that she three here there her hot
15 she and he had heard that other short heron here;

Skillbuilding

Only one letter changes in each word.

E. MINIMUM-CHANGE PRACTICE

16 dash hash sash lash last lost host hoss loss less
17 hall tall tale kale hale hole role dole dolt jolt
18 hero here hare hard hark lark dark dank rank rant

19 jeer seer seek leek leak teak tear teal seal real
20 horn torn tort fort fore fare hare hard hart dart
21 heat seat feat fear hear sear dear dean lean leak

F. NEW-KEY REVIEW

O 22 food noon soon fool nook root solo tool donor oho
R 23 err rear ardor dares freer rarer roar order erred
H 24 hash hardhat harsher hath shah harsh heath hashed

O 25 foot odor toot oho drool oleo too hoof rook drool
R 26 radar raker rooter rare arrest reader rafter sort
H 27 heathen hashes health hearth hoorah heather trash

O 28 dodo lost toro doors onto flood hooks roof honors
R 29 errata orator darker render rather tartar terrors
H 30 rehash hothead sheath thrash thresh handheld hash

G. CLAUSES

31 she folded the sheets and he held her hands free;
32 he heard an oath and told her to note the reason;
33 the odd raft had floated onto the north seashore;
34 then she joked that he had stolen the old shades;
    1 | 2 | 3 | 4 | 5 | 6 | 7 | 8 | 9 | 10

H. 1-MINUTE TIMED WRITING

Take two 1-minute timed writings. Let word wrap end each line. Press ENTER only at the end of line 36.

Goal: At least 12wpm/1'/3e

35 the jaded steno learned a hard lesson on the trek   10
36 to a tree;   12
    1 | 2 | 3 | 4 | 5 | 6 | 7 | 8 | 9 | 10

Enrichment • Lesson 3

A. NEW-KEY REINFORCEMENT

Type each line 2 times.

O
R
H

1 roost hotfoot solon forefoot loose offshoot odors
2 errs rater refer retro rotor harder roster resort
3 hardhats hasheesh hosanna hotshots rehashed flesh

O
R
H

4 nonfood shook forenoon stood torso onlooker hoots
5 darter terser horror roller eraser roarer errands
6 sheathed shoehorn aha thrasher handshake thrasher

O
R
H

7 shoot foothold forsooth noose stool rodeo tootles
8 narrator restorer tearjerker referral northerners
9 harshness horseshoe hotheaded shorthand threshold

O R H
O R H
O R H

10 rho ashore hoorah hero hereto shorts hoar hoarser
11 hoer holder hora horn honker forth horned shofars
12 frosh throes froth honor heron horror hoard honer

B. SHORT PHRASES

Type each line 2 times.

Do not type the colored vertical lines.

13 a loose shade|eats a short noodle|the rose thorns
14 a tattletale|she sat here|he often jostled a jerk
15 the rest of the lesson|thanks for the short looks

16 the oddest tattoos|those stolen forks|do not jerk
17 the shore floods|she flossed her teeth|jot a note
18 the earth shook hard|had a look|a tenth of a foot

C. CLAUSES

Type each line 2 times.

19 she shared her salad at the hotel near the shore;
20 three deer ran to the dark oak tree near the ark;
21 she had then also looked at the other ten horses;

22 she set all of the stolen art on that tall shelf;
23 take a seat near the dark settee and talk to her;
24 the teal sandals on her feet had soon fallen off;

25 the loose earth on the north and east had fallen;
26 ask her not to take the nonfat food to the stall;
27 the senator held a safe seat and soon left there;

New Keys

4

Goals

- Touch-type the I, LEFT SHIFT, and Period keys.
- Type at least 13wpm/1'/3e.

A. WARMUP

learned keys
concentration
easy

1 the soda jerks fell onto a stall and told a joke;
2 horseshoe northeast shorthand therefore threshold
3 half of an oak had torn and also half of a shelf;

New Keys

Keep the J finger at home as you reach for I.

Use the K finger.

B. THE **I** KEY

4 kkk kik kik iki iki iii aid die lei fit hit radii
5 jilt kid lit nit oil rid sits tie id if in is ilk
6 aid sin did fie kid jail kid lid nil tie oils ail
7 nine irises in a lei did die in a sink in a deli;

Use the A finger.

C. THE LEFT SHIFT KEY

To capitalize letters on the right half of the keyboard:

1. With the F finger at home, press and hold down the LEFT SHIFT key with the A finger.
2. Press the letter key to be capitalized.
3. Immediately release the LEFT SHIFT key and return fingers to the home-row position.

8   aaa Jaa Jaa Kaa Kaa Laa Laa Naa Iaa Oaa Jane Hank
9   Hans Hale Jade Jake Ian Kate Nan Oak Ian Hal Lara
10 Nan Halle Ian Karl Lara Lena Oates Jan Katie Lars
11 Neither Jake Hanks nor Nathan Karl is in Oakland;

Keep the J finger at home as you reach for the period.

Use the L finger.

D. THE . KEY

Follow these rules for spacing with periods:

- Do not space before a period.
- Space 1 time after a period following an abbreviation.
- Do not space after a period within an abbreviation.
- Space 1 time after each initial in a person's name.
- Space 1 time after a period ending a sentence in the middle of a paragraph. Do *not* space after a period at the end of a paragraph.

```
12  lll l.l l.l .l. .l. ... i.e. addl. intl. n.d. Jr.
13  Jan. Ill. a.k.a. N.J. Ind. anon. asst. N.H. Okla.
14  No. et al. i.e. I did. He is not. Ian ate. I sat.
15  J. L. Harris is in Okla. or Ill. for addl. tasks.
```

Skillbuilding

E. MINIMUM-CHANGE PRACTICE

```
16  sink link fink find kind kink link rink rind kind
17  file tile till kill sill silk silt lilt tilt tint
18  fail tail sail said laid lair hair hail nail rail

19  sill kill fill fall Falk talk tall Hall Hill Jill
20  list fist fish dish dash Nash Nast fast last Lash
21  Jane Lane Kane Kant rant rent Lent lint tint hint
```

F. NEW-KEY REVIEW

I
LEFT SHIFT
.
I LEFT SHIFT .

```
22  idiot initial kiddie raisin finish initiate if in
23  John Hall Lisa Jane Olaf Jill Joan Lois Joel Koto
24  H. I. J. K. L. N. O. n.d. Jr. i.e. No. Jan. asst.
25  Ida J. Harris; Indira K. Little; Lillian N. Iris;
```

G. SENTENCES

26 Neither Iris L. Harris nor Ida N. Jones is there.
27 In Orlando he had the aid of Nikita to finish it.
28 Lillian H. Little did not hide it inside the tin.
29 Inlaid tiles are on Oak Lane for Kristina to see.

    1 | 2 | 3 | 4 | 5 | 6 | 7 | 8 | 9 | 10

H. 1-MINUTE TIMED WRITING

Take two 1-minute timed writings.

 Goal: At least 13wpm/1′/3e

30 Lisa N. Jenkins had dined in Oakland. Lois had   10
31 to find her there.   13

    1 | 2 | 3 | 4 | 5 | 6 | 7 | 8 | 9 | 10

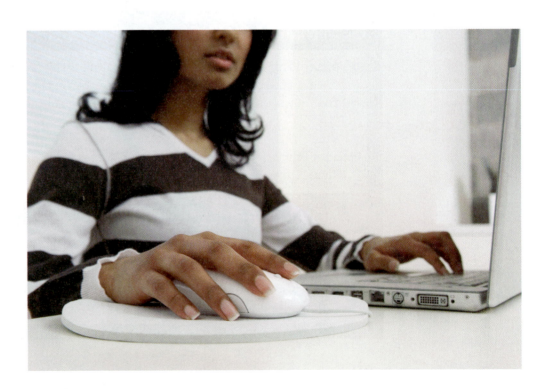

Enrichment • Lesson 4

Type each line 2 times.

| Left Shift
.

| Left Shift
.

| Left Shift
.

| Left Shift .
| Left Shift .
| Left Shift .

A. NEW-KEY REINFORCEMENT

1 aid air din fir fit hit ilk ink inn ire iris this
2 Joe Kid Les Ian Ned Ida Noe Lil Jon Ira Kent John
3 a.k.a. addl. Okla. N.J. N.H. n.d. intl. asst. Jr.

4 lid ail did fit tin tie sin oil irk if it is in I
5 Lee Joe Ida Ina Joel Leo John Koto Olaf I. N. Jai
6 anon. et al. i.e. Ill. Ind. Jan. n.d. No. Ltd. H.

7 idea iris nail dial edit into file sink soil hint
8 Jill Lisa Nina Lois Hall Jane Joel Hart Olaf Joan
9 I. J. K. L. N. O. Joe. H. Nie; Leo K. Kale; L. J.

10 Keith N. Harris; Irene I. Olson; Katie O. Hinder;
11 Hilario I. Oleans; Kristen N. Jai; Leila N. Jain;
12 Keiko O. Ikeda; Ida H. Jenkins; Lillie N. Little;

Type each line 2 times.

B. SHORT PHRASES

13 that diet soda; an inlaid tile; finish the tasks;
14 tried to aid her; a dirt floor; I. I. Johnson Jr.
15 initial on the fifth line; it is OK; hire Ida Li;

16 a fair deal; a kosher deli; kiss the thin kiddie;
17 other ideas; tidied the dens; inside this raisin;
18 H. and I. and J. and K. and L. and N. and O.; OK;

Type each line 2 times.

C. SENTENCES

19 Olla needs to freshen the tired look of the nook.
20 Keith did not find the softened toast in the tin.
21 I think either N.H. or N.J. is OK for the hotels.

22 Leo Jones insisted on the three lessons in there.
23 Iris Joel had fished here and had liked it a lot.
24 Leila sifted and stirred the soil that needed it.

25 Lois N. Henderson is a dentist there in Lakeland.
26 Ina has to attend the initial session in Oakland.
27 Jill had not finished the task so I assisted her.

New Keys

5

Goals

- Touch-type the B, U, and C keys.
- Type at least 14wpm/1′/3e.

A. WARMUP

learned keys   1   Jake Nort had not led a fast life; he had rested.

concentration   2   Hadassah Henderson Jonathan Jeanette Leonardo Lee

easy   3   Keith Idle and Henri did tie a fish to the dials.

New Keys

B. THE B KEY

Keep the A finger at home as you reach for B.

Use the F finger.

4   fff fbf fbf bfb bfb bbb label ebbs tidbits rebels

5   offbeat bib inkblot alb inbred job orb hotbed lab

6   babes barbs bobbin blab babble blob bobbed bobble

7   His best baseball and bat are near a blond table.

C. THE U KEY

Keep the Sem finger at home as you reach for U.

Use the J finger.

8   jjj juj juj uju uju uuu tau but dun euro fun huts

9   radius jut kudos flu nut out run sub tub flu aunt

10   luaus lulu tutus dufus undue usual bureau unusual

11   Kudos to Luke for the debut of his book on burns.

D. THE C KEY

Keep the A finger at home as you reach for C.

Use the D finger.

12   ddd dcd dcd cdc cdc ccc aces bobcat occur redcoat

13   deck ashcan ice bookcase talc inch dock arc discs

14   etch duck etch buck doc arc chic cacti cubic cock

15   Our church choirs can cancel our recitals on cue.

Skillbuilding

E. MINIMUM-CHANGE PRACTICE

16 buck luck lock rock rack race lace late Kate Kane
17 cube tube tune tone tine tint hint hind hand hard
18 curb carb cart dart dark lark Lars bars cars care

19 bout boat coat coal foal foul four tour hour sour
20 cure cute lute lube tube tune tone hone hose nose
21 bare barn bard lard lord cord curd card hard hark

F. NEW-KEY REVIEW

B
U
C
B U C

22 baker banjo bark basin bribe brake bond boast bit
23 unit uke urn use fuel hulk sun tusk house duo sub
24 cab chat carol chili check church condo cell aces
25 cub buck curb scuba scrub biscuit cubicle cutback

G. SENTENCES

26 Joe and Lee think the surf and turf is delicious.
27 Kent said a bunch of bandits robbed a local bank.
28 Unit costs of the industrial knob are reasonable.
29 Nine of the jurors can render the decisions soon.

H. 1-MINUTE TIMED WRITING

Take two 1-minute timed
writings.

Goal: At least
14wpm/1'/3e

30 Her old brick condo near Lake Huron has just the   10
31 features Luis needed.   14
    1 | 2 | 3 | 4 | 5 | 6 | 7 | 8 | 9 | 10

Enrichment • Lesson 5

A. NEW-KEY REINFORCEMENT

B 1 bans bar bud rib fib bad bin bat bee job ebb labs
U 2 dub jut run rubs sue but bud ours dud bun fur due
C 3 act can aces cab cat cod cot cad ice con cuts cue

B 4 babe debt bank able book snub blob boat both stab
U 5 euro haul Luke hush loud feud cure sour foul husk
C 6 ache duck cent each Nick cake inch fact lack care

B 7 abode board tribe boast beret burros brake rabbis
U 8 fruits audit crush abuse routes found ruler adult
C 9 catch crude acute clicks cross check chosen black

B U C 10 because buck butcher cube curb scuba subject club
B U C 11 cutback cubic cherub bucket biscuit bounce buckle
B U C 12 cubicle obscure brunch cubs curable scrub bunches

B. SHORT PHRASES

13 a brisk canter; because of us; a bunch of bananas
14 a rude subject; a tribe of Indians; choke a horse
15 the color of chalk; adults and children; a cherub

16 the noble cause; cost a fortune; a crust of bread
17 a unit of blood, a bleak outlook; hurt just a bit
18 black belt in karate; blue suede shoes; fur coats

C. SENTENCES

19 Little obscure cutbacks did not affect their job.
20 Her old cubicle is near the corner of the office.
21 Jack had a bacon biscuit and cola for his brunch.

22 Jed beat the odds because the disease is curable.
23 Haul the bucket of nuts and bolts to the shelter.
24 Look for the subject of the broken link to arise.

25 Just fill in the blank line and send it all back.
26 His adobe house near our house has not been sold.
27 One black briefcase is on the bureau in the hall.

Keyboarding: The Alphabet

New Keys

Goals

- Touch-type the RIGHT SHIFT, W, and M keys.
- Type at least 15wpm/1'/3e.

A. WARMUP

learned keys	1	Her brief research could land Kate her first job.
concentration	2	abundance incurable obstructs bucketful clubhouse
speed	3	Keith has both an auto and a bus but is not rich.

New Keys

Use the Sem finger.

B. THE RIGHT [SHIFT] KEY

To capitalize letters on the left half of the keyboard:

1. With the J finger at home, press and hold down the RIGHT SHIFT key with the Sem finger.
2. Press the letter key to be capitalized.
3. Immediately release the RIGHT SHIFT key and return fingers to the home-row position.

    4   ;;; A;; S;; D;; F;; Ali Sol Don Fido Eli Todd Ron
    5   Burr Cora Bo Che Alan Dick Sue Dot Chris Rob Ruth
    6   Bob Ana Don Blake Diane Bud Ann Rufus Rod Al Elon
    7   Diane S. Dickens likes the East Coast of Florida.

Use the S finger.

C. THE [W] KEY

    8   sss sws sws wsw wsw www bawls cobwebs dwarf fewer
    9   thwart kiwi awkward bulwark unwed owe Darwin swab
   10   two Kuwait bowwow owls news laws ewe haw how owns
   11   Wanda went to the World Wide Web for the lowdown.

Use the J finger.

D. THE KEY

12 jjj jmj jmj mjm mjm mmm am submit acme admit hems
13 Hoffman ohm him Hackman calm ammo unmet moms arms
14 ism Batman hums Newman Emma maim memos mime madam
15 Mamie can make a commitment to the mammal museum.

Skillbuilding

E. WORD BUILDING

16 A Al Ala Alan; D Do Don; R Ru Rut Ruth; m mu mum;
17 m mo mow; w wa war warm; M Ma Mac; w wh who whom;
18 m ma mai maim; e el elm; a ar arm; M Ma Mam Mama;

19 a ai aim; o oh ohm; s sw swa swam; T To Tod Todd;
20 M Mo Mom; w wh who whom; w wo wor worm; w wa war;
21 E Em Emm Emma; m ma mar; w wa war warm; M Mi Mia;

F. NEW-KEY REVIEW

RIGHT SHIFT   22 Adam Walt Carl Emma Rick Taft Ward Tate Rita Eric
W   23 news wire dawn owls wish awes dews town wake wolf
M   24 mill name demo home mast mind dime mini omen dome

RIGHT SHIFT   25 Will Aida Chad Erie Rome Tara Tess Ross Ewan Weir
W   26 wood twin bows bowl slaw know webs wool flaw claw
M   27 item mate mint room stem miss jamb dorm ammo lamb

RIGHT SHIFT   28 Alan Alma Webb Fern Ruhr Thad West Theo Fiji Cuba
W   29 fowl stew work stow whom crew wife crow wall wind
M   30 math mist team lima drum arms limo mean term monk

G. 1-MINUTE TIMED WRITING

Take two 1-minute timed writings. Press ENTER only at the end of line 32.

Goal: At least 15wpm/1'/3e

31 Then Barbra just left them at the house since the   10
32 men and women were awake.   15

    1 | 2 | 3 | 4 | 5 | 6 | 7 | 8 | 9 | 10

Enrichment • Lesson 6

Type each line 2 times.

RIGHT SHIFT
W
M

RIGHT SHIFT
W
M

RIGHT SHIFT
W
M

RIGHT SHIFT W M
RIGHT SHIFT W M
RIGHT SHIFT W M

Type each line 2 times.

A. NEW-KEY REINFORCEMENT

1 Anne Arab Dade Finn Sara Thor Tito Saul Fisk Dale
2 arrow crown dews word watch awe water towel award
3 aim number him album human dam alumni amend dream

4 Asia Wolf Baja Dana Ford Scot Toto Will Seth Demi
5 owner we row drawl bow elbow brawl towel who when
6 sum mob me arm elm macro aroma female month woman

7 Barb Bess Dodd Adam Shaw Finn Dean Shea Webb Earl
8 jewel waist straw law swine crowd war allow drown
9 man method Ms. mud crime hum admit am amuse armed

10 Awesome Somehow Swims Warmer Winsome Wisdom Warms
11 Twosome Swami Warmed Cutworm Dimwit Swarm Walkman
12 Wartime Snowman Woman Welcomes Swimmer Whom Women

B. SHIFT KEY PRACTICE

13 Jack Neal Shea Nell Jane Alan Dodd Jean Nero Jeff
14 Earl Alma Anne Ella Emil Thad Theo Emma Oahu Thor
15 Tito Kane Kate Kent Fiji Bill Finn Ural Bonn Fisk

16 Otto Urdu Ford Owen Uris Utah Fuji Laos Utes Rice
17 Hank Hans Rick Rita Hera Herb Mack Mali Chad Chen
18 Marc Wild Will Mari Cook Cuba Matt Wolf Wood Mead

C. SENTENCES

19 Mr. Taft admitted that his claim was turned down.
20 Ms. Wu used her Web cam and also browsed the Web.
21 Blossoms bloom when it rains twice in four weeks.
22 I wasted much time when I was in town last month.

D. PARAGRAPH TYPING

Type each paragraph 2 times, letting word wrap end each line for you.

23 Ms. Cara Fields listed Milwaukee Tech as her alma   10
24 mater on her resume. I think that she majored in   20
25 business administration and minored in science.   29

26 We rode in a sleek limousine from the hotel to   9
27 Jackson Hole and ate dinner at the Camelback   19
28 Restaurant. We both ordered seafood and wine.   28

29 The newest member of our firm is Ms. Caroline K.   10
30 Smith; she will start work tomorrow as our labor   20
31 relations assistant and will work in New Hall.   29

     1 | 2 | 3 | 4 | 5 | 6 | 7 | 8 | 9 | 10

New Keys

Goals

- Touch-type the X, P, and Tab keys.
- Type at least 16wpm/1'/3e.

A. WARMUP

learned keys	1	Ask Al and Jan to be in the room with Ms. Fuchs.
alternate hand	2	rituals socials downtown anthems dorms authentic
speed	3	Chris has to make an enamel dish for the mantel.

New Keys

Use the S finger.

B. THE X KEY

4 sss sxs sxs xsx xsx xxx ax ox fox box tax fix mix
5 axis jinx crux exam taxi exit hoax text coax flex
6 next lax inbox index sexism exhaust exists deluxe
7 The next wax exhibit will excite the anxious fox.

Use the Sem finger.

C. THE P KEY

8   ;;; ;p; ;p; p;p p;p ppp pi ape subplot mudpie pep
9   ashpit pips inkpad helps imps input opt apps warp
10 spa output up cowpea pa Alp top apes cap map cops
11 Pat put up a pinup that he ripped from the paper.

Use the A finger.

D. THE TAB KEY

The Tab key is used to indent paragraphs 0.5 inch. As shown on the next page, you can also align words in columns by pressing the Tab key.

Keep your F finger in home-row position as you quickly press the Tab key, and return your A finger to home-row position immediately after you press the Tab key.

Press TAB when you see the → symbol.

12	aah→	abs→	ace→	act→	add→	ado→	ads→	aft→	aha
13	aid→	ail→	aim→	air→	ale→	all→	alt→	amp→	and
14	ant→	ape→	app→	apt→	arc→	are→	ark→	arm→	art
15	ash→	ask→	asp→	ate→	auk→	awe→	awl→	awn→	axe

Skillbuilding

E. WORD BUILDING

```
16  p pr pro prop; b bo box; p pa pac pack; s se sex;
17  p pa pad; e ex exa exam; p pe pep; e ex exi exit;
18  f fo fox; p pi pin pint; p pa par part; w wa wax;

19  j ji jin jinx; r ra rap; p pi pin; t te tex text;
20  p po por port; f fi fix; p pl pla plan; m mi mix;
21  o op opt; f fl fle flex; p pu put; c co coa coax;
```

F. NEW-KEY REVIEW

X	22	box exile apex exec minx fox boxers ox inbox flux
P	23	pack dope pair ripe pest wipe plan sped jeep shop
TAB	24	is→ no→ on→ to→ we→ in→ he→ be→ at
X	25	expo wax next sax axed excess oxen maxi axle taxi
P	26	pain spam park upon pile bump plot apex camp whip
TAB	27	ad→ as→ do→ hi→ if→ it→ of→ or→ up
X	28	excuse tax expense reflex textbook except mailbox
P	29	palm hope part stop pine cope poem kept wrap deep
TAB	30	us→ so→ oh→ me→ id→ ho→ ha→ an→ am

G. 1-MINUTE TIMED WRITING

Take two 1-minute timed writings. Press ENTER only at the end of line 32.

 Goal: At least 16wpm/1′/3e

Note: The word counts in this book credit you with 1 stroke for each paragraph indention in a timed writing. The timed writing starts when you press the TAB key.

| 31 | Just ask the six of them to wait in place | 9 |
| 32 | for Brenda to complete that last job. | 16 |

   1 | 2 | 3 | 4 | 5 | 6 | 7 | 8 | 9 | 10

Enrichment • Lesson 7

A. NEW-KEY REINFORCEMENT

Type each line 2 times.

X
P
TAB

1 execute fixture exercise excuse mailbox exert tax
2 paper piper pauper prop pompom peep pope pulp pop
3 at→ is→ ho→ on→ to→ up→ in→ he→ be

X
P
TAB

4 lax maximum annex exception inexact examine extra
5 people pulpit pupil puppies pepper pump pinup opt
6 an→ as→ do→ hi→ if→ it→ of→ or→ we

X
P
TAB

7 example exclude experience except experts excuses
8 puppet pipe poplar up slipup rapper supper tiptop
9 us→ no→ so→ oh→ me→ id→ ha→ ad→ am

X, P, TAB
X, P, TAB
X, P, TAB

10 max→ mix→ cop→ tax→ pit→ pro→ pox→ hip→ lap
11 ape→ pad→ box→ cap→ fix→ pod→ cup→ tip→ rap
12 pep→ lax→ pet→ sip→ fox→ pun→ sax→ map→ wax

B. CORRESPONDING-FINGER PRACTICE

Type each line 2 times.

A and Sem
S and L
W and O

13 abase; fatal; axial; afar; area; ahead; ajar; Al;
14 else slap lets self list oils also lose last slam
15 word blow down owes flow show know whom crow work

D and K
E and I
R and U

16 dark dike eked kind deck kids disk skid desk duck
17 edit line bite nice bike side ripe cite tire deli
18 rule true burn sour four rule ours curb sure hour

C. SENTENCES

19 Paul was anxious to drop off the box of old maps.
20 The extra income Pam earned is exempt from taxes.
21 People expect excellent results on their laptops.
22 Please exit the plane and step on the purple box.

D. PARAGRAPH TYPING

Type each paragraph
2 times.

23   Just a few taxis were on the roads on that   9
24 black and cold late afternoon. I needed a map to   19
25 find the street to the second job consultation.   28

26   Blake used his own expertise to prepare the   9
27 report on the success of the annual fall flower   19
28 show. He reported that the show was a major hit.   28

29   We mixed up the names in random order so   8
30 that no one could know when he or she would be   18
31 called on to strum the banjo for the audience.   27

  1 | 2 | 3 | 4 | 5 | 6 | 7 | 8 | 9 | 10

New Keys

Goals

- Touch-type the Q, Comma, and G keys.
- Type at least 17wpm/1'/3e.

A. WARMUP

learned keys   1   Ned Black spotted the four women at that jukebox.

one hand   2   best jump card noun debt mink base pump read upon

speed   3   Six of their chaps spent their profit in Orlando.

New Keys

Use the A finger.

B. THE Q KEY

4   aaa aqa aqa qaq qaq qqq aquas acquit equals pique

5   kumquat banquet croquet torque squad bouquet quip

6   quad quid pique quaff equip quiet quit quack quod

7   Quin quoted from his unique request for a quorum.

Use the K finger.

C. THE , KEY

Space 1 time after a comma (but not before). However, do not space after a punctuation mark or word that ends a line; instead, immediately press ENTER.

8   kkk k,k k,k ,k, ,k, ,,, ma, cab, arc, ad, be, of,

9   oh, ask, Al, am, pin, too, up, ore, is, eat, emu,

10   ho, box; Al, Bo, Ed, Jo, Di, or I; a, b, c, or d;

11   Li, Ed, and I wrote, proofread, and formatted it.

Use the F finger.

D. THE G KEY

12   fff fgf fgf gfg gfg ggg ages edge begs afghan egg

13   dig ginkgo alga Eng cog popgun urge disgust outgo

14   bug gag gang gouge aging gongs gauge gorged going

15   Greg Rigg is going to see ping pong in Hong Kong.

Skillbuilding

E. BACKSPACE-KEY PRACTICE

Type each word as shown until you reach the backspace sign (←). Then backspace 1 time and replace the previously typed character with the one shown; for example, in line 16, *gale* becomes *gall*.

16	gale←l at←n gag←p had←m he←i bad←n if←n ad←h or←n
17	gut←n mask←h big←n me←u her←m dire←k slaw←p age←o
18	us←p die←m as←n box←o of←h kit←n hut←m mad←n it←n

F. NEW-KEY REVIEW

Q 19 banquet quotas squalor square quote quail bouquet
, 20 ago, rub, can, pop, jag, lax, men, owe, air, fun,
G 21 blog sign gold sing drag edge good wing gain high

Q 22 liquid quid request squid quark queen clique quit
, 23 one, lag, ton, aid, sex, two, ear, jar, use, new,
G 24 logo rage cage glad ring huge guru long urge gate

Q 25 croquet quarrel sequel quilt quarter equator quip
, 26 own, aim, ten, let, cap, its, our, ask, kin, bad,
G 27 goal king glow golf wage drug grow page grew gift

G. SENTENCES

28 Gus was quick to go to Quebec, Canada, in August.
29 He began to quarrel, argue, and quibble about it.
30 Gosh, Peg sighed at the quietness at the equator.

31 Bring the unique graph, ledger, and plaques here.
32 Grace brought a gold liqueur to the golf banquet.
33 Megan quit using that croquet equipment long ago.

H. 1-MINUTE TIMED WRITING

Take two 1-minute timed writings.

Goal: At least 17wpm/1'/3e

34	Just ask Phil to quit making that big racket	9
35	and, in addition, to fix the wood pipe.	17

  1 | 2 | 3 | 4 | 5 | 6 | 7 | 8 | 9 | 10

Enrichment • Lesson 8

Type each line 2 times.

A. NEW-KEY REINFORCEMENT

Q
1 equals quirk squid quote quest squat unique quick
,
2 ajar, jeeps, jump, joke, joins, jerk, junk, just,
G
3 agents range align cargo right guides judge globe

Q
4 squad quits equip quads liquid quiet square quota
,
5 book, kick, kind, like, risks, pack, neck, keeps,
G
6 grants light fight angles grasp great dough agree

Q
7 quarts quilt squab queen quips squeal quail quite
,
8 apex, oxen, taxi, coax, jinx, axles, text, exams,
G
9 gains begins images grade might doing being greed

B. VERTICAL REACHES

Type each line 2 times.

Up Reaches
10 at atlas match later plate water batch fatal late
11 dr drums draft drift drawn drain drama dress drab
12 ju jumps juror junks jumbo julep judge juice just

Down Reaches
13 ca cadet cable cabin camel cameo cards carts cash
14 nk trunk drink prank rinks brink drank crank sink
15 ba baked batch badge bagel banjo barge basis bank

C. ROW PRACTICE

Type each line 2 times.

Top Row
16 We were to take our trucks to Pete at the window.
17 There were two tired people at the hut in Warsaw.
18 Please write to their home to tell Tom in a week.

Home Row
19 Jake asked his dad for small red flags in Dallas.
20 She is glad he added a dash of salt to the salad.
21 Dale said she sold her glasses at that fall sale.

Bottom Row
22 He can come to the annex in Macon to meet Maxine.
23 Their maximum number from Mexico can come to box.
24 Mabel Baxter connected with the Nixons in Benson.

New Keys

Goals

- Touch-type the V, Y, and Z keys.
- Type at least 18wpm/1'/3e.

A. WARMUP

learned keys   1 The quick boxing warden jumped and flipped sides.
one hand   2 were lion card hump base join feat hook axes hulk
speed   3 A half bushel of corn was thrown to the big duck.

New Keys

Use the F
finger.

B. THE V KEY

4 fff fvf fvf vfv vfv vvv avows obvious advice even
5 five salve Humvee anvil doves curved outvoted luv
6 vie event Van vat vie vexes vim vet vow via vivid
7 Eva and Vi visited the vast civic event in Provo.

Use the J
finger.

C. THE Y KEY

8 jjj jyj jyj yjy yjy yyy aye by icy dyes eyes defy
9 gym shy sky fly my any boys spy cry busy sty guys
10 ivy dewy sexy buy guy joy pay way yes yew you yet
11 Kelly may buy the forty gray kayaks for the navy.

Use the A
finger.

D. THE Z KEY

12 aaa aza aza zaz zaz zzz daze subzero czar adz fez
13 zigzagged biz unzip cozy ditz ouzo frowzy analyze
14 buzz pizzazz fuzzy jazz abuzz zit gaze razzmatazz
15 Zeke rented a cozy Mazda from Hertz in the plaza.

Skillbuilding

E. SPACE BAR PRACTICE

16 a b c d e f g h i j k l m n o p q r s t u v w xyz
17 an as be by go in is it me no of or to we ad Al I
18 ah am at do he hi but id if ma my on so up us for

19 Do not go to Ada or Ida for work every day or so.
20 I am sure he can go with you if he has some time.
21 He is to be at the car by the time you get there.

F. NEW-KEY REVIEW

V   22 cove gave vane love vein ever verb vast avow oven
Y   23 army ally city many copy navy gray away yell only
Z   24 buzz whiz gaze quiz zinc fez zeal fizzy zany daze

V   25 dove five vain diva over vest have vote vent move
Y   26 clay envy baby type Tony hype pays myth pony easy
Z   27 lazy ooze zips zero size daze Hazel zoo zoom jazz

V   28 five save even view dive veto void live vine avid
Y   29 busy lady play typo body holy defy nosy vary boxy
Z   30 gaze zest hazy cozy zone zaps ziti haze wiz dozen

G. SENTENCES

31 Hazel gave Zeke some advice on verbs and adverbs.
32 You really need to try out your new frozen pizza.
33 Forty or fifty of you have yet to give any money.

34 I eyed the dazzling piece made of topaz and onyx.
35 You have to visit my newest exhibit in Las Vegas.
36 Zelda vividly gazed at the ritzy piazza in Provo.

H. 1-MINUTE TIMED WRITING

Take two 1-minute timed writings.

 Goal: At least 18wpm/1'/3e

37   David quickly spotted those four old women   9
38 who were just dozing over in the new jury box.   18

   1 | 2 | 3 | 4 | 5 | 6 | 7 | 8 | 9 | 10

Enrichment • Lesson 9

Type each line 2 times.

A. NEW-KEY REINFORCEMENT

V
Y
Z

1 cover value level movie never drive advice clever
2 bylaw entry money every angry needy anyway typify
3 craze seize klutz unzip dizzy zesty zealot wizard

V
Y
Z

4 grave valid avoid solve rival voice device avenue
5 lucky annoy maybe decay imply dirty heyday yearly
6 pizza dozen razor blaze ritzy hazel guzzle sizzle

V
Y
Z

7 cover prove never event leave civic behave divide
8 decoy hurry carry glory diary empty byways mayday
9 ozone prize amaze zebra gauze froze puzzle nozzle

B. COMMON LETTER COMBINATIONS

Type each line 2 times.

Word Beginnings

10 comply comedy combat coming common commit compels
11 forget forbid forced forest formal former formats
12 permit perils peruse perish period person peruses
13 subtle submit subdue subtly suburb sublet subways

Word Endings

14 enable liable nimble edible doable usable jumbles
15 joyful fitful useful armful sinful lawful boxfuls
16 caring typing losing hiring seeing having rulings
17 action option notion vision region nation motions

C. PARAGRAPH TYPING

Type each paragraph 2 times.

18   Back in July, we were authorized to acquire   9
19 five boxes of green letterhead stationery. That   19
20 amount should be ample for the entire year.   27

21   Kate took a quick jet to Phoenix, Arizona,   9
22 to enjoy the weather and to have time to begin   19
23 fall duties with the Girl Scouts of America.   27

24   Please just fix the copier quickly so that   9
25 we can minimize our downtime and get productivity   19
26 back in shape. We have to meet our monthly quota.   29

   1 | 2 | 3 | 4 | 5 | 6 | 7 | 8 | 9 | 10

Review

Goals

- Reinforce key reaches.
- Type at least 19wpm/1'/3e.

A. WARMUP

alphabet	1	Five boxing wizards jumped quickly into the ring.
shift keys	2	Mr. Ho and Ms. Yu let Al, Bo, Ed, Jo, and Ty eat.
speed	3	Dick may air the new anthem on the eighth of May.

Skillbuilding

B. REVIEW: A–D

4 alpaca acacia banana cabana armada azalea pajamas
5 Bob bobbin babble bubble blubber bumblebee bobble
6 Cy cyclic concentric eclectic climactic eccentric
7 do added daddy addled nodded doodad dodged kidded

C. REVIEW: E–H

8 epees eerie emcees geese levee peeve tepee beeper
9 fisticuffs fluffy foodstuff liftoff falloff fluff
10 groggy eggnog giggle baggage gauging digging gigs
11 hitchhike high hashish hashes highlight Chihuahua

D. REVIEW: I–L

12 idiotic bikini if illicit inhibit initial militia
13 jobs jog jam jar jaws jay jet jig jut jog jot joy
14 kick kinky kook knock key kayak khaki kiosk knack
15 lull locally fulfill loyally lullaby ill billfold

E. REVIEW: M–P

16 mommy mammal mummy mammoth medium maximum minimum
17 nanny cannon inning antenna canning pennant ninny
18 outdoor outlook offshoot option onlooker orthodox
19 peppy poppy puppies pepper popped puppets propped

F. REVIEW: Q–T

20 quip aqua equal quay quid equip quip quit Quakers
21 rarer errors horror mirror terror arrears barrier
22 sass sissy Swiss assess says assets assist senses
23 tattoo attest tattle attempt tilt attract statute

G. REVIEW: U–X

24 unusual gurus usurious luau luxurious sunup undue
25 valve viva savvy verve vivid evolve revive velvet
26 widows willow window awkward swallow wows walkway
27 ax ox box fix fox hex lax mix nix sax sex tax tux

H. REVIEW: Y–Z, COMMA, PERIOD

28 yearly byway gypsy pygmy shyly anyway payday your
29 zigzag buzz pizzazz jazz fuzzy pizza buzzer zesty
30 am, we, in, is up, an, to, be, no, do, my, go, it
31 Mr. Ms. Dr. Mrs. Esq. Inc. pp. Nos. Wed. Oct. Pa.

I. 1-MINUTE TIMED WRITING

Take two 1-minute timed writings.

Goal: At least 19wpm/1'/3e

32   Back in June, we delivered oxygen equipment   9
33 of odd sizes to the new hospital near Ogden,   18
34 Utah.   19

   1 | 2 | 3 | 4 | 5 | 6 | 7 | 8 | 9 | 10

Enrichment • Lesson 10

Type each line 2 times.

A. REVIEW: A–E

1 Allan asked Alma Adams to fly to Alaska and Asia.
2 Both Barbara and Robb bought a rubber basketball.
3 Carly can accept a classic car at a Cairo clinic.
4 Dade suddenly dined in the dark diner in Detroit.
5 Reeves said Eddie edited the entire eleven texts.

Type each line 2 times.

B. REVIEW: F–J

6 Five friars focused on the four offensive fables.
7 George gave the bag of green grapes to Gina Gaye.
8 Haughty Hugh hoped Hal had helped Seth with this.
9 Iris liked to pickle pickles in the acidic brine.
10 Jo Jones joined a junior jogging team in pajamas.

Type each line 2 times.

C. REVIEW: K–O

11 Ken kept a sleek kayak for the ski trek to Akron.
12 Luella played a well-planned ball game in Lowell.
13 I made more money on many markups of the pompoms.
14 Ned and Ginny knew ten men in a main dining room.
15 Opal Orr opened four boxes of oranges at the zoo.

Type each line 2 times.

D. REVIEW: P–T

16 Pat paid to park the plane at the pump in Pompey.
17 Quincy quickly quit his quarterly quiz in Quebec.
18 Robin carried four rare rulers into that library.
19 Sam signed, sealed, and sent six leases to Jesse.
20 Matt caught the little trout near Twelfth Street.

Type each line 2 times.

E. REVIEW: U–Z

21 Uncle Rubin urged Judy to go see a guru in Utica.
22 Vivian moved to veto five voice votes in Ventura.
23 Walt waited while Wilma went to Watts for a week.
24 Alexi mixed sixty extra extracts exactly as told.
25 Yes, your young son plays cymbals anyway at Yale.
26 Liza saw the zany zebras zigzag in the Ozark zoo.

1 | 2 | 3 | 4 | 5 | 6 | 7 | 8 | 9 | 10

Keyboarding: Numbers and Symbols

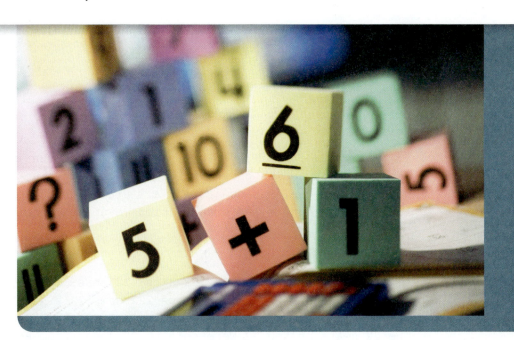

New Keys

Goals

- Touch-type the -, 2, and 9 keys.
- Type at least 19wpm/2'/5e.

A. WARMUP

alphabet | 1 | Big July earthquakes confounded the zany experimental vows.
concentration | 2 | uncommunicativeness departmentalization electrocardiography
easy | 3 | It is the duty of the busy ensigns to dismantle the panels.

New Keys

B. THE ▮ KEY

Keep the J finger in home-row position.

Use the Sem finger.

Do not space before or after a hyphen.

4 ;;; ;p; ;-; ;-; -;- -;- --- no-no to-do mix-up run-in X-ray
5 pop-up sit-in add-on get-go set-to can-do U-turn up-to-date
6 Jo Dye-Lee, a well-to-do jack-of-all-trades, had a boo-boo.
7 Le-Sam is a shut-in who drank a pick-me-up from the get-go.

C. THE 2 KEY

Keep either the A or F finger in home-row position.

Use the S finger.

8   sss sws s2s s2s 2s2 2s2 222 22 sets; 22 seas; 2 sons; 2 men
9   222 suns 22 subs 222 sins 22 saps 222 saws 22 sips 222 sirs
10 He got 22 pens, 22 pads, 22 pencils, and 22 clips on May 2.
11 The 22 seats in Row 22 were sold to 22 coeds from Room 222.

D. THE 9 KEY

Keep the Sem finger in home-row position.

Use the L finger.

12 lll lol l9l l9l 9l9 9l9 999 9 laws; 99 lots; 9 lies; 9 laps
13 99 labs 9 keys 9,992 kits 299 leis 999 legs 99 logs 29 lips
14 She moved from 929 29th Street to 922 92nd Avenue on May 9.
15 On May 9, the 99 men and 29 women baked 9 pies and 9 cakes.

Skillbuilding

E. NEW-KEY REVIEW

16 29-22 majority; 99-92 lead at half-time; 929 one-way roads;
17 92 cave-ins; 99 walk-ins; 92 up-to-date items; 22 tune-ups;
18 299 sign-ups; 929 fill-in-the-blank questions; 99 push-ups;
19 929 look-alikes; 922 go-getters; 29 T-shirts; 292 boo-boos;

F. PROGRESSIVE PRACTICE: ALPHABET

Follow the GDP software directions for this exercise to improve keystroking accuracy.

G. TECHNIQUE PRACTICE: HYPHEN

Make a dash by typing two hyphens with no space before, between, or after (lines 21 and 24). Note: Microsoft Word (but not the GDP software) automatically converts two hyphens into a formatted dash (—).

20   Larry will go to the next tennis tournament. I am
21 positive that he--like Lane--will find the event to be a
22 first-class sports event. If he can go, I will get all of
23 us first-rate seats.
24   Larry--but not Ella--enjoys going to tournaments that
25 are always first-rate, first-class sporting events.

Take three 12-second timed writings on each line. The scale below the last line shows your wpm speed for a 12-second timed writing.

H. 12-SECOND SPEED SPRINTS

26 Jan owns a pair of old gowns and a new hat she got from me.
27 He may go with us to the giant dock down by the handy lake.
28 His civic goal for the city is for them to endow the chair.
29 I may make us one set of maps to aid us when we visit them.
`' ' ' ' 5 ' ' ' 10 ' ' ' 15 ' ' ' 20 ' ' ' 25 ' ' ' 30 ' ' ' 35 ' ' ' 40 ' ' ' 45 ' ' ' 50 ' ' ' 55 ' ' ' 60`

Take two 2-minute timed writings.

Goal: At least 19wpm/2'/5e

I. 2-MINUTE TIMED WRITING

30   Zachary just paid for six seats and quit because he   11
31 could not get the views he required near the middle of the   22
32 field. In August he thinks he may go to the ticket office   34
33 to purchase tickets.   38
`   1  |  2  |  3  |  4  |  5  |  6  |  7  |  8  |  9  |  10  |  11  |  12`

Enrichment • Lesson 11

Type each line 2 times.

A. NEW-KEY REINFORCEMENT

1 29-92 99-22 92-29 22-99 99-92 22-92 22-29 29-99 22-92 99-29
2 99-29 29-92 92-29 22-99 99-22 99-92 22-92 29-99 22-92 22-29
3 99-22 29-92 99-92 22-92 92-29 22-99 22-92 99-29 22-29 29-99

4 99 also-rans; 29 set-asides; 92 cure-alls; 29 two-by-fours;
5 92 free-for-alls; 29 do-it-yourselfers; 22 merry-go-rounds;
6 292 look-alikes; 929 flip-flops; 292 I-beams; 922 A-frames;

7 She had 92 pens, 29 pads, 99 pencils, 29 clips and 2 notes.
8 To dry-clean the 92 suits, use the 229 high-pressure hoses.
9 Only 22 off-the-record comments were heard from 292 people.

10 The 29 high-ranking men had to attend 22 black-tie affairs.
11 Over 99 part-time jobs were posted at the all-day job fair.
12 Use a 92-29 ratio in the 9-liter container on September 29.

B. ROW PRACTICE

Type each line 2 times.

Top Row

13 uproot Peter treetop typewriter witty purity quieter tiptoe
14 equity Europe prettier teeter quitter troop tutor write wee

Home Row

15 Dallas salads flask gassed ladled leash saddle shall shakes
16 slash ladles flakes flesh safes Allah salsa faked jags fall

Bottom row

17 Amman anemic annexing numb Venice menace examine Mexico ebb
18 Nancy convey become combat machine convene inn Manchu comma

C. PARAGRAPH TYPING

Type each paragraph 2 times.

19   This note is just to confirm my order on the basis of 11
20 the prices you quoted me on the phone. Let me know when you 23
21 ship five dozen boxes of staples for my light-duty machine. 35

22   Yes, I will be quite pleased to have you see the house 11
23 next week on Wednesday, if convenient. I feel sure you will 23
24 think it is just as great a prize as your main residence.   34

25   If we are to have an exciting project of any real size 11
26 this year, we need a more vigorous chair for it, so I will 23
27 request that you serve. I hope that will be okay with you. 35

   1 | 2 | 3 | 4 | 5 | 6 | 7 | 8 | 9 | 10 | 11 | 12

New Keys

Goals

- Touch-type the 8, 5, and ' keys.
- Type at least 20wpm/2'/5e.

A. WARMUP

alphabet   1   Dr. Jekyll vowed to finish zapping the quixotic bumblebees.
one hand   2   secret hominy dew hip beasts nonunion edge monk staff nylon
easy   3   Pamela may use a kayak and map to come to the old city dam.

New Keys

Use the K finger.

B. THE 8 KEY

4   kkk kik k8k k8k 8k8 8k8 888 88 kits; 88 kegs; 8 kin; 8 keys
5   828 kites 982 kings 828 kids 988 kilts 828 knees 998 knocks
6   On July 28, I saw 88 cats, 82 dogs, 88 birds, and 28 foxes.
7   Of the 828 people, 28 were at the free-for-all on April 28.

Use the F finger.

C. THE 5 KEY

8   fff frf f5f f5f 5f5 5f5 555 5 fans; 5 fibs; 5 figs; 58 firs
9   5 figs 5 foes 5 tins 5 taps 55 tons 58 bays 85 bids 95 boys
10   Just call me at 585-555-5955 or on my cell at 585-555-5585.
11   The 585 men, 952 women, and 852 children left on August 25.

Use the Sem finger.

D. THE ' KEY

12   ;;; ;'; ;'; ';' ';' ''' he'd; I've; Al's; it's; she's; I'll
13   all's can't cont'd dep't gov't we'll you're I'll lad's we'd
14   It's too bad that he'd eaten Kate's dessert at Abe's Diner.
15   I'm sure he won't mind if Joe's car isn't in Alan's garage.

Skillbuilding

E. NEW-KEY REVIEW

16 Li's 85-58 lead; Moe's and Bob's 82 ads; I'll take 59 bids;
17 Bob's sister can't type 85 wpm; 8585 East 85th Lane; 89-58;
18 pages 558-582; call her at 858-555-8958; 558 part-time ads;
19 Invoice 88-595; Apt. 58-B; I'll be in Room 588-D; May 5-28;

F. SUSTAINED PRACTICE: CAPITALS

Take a 1-minute timed writing on the boxed paragraph to establish your base speed. Then take a 1-minute timed writing on the following paragraph. As soon as you equal or exceed your base speed on this paragraph, move to the next, more difficult paragraph.

20   Even though he was only about thirty years old, Jason   11
21 knew that it was not too soon to begin thinking about his   23
22 retirement. He learned that many things were involved.   33

23   Even without considering the uncertainty of social   10
24 security, Jason knew that he should plan his career moves,   22
25 so he opened a new Individual Retirement Account in May.   34

26   When he became aware that The Longman Company would   11
27 match his contributions, Jason asked the Payroll Department   23
28 to open a retirement account for him with the Coplin Group.   34

29   He also learned that The Longman Company retirement   11
30 plan and his Individual Retirement Plan are all deferred   22
31 savings. Then, Jason purchased New Venture Group mutuals.   33

    1 | 2 | 3 | 4 | 5 | 6 | 7 | 8 | 9 | 10 | 11 | 12

G. 2-MINUTE TIMED WRITING

Take two 2-minute timed writings.

Goal: At least 20wpm/2'/5e

32   Jack and Alex ordered six pizzas at a price that was   11
33 quite a bit lower than was the one they ordered yesterday.   23
34 They will order from the same place tomorrow for the party   34
35 they are wanting to provide.   40

    1 | 2 | 3 | 4 | 5 | 6 | 7 | 8 | 9 | 10 | 11 | 12

Enrichment • Lesson 12

Type each line 2 times.

A. NEW-KEY REINFORCEMENT

1 Mary's pages 58-85; John's 2,585 sales; 8858 O'Hara Street;
2 Call me at 858-555-8258; I'm in Room 859-B; Al's 58 errors;
3 cont'd on p. 285; 29,858 employees; 825 boys and 589 girls;

4 Pacers' final score of 89-82; May 28, '99; go to Room 2858;
5 Take I-85 to 92-B; Apt. 28-C; I'm 28.5 years old. He's out;
6 A tie score of 58-58; I'm out; the combination is 28-95-85;

Type each line 2 times.

B. ALPHABET PRACTICE

7 A Jack in the Box quickly varied its menu with fudge pizza.
8 Ban all foul toxic smog which can quickly jeopardize lives.
9 Five or six big jet planes zoomed quickly by the old tower.

10 Grumpy wizards made toxic brew for Jack and the evil queen.
11 If fog makes Max shiver, quickly zip down and buy a jacket.
12 Just keep examining every low bid quoted for zinc etchings.

13 Six crazy kings vowed to abolish my quite pitiful projects.
14 The jobs of waxing linoleum frequently peeved chintzy kids.
15 Weekly magazines request help for and by junior executives.

Type each paragraph 2 times.

C. PARAGRAPH TYPING

16   When I was at the gym today, I met Bill Saxon, the   10
17 former Jets quarterback. Bill is leaving football and needs 22
18 a job like the one we have open in hazardous control.   33

19   Folks do not want to live near airports because of   10
20 the extreme racket of the planes. The roar and whine as a   22
21 jet zooms by cannot be equaled by ten giant bulldozers.   33

22   If you accept this job, as we hope, please plan to   10
23 arrive next week so that we may zero in on those fashion   22
24 shows we have in Denver, Boston, Raleigh, and Quebec.   32

25   This is in response to your inquiry about Elizabeth   11
26 Jones. Ms. Jones worked for us for six years. We were sorry 23
27 to lose her to a company that gave her a larger salary.   34
        1 | 2 | 3 | 4 | 5 | 6 | 7 | 8 | 9 | 10 | 11 | 12

New Keys

13

Goals

- Touch-type the 4, 7, and : keys.
- Type at least 21wpm/2'/5e.

A. WARMUP

alphabet

practice: *f* and *g*

easy

1 Prized waxy jonquils choked the weeds in the big farm vats.
2 gruff fig finger flag frogs gift golf gulf goofs fogs flags
3 The new formal audit may be paid for by the downtown firms.

New Keys

Use the F finger.

B. THE 4 KEY

4 fff frf f4f f4f 4f4 4f4 444 4 fans; 4 fibs, 4 figs, 44 firs
5 4 figs 4 foes 4 tins 4 taps 44 tons 49 bays 45 bids 94 boys
6 The 44 men and 54 boys used 494 liters in 42 days on May 4.
7 Please add Items 428, 84, 944, 42, and 488 to Order 44-482.

Use the J finger.

C. THE 7 KEY

8 jjj juj j7j j7j 7j7 7j7 777 77 jugs; 7 jets; 7 jars; 7 jabs
9 74 jays 47 jobs 77 jots 74 hams 74 hats 47 hits 77 hugs 777
10 I bought Item 74 that weighs 47 pounds 7 ounces on June 27.
11 Allen covered pages 472-479, and Sue covered pages 277-789.

Use the Sem finger.

D. THE : KEY

The colon is the shift of the semicolon key. Do not space before or after a colon used with numbers. Space 1 time after a colon following a word except at the end of a line.

12 ;;; ;:; ;:; ;j: ;j: ::: 7:47 a.m.; 47:74 odds; Dear Mr. Ng:
13 Dr. Poole: Ms. Shu: Mr. Rose: Mrs. Tam: Dear Ed: Dear John:
14 Dear Johnny: Let's meet at 2:45 to discuss the 57:47 ratio.
15 Do not forget the Date:, To:, From:, and Subject: headings.

Skillbuilding

E. NEW-KEY REVIEW

16 The 47 managers had 74 tickets for the 4:47 game on May 24.
17 as follows: these people: this motion: here it is: Dear Jo:
18 Ed's 97-42 lead at 4:25 p.m.; pages 477-747; a 747 jet; Hi:

PRETEST » PRACTICE » POSTTEST

PRETEST
Take a 1-minute timed writing.

F. PRETEST: Common Letter Combinations

19   The condo committee was hoping the motion would not be   11
20 forced upon it, realizing that viable solutions ought to be   23
21 developed. It was forceful in seeking a period of time.   34
        1 | 2 | 3 | 4 | 5 | 6 | 7 | 8 | 9 | 10 | 11 | 12

PRACTICE
Speed Emphasis:
  If you made 2 or fewer errors on the Pretest, type each *individual* line 2 times.
Accuracy Emphasis:
  If you made 3 or more errors, type each *group* of lines (as though it were a paragraph) 2 times.

G. PRACTICE: Word Beginnings

22 for forum forge forced forgot formal forest foreign forerun
23 con conks conic consul confer convey convex contact concern
24 per perks peril person period perish permit percale percent

H. PRACTICE: Word Endings

25 ing tying hiking liking edging bowing hoping having nursing
26 ble fable pebble treble tumble viable dabble fumble fusible
27 ion union legion nation region motion potion option bastion

POSTTEST
Repeat the Pretest timed writing and compare performance.

Take two 2-minute timed writings.

I. POSTTEST: Common Letter Combinations

J. 2-MINUTE TIMED WRITING

28   Jim told Bev that they must keep the liquid oxygen   10
29 frozen so that it could be used by the new plant managers   22
30 tomorrow. The oxygen will then be moved quickly to its new   34
31 location by transport or rail on Tuesday.   42
        1 | 2 | 3 | 4 | 5 | 6 | 7 | 8 | 9 | 10 | 11 | 12

Goal: At least 21wpm/2'/5e

Enrichment • Lesson 13

Type each line 2 times.

A. NEW-KEY REINFORCEMENT

1 Jill bought 29 tickets for the 8:25 or 7:45 show on July 5.
2 Maxine called from 777-555-4278 or 777-555-4279 for Martin.
3 Jackson sold 85 tires, 94 air filters, and 247 oil filters.

4 Flight 4789B departed at 8:45 a.m. and arrived at 9:25 p.m.
5 I'm moving from 4529 East Rogers to 4725 East Eaton in May.
6 Only 247 men and 74 women attended the orientation at 8:45.

7 Ty: Flight 982 on the 747 jet departs at 2:45 on August 27.
8 On November 24-27, we were open from 7:45 a.m. to 9:45 p.m.
9 The 89 men then drove 774 miles on Route 47-B and Route 77.

Type each line 2 times.

B. SUBSTITUTION ERRORS

10 r-t hurt trot trite Trent treat tutor tort trust rotate try
11 m-n mend mine norm unman many naming morn manual hymn amend
12 o-i void silo olio Ohio into icon coin polio folio boil oil

13 a-s tasks visas sodas seams scans areas bases sales say has
14 s-d suds soda sides sheds dusts dudes dosed desks deeds sad
15 r-e rear refer every erred enter emery elder Erie eerie red

16 v-b visible brave bovine vibe livable above bevy bevel verb
17 w-e endow wade wee ewe wide dew wed elbow we where were wet
18 f-g flags fogs gruff goof gulf golf gift frog flag fang fig

Type each paragraph 2 times.

C. PARAGRAPH TYPING

19   The senator quietly voted to legalize marijuana but 11
20 drew the line at making it easily available to teens. He 22
21 also voted for new price controls on all foreign exports. 33

22   The anxious job applicant inquired about the size of 11
23 the firm's overseas business. He also wanted to know the 22
24 weekly sales of gas and other petroleum products to China. 34

25   I jotted down all the questions I wanted to ask the 11
26 five energy czars the next time I met with them. They were 23
27 in town for the big expo being held at the city arena. 33

28   Three weekly magazines requested help for the junior 11
29 executives in the software industry. By now, they must have 23
30 received many responses from their readers and subscribers. 35

    1 | 2 | 3 | 4 | 5 | 6 | 7 | 8 | 9 | 10 | 11 | 12

New Keys

Goals

- Touch-type the 6, 3, and / keys.
- Type at least 22wpm/2'/5e.

A. WARMUP

alphabet   1 Max did not become eloquent over a zany gift like jodhpurs.
frequent digraphs 2 te tee ate byte tell tea termite ten Ute tent teed teen Ted
easy   3 The auditor's panel had the right to risk a firm's profits.

New Keys

Use the J finger.

B. THE 6 KEY

4 jjj jyj j6j j6j 6j6 6j6 666 66 jugs; 6 jets; 6 jars; 6 jabs
5 64 jays 46 jobs 66 jots 67 hams 76 hats 46 hits 67 hugs 666
6 Tom Quin left at 6:26 p.m. on Train 66 to travel 626 miles.
7 There were 56,646 people in Bath and 26,269 in Hale in May.

Use the D finger.

C. THE 3 KEY

8 ddd ded d3d d3d 3d3 3d3 333 33 dots; 3 dies; 3 dips; 3 days
9 332 days 36 dogs 63 does 73 duds 37 dies 3:39 p.m.; 323-373
10 The 33 vans moved 36 cases in less than 33 hours on July 3.
11 Please add 55 to 753 and subtract 73 to get a total of 735.

Use the Sem finger.

D. THE / KEY

Do not space before or after the slash—unless it is the last character of an expression (line 15).

12 ;;; ;/; ;/; /;/ /;/ /// a/an and/or at/about bad/badly I/me
13 both/each disc/disk farther/further fewer/less like/such as
14 On 6/2/99, you asked him/her if he/she selected true/false.
15 Visit http://gdpkeyboarding.com/ for any questions/answers.

Skillbuilding

E. NEW-KEY REVIEW: 6, 3, AND SLASH KEY

16 In 6 months, he had walked 36 miles and/or driven 63 miles.
17 I realize that 3/6 of the 66 shipments equals 33 shipments.
18 He was born in New York on 6/3/36 and died there on 6/6/63.
19 Lucille bought 36 his/her towels on 3/3 with terms of n/29.

F. NUMBER-KEY REVIEW: 2, 4, 5, 7, 8, AND 9

20 My staff of 24 worked a total of 87 hours on Project 598-B.
21 Ed's instructor assigned pages 549-782 to be read by May 2.
22 From 2:45 p.m. until 5:45 p.m., I'll be typing in Room 987.
23 Let's visit her at 592 North Elm, Apt. 47, on September 28.

G. TECHNIQUE PRACTICE: SHIFT KEY

Type each line 2 times. After striking the capitalized letter, return the SHIFT key finger immediately to home-row position.

24 Alex Bly and Clara Dye wed. Ella Fochs and Gil Hall talked.
25 Ida Jackson met Kay Lang for a fast lunch at Mamma Nancy's.
26 Otis Pike should call Quint Richards about Sophia Townsend.
27 Ulrich Volte will take Winona Xi to visit Yadkin in Zurich.

H. PROGRESSIVE PRACTICE: ALPHABET

Follow the GDP software directions for this exercise to improve keystroking speed.

I. 2-MINUTE TIMED WRITING

Take two 2-minute timed writings.

 Goal: At least 22wpm/2'/5e

28   Jack scheduled a science quiz next week for Gregory,   11
29 but he did not let him know what time the exam was to be   22
30 taken. Gregory must score well on the exam in order to be   34
31 admitted to the class at the private Mount Academy.   44
　　　1 | 2 | 3 | 4 | 5 | 6 | 7 | 8 | 9 | 10 | 11 | 12

Enrichment • Lesson 14

Type each line 2 times.

A. NUMBER-KEY REINFORCEMENT

1 The 375 cars traveled 847 miles and used 45 gallons of gas.
2 My staff of 24 worked 48 hours a week from May 6 to May 29.
3 The 6 teams comprised 69 girls and 7 boys and left at 9:45.

4 The 37 men visited the 45 women at 3:25 p.m. on October 26.
5 Larry's 29 basketball players scored 467 points on 6/23/99.
6 The 23 workers packed 87 cartons, which weighed 389 pounds.

Type each line 2 times. Type the 3-letter word, backspace, and type the new letter. Thus, *rat* becomes *ram*.

B. TECHNIQUE PRACTICE: BACKSPACE KEY

7 rat←m gut←m are←m tip←n rut←n pat←n gut←n did←n bit←n ale←l
8 ash←k woo←k pat←l cot←n fit←n mat←n put←n tap←n wit←n ton←o
9 elk←m ill←k air←l bat←n fur←n owe←n rat←n air←m get←m sin←p
10 inn←k ire←k ilk←l but←n dot←n ink←n pet←n hat←m hit←m air←l

Take three 12-second timed writings on each line. The scale below the last line shows your wpm speed for a 12-second timed writing.

C. 12-SECOND SPEED SPRINTS

11 The doe and buck by the old lake may dig up the giant oaks.
12 It is a shame she works such an odd bowl into her art work.
13 Jake moved to amend the law to let the worker take the job.
14 He may sign over the title to his autos when he is in town.
` ' ' ' '5' ' ' '10' ' ' '15' ' ' '20' ' ' '25' ' ' '30' ' ' '35' ' ' '40' ' ' '45' ' ' '50' ' ' '55' ' ' '60`

Type each paragraph 2 times.

D. PARAGRAPH TYPING

15   My boss knew that her expert eloquence was just a big   11
16 hazard to effective teamwork, so he asked her to tone down   23
17 her remarks when giving her opinions on our progress.   33

18   Six of the female employees quietly gave back their   11
19 prizes to the judge because they did not agree with his   22
20 decisions regarding the basis for making his decisions.   33

21   Please, just be very quick and careful when you fix   11
22 the size of the tables in your annual report. You should   22
23 get Margaret to help you proofread your final report.   33

24   Our firm should ban all foul toxic smog because it   10
25 can quickly jeopardize the lives of our workers and their   22
26 families. I hope the board will make this decision soon.   33
    1 | 2 | 3 | 4 | 5 | 6 | 7 | 8 | 9 | 10 | 11 | 12

Review

15

Goals

- Type at least 23wpm/2'/5e.

A. WARMUP

alphabet | 1 Jack amazed a few girls by dropping the antique onyx vases.
alternate-hand words | 2 half height right penalty with visit social lens rigid snap
easy | 3 My mangy dog then ran to his bowl in the den to take a sip.

Skillbuilding

B. NUMBER-KEY REVIEW

4 I sent 72 jars, 89 cans, 29 boxes, and 32 bags to 33 homes.
5 The 494 students partied at 576 Dale and then at 5896 Park.
6 We got seats 27, 25, 28, 67, and 79 for the August 98 game.

7 Open Rooms 325, 343, 467, and 456 with Master Key No. 65-7.
8 The equipment shed was 267 by 278 feet, not 289 by 93 feet.
9 Mail the 378 packages to 548 East 65th Lane, not to 46 Elm.

C. PUNCTUATION REVIEW

. | 10 Go to Reno. Drive to Yuma. Call Mary. Get Samuel. See Cory.
, | 11 We saw Nice, Paris, Bern, Rome, Munich, Bonn, and Shanghai.
; | 12 Type the memo; read my report; get pens; get paper; see me.

:- | 13 Dear Aldo: Read these pages by 9:45: 2-9, 26-35, and 45-78.
' | 14 Ted's car and Ann's truck took the Hills' kids to Shoney's.
/ | 15 My aunt/best friend was born on 6/22/37 and died on 9/2/95.

D. PROGRESSIVE PRACTICE: ALPHABET

Follow the GDP software directions for this exercise to improve keystroking accuracy.

E. TECHNIQUE PRACTICE: TAB KEY

Press TAB where you see the → symbol.

```
16  Kim→ apt→ Mac→ art→ Nat→ Meg→ ads→ arm→ all→ ado→ Joy
17  Orr→ awl→ Jan→ Ida→ Moe→ Lin→ zap→ Joe→ zed→ ark→ awe
18  Kai→ Lev→ add→ ask→ Mom→ Uri→ Jeb→ Nan→ aid→ Lot→ amp
19  Jay→ Hal→ Ima→ Ira→ ail→ aim→ Ian→ Max→ Pat→ Liv→ Jim
```

F. TECHNIQUE PRACTICE: SPACE BAR

```
20  A toy dog in the pen is apt to be a big hit at the new gym.
21  We may go to the zoo for the day if the sun is not too hot.
22  Eli and Max may use a map to see how to get to the new pub.
23  If it is to be, it is up to you and Ben to do it for a fee.
```

G. 2-MINUTE TIMED WRITING

Take two 2-minute timed writings.

 Goal: At least 23wpm/2'/5e

```
24        Jeff Melvin was quite busy fixing all of the frozen     11
25  pipes so that his water supply would not be stopped. Last     22
26  winter Jeff kept the pipes from freezing by wrapping them     34
27  with an insulated tape that protected them from snow and     45
28  ice.                                                          46
       1  |  2  |  3  |  4  |  5  |  6  |  7  |  8  |  9  |  10  |  11  |  12
```

Enrichment • Lesson 15

Type each line 2 times.

A. NUMBER-KEY REINFORCEMENT

1 Just call me at 275-555-8346 or on my cell at 748-555-9292.
2 I bought Item 536 that weighs 45 pounds 6 ounces on May 27.
3 She moved from 859 36th Street to 734 82nd Avenue on May 5.

4 On July 26, I saw 67 cats, 92 dogs, 83 birds, and 49 foxes.
5 Please add Items 526, 73, 989, 24, and 453 to Order 56-627.
6 The 587 police met at 2:25 a.m. with 89 agents in Room 324.

Type each line 2 times.

B. ALPHABET PRACTICE

7 A campus TV quiz just asks why gold is buried at Fort Knox.
8 Crazy Fredrick bought Jane many very exquisite opal jewels.
9 All questions asked by five watch experts amazed the judge.

10 Jack quietly gave the dog owners most of his prized boxers.
11 Fred specialized in the job of making very quaint wax toys.
12 Six big devils from Japan then quickly forgot how to waltz.

Take three 12-second timed writings on each line. The scale below the last line shows your wpm speed for a 12-second timed writing.

C. 12-SECOND SPEED SPRINTS

13 He may go with us to the giant dock down by the handy lake.
14 The doe and buck by the old bush may dig up the giant oaks.
15 Ken had a dish of lamb and cut up a mango and a ripe mango.
16 Kay may visit the big island in May when she is down there.
     ' ' ' '5' ' ' '10' ' ' '15' ' ' '20' ' ' '25' ' ' '30' ' ' '35' ' ' '40' ' ' '45' ' ' '50' ' ' '55' ' ' '60

Type each paragraph 2 times.

D. PARAGRAPH TYPING

17   Please ship to me by freight sixty dozen quart jars   11
18 and twelve dozen black pans for the opening of our newest   22
19 appliance store in the coming weeks in North Carolina.   33

20   Mr. Dave Jones, the defense attorney, quickly spotted   11
21 four women dozing in the jury box. He moved to have the   22
22 judge quickly declare a mistrial and dismiss the jurors.   33

23   Back in June, our company delivered oxygen equipment   11
24 of odd sizes to the county hospital. It has already been   22
25 installed and is working properly in the emergency room.   33

26   I saw the four brown foxes who were quickly jumping   11
27 over the lazy dogs that were resting out back. The dogs did 23
28 not even open their eyes but continued sleeping heavily.   34
       1 | 2 | 3 | 4 | 5 | 6 | 7 | 8 | 9 | 10 | 11 | 12

Keyboarding: Numbers and Symbols

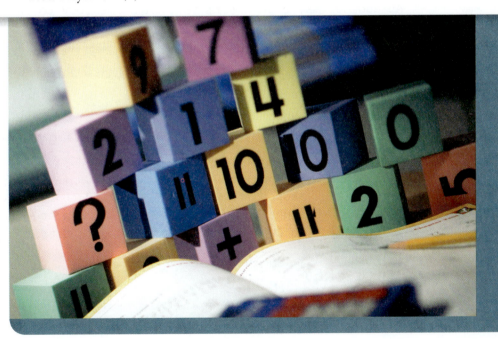

New Keys

Goals

- Touch-type the &, $, and 0 keys.
- Type at least 24wpm/2′/5e.

A. WARMUP

alphabet	1	Jack's man found exactly a quarter in the woven zipper bag.
concentration	2	oversimplifications nonrepresentational professionalization
easy	3	An auditor may sign a form that may name Toby to the panel.

New Keys

Use the J finger.

B. THE & KEY

The ampersand key (the sign for *and*) is the shift of 7. In normal narrative writing, space 1 time before and after the ampersand.

    4 jjj juj j&j j&j &j& &j& &&& Max & Dee & Sue & Tom & Rex & I
    5 Brown & Sons shipped to May & Lee and also to Dye & Pearce.
    6 John & Loo brought a case against May & Green and Li & Won.
    7 Von & Trapp and Den & Sax were joined by Contreras & Duran.

Use the F finger.

C. THE $ KEY

The dollar sign is the shift of 4. Do not space between the dollar sign and the following number.

    8 fff frf f$f f$f f f $$$ $44 $434.44 $4,444 $456 $492.85
    9 He paid $48, $64, and $94 for the chairs plus $48 shipping.
    10 Last season's concert tickets were $35, $45, $75, and $255.
    11 If you add $48.62, $49.93, and $324.42, you'll get $422.97.

Keep the J finger in
home-row position.

**Use the
Sem finger.**

D. THE 0 KEY

12 ;;; ;p; ;0; ;0; 0;0 0;0 000 00 2:00; 3:00; 4:00; 5:00; 6:30
13 The 80 men met at 3:05 with 20 agents in Room 90 on May 20.
14 I paid $40.05 for 20 pens and $50.50 for 30 pads on May 30.
15 The firm of Mori & Itou at 200 Broad Street owes us $8,000.

Skillbuilding

E. NEW-KEY REVIEW

16 $20.50 & $380.65 & $90.20 & $40.50 & $30.40 & $247.50 & $80
17 We hired Rizzo & Kelly for $20,000 to help Diamond & Green.
18 Arn & Sons owed us $4,000 and paid us only $250.50 in July.
19 Call Penn & Ames at 800-555-2040 and ask about the $48,000.

F. PACED PRACTICE

Follow the GDP software directions for this exercise to improve keystroking speed
and accuracy.

G. TECHNIQUE PRACTICE: SHIFT KEY

20 Ann Bonn asked for lunch. Colin Dix and Elaine Fochs moved.
21 Glen Hans filed as Iris James typed. Les Kay talked loudly.
22 Maya Nevins and Orin Parks tried. Quinn Roberts lost a bet.
23 Skye Tynch sat. Uriah Vin and Winn Xung ate. Yosef Zoe hid.

H. PROGRESSIVE PRACTICE: ALPHABET

Follow the GDP software directions for this exercise to improve keystroking speed.

I. 2-MINUTE TIMED WRITING

Take two 2-minute timed
writings.

Goal: At least
24wpm/2'/5e

24   Ginny quit her zoo job seven days after she learned   11
25 that she was expected to travel to four zoos in the first   22
26 month of work. After she had quit her job, she found an   34
27 excellent position that did not require her to be away   48
28 from home so much.

    1 | 2 | 3 | 4 | 5 | 6 | 7 | 8 | 9 | 10 | 11 | 12

Enrichment • Lesson 16

Type each line 2 times.

&
$
0
& $ 0

A. NEW-KEY REVIEW

1 Ali & Wu; Ash & Li; Cho & Ng; Day & Ivy; Gil & Ray; Ho & Yu
2 $234.56 and $78.54 and $463.38 and $23,896.25 and $4,993.39
3 20 and 30 and 40 and 50 and 60 and 70 and 80 and 90 and 200
4 Ott & Orr owed $5,000 to me; they owed $7,000 to Jay & Poe.

B. SUSTAINED PRACTICE: SYLLABIC INTENSITY

Syllabic intensity refers to the average number of syllables per word in a passage. The higher the syllabic intensity, the more difficult the passage is to type.

Take a 1-minute timed writing on the boxed paragraph to establish your base speed. Then take a 1-minute timed writing on the following paragraph. As soon as you equal or exceed your base speed on this paragraph, move to the next, more difficult paragraph.

5	One should always attempt to maintain good health. As	11
6	the first step in keeping good health, one should avoid the	23
7	habit of smoking. Volumes have been written on this topic.	35

8 A second habit that will help maintain your health for 11
9 decades is consuming an appropriate amount of water, day in 23
10 and day out. Most doctors recommend eight glasses a day. 34

11 Making exercise a habit is another important trait for 11
12 staying in good health. Most experts agree that spending a 23
13 few minutes a day in regular, vigorous exercise is helpful. 35

14 A final habit of importance is maintaining appropriate 11
15 body weight. The key to maintaining weight is developing a 23
16 positive eating pattern. Calculating calories is helpful. 34

   1 | 2 | 3 | 4 | 5 | 6 | 7 | 8 | 9 | 10 | 11 | 12

C. PARAGRAPH TYPING

Type each paragraph 2 times.

17 Jack typed a requisition for white moving boxes of 10
18 various sizes--some long and some short. He will need them 22
19 when we move into our new headquarters sometime next month. 34

20 My grandfather picked up a quartz and onyx necklace 11
21 for my grandmother at the bazaar. He knew that she loved 22
22 jewelry, and he was eager to give it to her on Christmas. 33

23 Jeff had his size, which helped him quickly win over 11
24 Gene in the boxing match. He won based on both his size and 23
25 his abilities as a boxer. My school was quite proud of him. 35

   1 | 2 | 3 | 4 | 5 | 6 | 7 | 8 | 9 | 10 | 11 | 12

New Keys

Goals

- Touch-type the 1, ?, and @ keys.
- Type at least 25wpm/2'/5e.

A. WARMUP

alphabet 1 Many big jackdaws quickly zipped over those empty fox pens.
one hand 2 street unholy sad you stated monopoly seat pink treat unpin
easy   3 Duane may try to fix the auditory problems in the city gym.

New Keys

Keep the F finger in
home-row position.

Use the A
finger.

B. THE 1 KEY

4 aaa aqa a1a a1a 1a1 1a1 111 11 ants; 11 asps; 1 aim; 11 ads
5 Sam left here at 1:11, Susan at 6:11, and Don at 11:11 a.m.
6 Erich had moved from 1010 Main Street to 1101 Main in 1990.
7 Sarah left at 11:00 a.m. on Train No. 11 to go 1,100 miles.

Use the
Sem finger.

C. THE ? KEY

The question mark is the shift of the slash. Space 1 time after a question mark.

8 ;;; ;/; ;?; ;?; ?;? ?;? ??? Who? What? When? Where? Why me?
9 May I? Why not? Who called? Need a job? Which one? Is it I?
10 Who's there? Any questions? Yes? Need some help? Who cares?
11 Is it 11:00? Was it held on 11/11/09? Where is 1101 W. Elm?

Use the S finger.

D. THE @ KEY

The at sign is the shift of 2. Space 1 time before and after the at sign except when it is used in an e-mail address (lines 13 and 15).

12 sss sws s@s s@s @s@ @s@ @@@ Buy 15 @ $41.01 and 11 @ $3.15.
13 E-mail me at jfox@tmu.edu or at jfox01@aol.com on April 11.
14 Order 12 pens @ $14, 185 pads @ $16, and 110 clips @ $2.50.
15 Can you e-mail Roger at rlowe@umn.edu to order 250 @ $1.15?

Skillbuilding

E. NEW-KEY REVIEW

16 Who knows if Randy's e-mail address is rjoyner@hotmail.com?
17 Should she buy 150 shares @ $11.50 and 200 shares @ $11.25?
18 Did she change her e-mail address to dcberkow011@yahoo.com?
19 Did Beverly try cokeefe011@vmu.edu or caroleoke101@msn.com?

F. TECHNIQUE PRACTICE: BACKSPACE KEY

Directions: Type the 3-letter word, backspace, and type the new letter.

20 bud←m gig←n dew←n rag←m tad←n own←l get←m tie←n toe←n
21 car←p hoe←g yea←n pie←n vat←n hug←m rug←m pod←i per←p
22 job←y yaw←m bus←y pad←l lad←p the←y nag←p fur←n nub←n
23 fad←n max←y jag←m fig←n ice←y oaf←k add←o mow←p log←o

G. MAP+: ALPHABET

Follow the GDP software directions for this exercise to improve keystroking accuracy.

H. 2-MINUTE TIMED WRITING

Take two 2-minute timed writings.

Goal: At least 25wpm/2'/5e

24   From the tower John saw that those six big planes   11
25 could crash as they zoomed quickly over treetops on their   22
26 way to the demonstration that was scheduled to begin very   33
27 soon. We hope there are no accidents and that the pilots   45
28 reach the airport quickly.   50
    1 | 2 | 3 | 4 | 5 | 6 | 7 | 8 | 9 | 10 | 11 | 12

Enrichment • Lesson 17

A. NEW-KEY REINFORCEMENT

Type each line 2 times.

1

?

@

1 ? @

1 Adam moved from 1101 Oak Lane to 2110 11th Street on May 1.
2 Who knows? Does Karina? Cloris? Gamal? How about Salvatore?
3 Order 328 @ $4.50 and 390 @ $16.75 from renees@comcast.net.
4 Whose address is luan111@msn.com? Whose is wells101@cc.com?

B. NUMBER PRACTICE

Type each line 2 times.

5 we 23 ere 343 wry 246 woe 293 ask 128 lay 916 did 383 to 59
6 err 344 I 8 it 85 quit 1785 pup 070 pre 043 rip 480 tie 583
7 yew 632 quip 1780 ow 92 ire 843 per 034 pry 046 is 82 do 39

PRETEST » PRACTICE » POSTTEST

PRETEST
Take a 1-minute timed writing.

C. PRETEST: Close Reaches

```
 8      Casey hoped that we were not wasting good grub. After  11
 9  the sun went down, he swiftly put the oleo and plums in the 23
10  cart. Bart opened a copy of an old book; Grant had a swim.  35
        1 | 2 | 3 | 4 | 5 | 6 | 7 | 8 | 9 | 10 | 11 | 12
```

PRACTICE
Speed Emphasis:
   If you made no more than 2 errors on the Pretest, type each *individual* line 2 times.
Accuracy Emphasis:
   If you made 3 or more errors, type each *group* of lines (as though it were a paragraph) 2 times.

D. PRACTICE: Adjacent Keys

```
11  op hope flop open mops rope opera droop scope copier trophy
12  we west owed went weld weep weigh weary wedge wealth plowed
13  rt hurt port cart dirt fort court party start hearty parted
```

E. PRACTICE: Consecutive Fingers

```
14  un tune spun unit dune punt under prune sunny hunter uneasy
15  gr grow grim grab grub grew great graze gripe greasy grassy
16  ol role oleo pool sold hole troll folly polka stolen oldest
```

POSTTEST
Repeat the Pretest timed writing and compare performance.

F. POSTTEST: Close Reaches

18

New Keys

Goals

- Touch-type the % ( ) and # keys.
- Type at least 26wpm/2'/5e.

A. WARMUP

alphabet 1 My woven silk pajamas can be exchanged for the blue quartz.

practice: *s* and *d* 2 ads sad deeds desks dosed dudes dusts sheds sides soda suds

easy 3 Her ruby handiwork is fine, and she is so proficient at it.

New Keys

Use the F finger.

B. THE % KEY

Percent is the shift of 5. Do not space between the number and the percent sign.

4 fff frf f%f f%f %f% %f% %%% 10% 9% 8% 7% 6% 5% 4% 3% 2% 10%
5 Rob quoted rates of 8%, 9%, 10%, 11%, and 12% on the bonds.
6 Sandy scored 82%, Jan 89%, Ken 90%, and me 91% on the exam.
7 Only 55% scored 75% or higher, and 8% scored 90% or higher.

**Use the L finger on (.
Use the Sem finger on).**

C. THE (AND) KEYS

Parentheses are the shifts of 9 and 0. Do not space between the parentheses and the text within them.

8 lll lol l(l l(l (l((l((((;;; ;p; ;); ;););));)))) (a)
9 Please ask (1) Al, (2) Pat, (3) Ted, (4) Dee, and (5) Lise.
10 He'll (a) take two aspirin, (b) go to bed, and (c) rest up.
11 Rosa's (a cafe) had fish (shad) on the menu today (Monday).

Use the D finger.

D. THE # KEY

The # sign stands for *number* if it comes before a figure and *pounds* if it comes after a figure. It is the shift of 3. Do not space between the # sign and the number.

12 ddd ded d#d d#d #d# #d# ### #3 #33 #333 33# 83#; 37# of #83
13 Write down 330# of #200 and 380# of #400 using a #2 pencil.
14 We sat in seats #12, #34, #56, #65, and #66 at the concert.
15 Please use 50# lined paper for #373 and 30# paper for #374.

Skillbuilding

E. NEW-KEY REVIEW

16 Policy 8(b) says to load Truck #48 with 2,000# of 50% sand.
17 We need 85# of #2 grade ore (aluminum) and 45# of #3 grade.
18 Nearly 60% of the males and 50% of the females chose #5738.
19 Just stress (a) speed 50% of the time and (b) accuracy 50%.

F. PROGRESSIVE PRACTICE: NUMBERS

Follow the GDP software directions for this exercise to improve keystroking speed.

G. TECHNIQUE PRACTICE: SPACE BAR

20 Eli and Max may use a map to see how to get to the new pub.
21 A toy dog in the pen is apt to be a big hit at the new gym.
22 If it is to be, it is up to you and Ben to do it for a fee.
23 We may go to the zoo for the day if the sun is not too hot.

Take two 2-minute timed writings.

Goal: At least 26wpm/2'/5e

H. 2-MINUTE TIMED WRITING

24   Max had to make one quick adjustment to his television 11
25 set before the football game began. The picture during the 23
26 last game was fuzzy and hard to see. If he cannot fix the 35
27 picture, he may have to purchase a new television set; and 46
28 that may be difficult to do. 52

    1 | 2 | 3 | 4 | 5 | 6 | 7 | 8 | 9 | 10 | 11 | 12

Enrichment • Lesson 18

A. NEW-KEY REINFORCEMENT

1 Of the 85% of the alumni here, 9% gave 28% and 6% gave 25%.
2 Just (a) stop, (b) look, and (c) listen to her (Iphigenia).
3 Please record 33# of #200 and 38# of #400 on the #20 paper.
4 Only 15% of them (the attendees) ordered 30# of item #5011.

Type each line 2 times.

%
( )
#
% ( ) #

B. NUMBER PRACTICE

5 we 23 ort 945 rep 430 pot 095 toy 596 yip 680 yow 692 it 85
6 tee 533 ore 943 weep 2330 pop 090 poi 098 top 590 quit 1785
7 quip 1780 tip 580 woo 299 try 546 out 975 pro 049 quay 1716

Type each line 2 times.

C. SUSTAINED PRACTICE: NUMBERS

Take a 1-minute timed writing on the boxed paragraph to establish your base speed. Then take a 1-minute timed writing on the following paragraph. As soon as you equal or exceed your base speed on this paragraph, move to the next, more difficult paragraph.

8   Michael learned through firsthand experience last week   11
9 that the cost of a week at the beach varies a great deal.   23
10 He says that a rowboat would be about right for his money.   34

11   His Uncle Bo told him that when he was his age, he had   11
12 rented a small cabin for the huge sum of $105 for one week.   23
13 For $23 more, he rented a small boat and outboard motor.   34

14   Then Uncle Bo went on to say that when he rented the   11
15 same cabin last year, the cost had gone up to either $395   22
16 or $410. Boat and motor rentals now cost from $62 to $87.   34

17   Aunt Kate said that she and her husband will be paying   11
18 either $1,946 or $2,073 for a week's sailing on the 53-foot   23
19 yacht. The boat has a 4-person crew and was built in 2006.   35

    1 | 2 | 3 | 4 | 5 | 6 | 7 | 8 | 9 | 10 | 11 | 12

D. PACED PRACTICE

Follow the GDP software directions for this exercise to improve keystroking speed and accuracy.

E. PARAGRAPH TYPING

Type each paragraph 2 times.

20   I saw five or six of the big jet planes zoom quickly   11
21 over an old tower by the side of the road. They were flying   23
22 in formation and created a beautiful display for everyone.   34

23   Brown jars of an acidic mixture prevented the solution   11
24 from freezing so quickly. It took about four days for it to   23
25 freeze solid; then we could store it in the lab's freezer.   35

    1 | 2 | 3 | 4 | 5 | 6 | 7 | 8 | 9 | 10 | 11 | 12

New Keys

Goals

- Touch-type the " ! and * keys.
- Type at least 27wpm/2′/5e.

A. WARMUP

alphabet

1 The jinxed wizards plucked the ivy stem from the big quilt.

frequent digraphs

2 on bon con none noon don ion one son ton won onto moon font

easy

3 Jan and her son may make a bowl of fish and a cup of cocoa.

New Keys

Use the Sem finger.

B. THE " KEY

The quotation key is the shift of the apostrophe. Do not space between quotation marks and the text they enclose.

4 ;;; ;"; ;"; ";" ";" """ "Thanks," he said, "I needed that."

5 I read her article, "Freaking Out," and said, "It is great."

6 "Those were wonderful," Fidel said. "I'll take seven more."

7 Juan wanted to know if the name was "Roberto" or "Roberta."

Use the A finger.

C. THE ! KEY

The exclamation mark is the shift of 1. Space 1 time after an exclamation mark.

8 aaa aqa a!a a!a !a! !a! !!! Wow! Now! Go! Stay! Sit! Nurse!

9 Put it down! Do not move! Leave it there! Get out! Move it!

10 Ouch! That hurt! Let's roll! Incredible! Hang in there! No!

11 Congratulations! That was great! Don't shoot! Oh, no! Help!

Use the K finger.

D. THE KEY

The asterisk is the shift of 8. Do not space before the asterisk but space 1 time after the asterisk.

```
12  kkk kik k*k k*k *k* *k* *** p. 18* as follows:* Note* etc.*
13  An * may be used to indicate a footnote at the page bottom.
14  In the footnote itself, do not leave any space after the *.
15  Did he really call Mr. Baines a *****? Wow! That was awful!
```

Skillbuilding

E. NEW-KEY REVIEW

```
16  The right word* was "parenthesis" instead of "parentheses."
17  "Wow!" Aki said, "That* was an amazing display! Go see it."
18  "Only one* was allowed in," said Jin. "It was Mr. Mystery."
19  The source* was absolutely reliable! "I agree," Yaron said.
```

F. MAP+: NUMBERS

Follow the GDP software directions for this exercise to improve keystroking accuracy.

G. PLACEMENT OF QUOTATION MARKS

1. The closing quotation mark is always typed *after* a period or comma (line 20) but *before* a colon or semicolon (line 21).
2. The closing quotation mark is typed *after* a question mark or exclamation point if the quoted material itself is a question or an exclamation (line 22). Otherwise, the quotation mark is typed *before* the question mark or exclamation point (line 23).

```
20  "Hi, there," I said. "My name is Karen, and I am new here."
21  James said, "I'll mail the check tomorrow"; but he did not.
22  Raheem read the article "Will They Succeed on the Economy?"
23  Did Anne say, "We won"? I was shocked when Juan said, "Me"!
```

H. PACED PRACTICE

Follow the GDP software directions for this exercise to improve keystroking speed and accuracy.

I. TECHNIQUE PRACTICE: TAB KEY

Press TAB where you see the →.

24 Orr→	Ike→	zoo→	Jon→	apt→	Pat→	ado→	zap→	Ned→	asp→	zag
25 Jan→	Lev→	Kit→	Ida→	Joy→	ads→	Joe→	ago→	Ima→	are→	ace
26 Mac→	Jim→	ate→	Lou→	Mia→	zed→	add→	Pia→	Moe→	Lot→	Jay
27 zip→	Obi→	Mom→	aft→	Job→	age→	Ham→	Ott→	awl→	art→	Hsu

J. 2-MINUTE TIMED WRITING

Take two 2-minute timed writings.

 Goal: At least 27wpm/2'/5e

```
28      Topaz and onyx rings were for sale at very reasonable   11
29  prices last month. When Jeanette saw the rings with these    23
30  stones, she quickly bought them both for her sons. These     34
31  jewels were difficult to find, and Jeanette was pleased      45
32  she could purchase those rings when she did.                 54
        1 | 2 | 3 | 4 | 5 | 6 | 7 | 8 | 9 | 10 | 11 | 12
```

Strategies for Career Success

Being a Good Listener

Silence is golden! Listening is essential for learning, getting along, and forming relationships.

Do you tend to forget people's names after being introduced? Do you look away from the speaker instead of making eye contact? Do you interrupt the speaker before he or she finishes talking? Do you misunderstand people? Answering yes can indicate poor listening skills.

To improve your listening skills, follow these steps. *Hear the speaker clearly.* Do not interrupt; let the speaker develop his or her ideas before you speak. *Focus on the message.* At the end of a conversation, identify major items discussed. Mentally ask questions to help you assess the points the speaker is making. *Keep an open mind.* Do not judge. Developing your listening skills benefits everyone.

Your Turn: Assess your listening behavior. What techniques can you use to improve your listening skills? Practice them the next time you have a conversation with someone.

Enrichment • Lesson 19

Type each line 2 times.

"
!
*
" ! *

A. NEW-KEY REINFORCEMENT

1 "If we go," Arif said, "we will need to find a substitute."
2 Goodness! I can't believe that! He must have been in shock!
3 The real reason* may never be known about those strangers.*
4 "Umberto's exact remarks* were shocking, to say the least!"

PPP — PRETEST » PRACTICE » POSTTEST

PRETEST
Take a 1-minute timed writing.

PRACTICE
Speed Emphasis:
If you made no more than 2 errors on the Pretest, type each *individual* line 2 times.
Accuracy Emphasis:
If you made 3 or more errors, type each *group* of lines (as though it were a paragraph) 2 times.

POSTTEST
Repeat the Pretest timed writing and compare performance.

B. PRETEST: Discrimination Practice

5   Few of us were as lucky as Bev was when she joined us   12
6 for golf. She just dreaded the look of the work crew when   24
7 she goofed. But she neatly swung a club and aced the hole.   36
    1 | 2 | 3 | 4 | 5 | 6 | 7 | 8 | 9 | 10 | 11 | 12

C. PRACTICE: Left Hand

8 vbv behaves verb bevy vibes bevel brave above verbal bovine
9 wew dewdrop west weep threw wedge weave fewer weight sewing
10 ded precede deed seed bride guide dealt cried secede parted

D. PRACTICE: Right Hand

11 klk kindle kiln lake knoll lanky locks liken kettle knuckle
12 uyu untidy buys your usury unity youth buoys unruly younger
13 oio iodine coin lion oiled foils foist prior oilcan iodized

E. POSTTEST: Discrimination Practice

Type each paragraph 2 times.

F. PARAGRAPH PRACTICE

14   Only a very few phlox grew or even bloomed just in   10
15 back of my old zinc quarry. I think the reason was that the   22
16 zinc had leached into the soil, making plants hard to grow.   34
17   She promptly judged the antique ivory buckles that   10
18 were made for the county fair. They won a prize. Next, we   22
19 moved on to judging the cakes and pies, which we all liked.   34
    1 | 2 | 3 | 4 | 5 | 6 | 7 | 8 | 9 | 10 | 11 | 12

Review

Goals

- Type at least 28wpm/2'/5e.

A. WARMUP

alphabet   1 West quickly gave Bert handsome prizes for six juicy plums.
number/symbol 2 gilp@comcast.net (11%) Ng & Ma 4/5 No! $13.86 *Est. #20-972
easy   3 Rodney may risk half of his profits for the old oak mantel.

Skillbuilding

B. NUMBER-KEY REVIEW

4 With 37,548 fans screaming, we won the game 10-9 on May 26.
5 He went to Rome on May 30, 1975, and left on July 24, 1986.
6 Seats 10, 29, 38, 47, and 56 are still unsold for tomorrow.
7 Our store will be open from 7:30 to 9:45 on February 18-26.

8 The 29 teachers and 754 students arrived at 8:30 on May 16.
9 Call 555-3190 and clarify our $826.47 charge for equipment.
10 Order No. 3874 for $165.20 did not arrive until October 19.
11 Al's sales for the last month went from $35,786 to $41,290.

C. PUNCTUATION REVIEW

.
?
!
,

12 Stand here. Sit down. Rest a minute. Relax. Breathe deeply.
13 Can it wait? Why not? Can he drive? Where is it? Who knows?
14 No! Stop! Don't look! Watch out! Move it over! Jump! Do it!
15 Inga, Lev, and I worked, rested, and then worked some more.

;
:
-

16 First, read the directions; next, practice; and then build.
17 Be on call at these times: 9:30, 12:30, 2:30, and 3:30 p.m.
18 It was a once-in-a-lifetime experience for Kay Jones-Lange.

'
/
"

19 It's Lynn's job to cover Maria's telephone when she's gone.
20 Two/thirds of us and one/fourth of them came on 12/10/2009.
21 I watched "Meet the Mets" and "Yankee Power" on the screen.

D. SYMBOL REVIEW

@
#
$
%

22 Order 12 items @ $114, 9 @ $99, and another 18 items @ $87.
23 My favorite seats for this year are #92, #83, #74, and #65.
24 She received quotes of $48, $52, and $76 for the old radio.
25 Ramos scored 93% on the test, Sue had 88%, and Al made 84%.

&
*
( )

26 Rudd & Sons bought their ten tickets from Cross & Thompson.
27 The * sign, the asterisk, is used for reference purposes.**
28 The typist is (a) speedy, (b) accurate, and (c) productive.

E. MAP+: SYMBOLS

Follow the GDP software directions for this exercise to improve keystroking accuracy.

F. 12-SECOND SPEED SPRINTS

Take three 12-second timed writings on each line. The scale below the last line shows your wpm speed for a 12-second timed writing.

29 Kay and she may both visit us in May when they are in town.
30 She may go with me to the city to visit my son and his pal.
31 His body of work may charm the guests who visit the chapel.
32 That new city law may help us to fish for cod on the docks.
' ' ' ' 5 ' ' ' 10 ' ' ' 15 ' ' ' 20 ' ' ' 25 ' ' ' 30 ' ' ' 35 ' ' ' 40 ' ' ' 45 ' ' ' 50 ' ' ' 55 ' ' ' 60

G. 2-MINUTE TIMED WRITING

Take two 2-minute timed writings.

 Goal: At least 28wpm/2'/5e

33   Jake or Peggy Zale must quickly fix the fax machine   11
34 so that we can have access to regional reports that we   22
35 think might be sent within the next few days. Without the   33
36 fax, we will not be able to finish all our monthly reports   45
37 by the deadline. Please let Peggy know of any problems.   56
   1 | 2 | 3 | 4 | 5 | 6 | 7 | 8 | 9 | 10 | 11 | 12

Enrichment • Lesson 20

A. SUSTAINED PRACTICE: SYMBOLS

Take a 1-minute timed writing on the boxed paragraph to establish your base speed. Then take a 1-minute timed writing on the following paragraph. As soon as you equal or exceed your base speed on this paragraph, move to the next, more difficult paragraph.

1   It was quite normal that Patty was somewhat nervous as   11
2 she entered the college building. After four years of work   23
3 as a clerk, she was here to take the college entrance exam.   35

4   Just as you have likely done, Patty took her #2 pencil   11
5 and began to fill in the score sheet. A test administrator   23
6 (Mr. Graham) had said that a grade of 75% would be passing.   35

7   Patty had come to Room #68 (a large lecture hall) from   11
8 the Stone & Carpenter accounting firm. It's a "mighty long   23
9 hike," and almost 100% of the examinees were already there.   35

10   For a $25 fee, everyone in Room #68 (the test site)   11
11 answered the "moderately difficult" true-false or A/B/C/D   23
12 questions; 40% had used the Dun & Bradstreet study guide.   34

    1 | 2 | 3 | 4 | 5 | 6 | 7 | 8 | 9 | 10 | 11 | 12

B. TECHNIQUE PRACTICE: ENTER KEY

Type each line 2 times. Type each sentence on a separate line by pressing ENTER after each sentence.

13 Ed saw her. Ah. What? We do. Speak. Stop. Go. No. Begin it.
14 Thanks. Stop. Why not? See? Get it? Who, me? Well? She can.
15 See me. Who? Read it. What? Really! Why me? So soon? Do it.
16 Who knew? Enough? What is it? Go now. She did. Why not? So?

C. NUMBER PRACTICE

Type each line 2 times.

17 we 23 pro 049 too 599 wit 285 toe 593 wet 235 eye 363 IQ 81
18 pit 085 opts 9052 wow 292 quiz 1781 pep 030 pow 092 tow 592
19 you 697 tors 5942 ewe 323 tot 595 ere 343 wry 246 quit 1785

D. PARAGRAPH TYPING

Type each paragraph 2 times.

20   A campus TV quiz show just asked one contestant why   11
21 gold was buried at Fort Knox. No one knew the answer, so   22
22 they moved on to the business category, which was easier.   33

23   A few of the black taxis drove up the major road on   11
24 the hazy night. Because the hour was so late, they could   22
25 not find passengers needing rides, so they quickly left.   33

26   Jay took a big quiz and exam even though he suffered   11
27 a lower back pain that forced him to be very careful with   22
28 how he moved during the test. Fortunately, he aced it.   33

    1 | 2 | 3 | 4 | 5 | 6 | 7 | 8 | 9 | 10 | 11 | 12

Supplementary Lesson: Ten-Key Numeric Keypad

Goals

- Touch-type the ten-key numeric keypad keys.

New Keys

A. THE , , AND KEYS

To input numbers using the ten-key numeric keypad, you must activate the NUM LOCK (Numeric Lock) key. Usually, an indicator light signals that the NUM LOCK is activated.

On the keypad, 4, 5, and 6 are the home-row keys. Place your fingers on the keypad home row as follows:

- J finger on 4
- K finger on 5
- L finger on 6

On most computers, there is a raised line or dot on the 5 key to help you easily locate the home-row position when using the keypad.

Use your Sem finger to control the ENTER key. For the exercises in A–F that follow:

1. Ensure that NUM LOCK is activated.
2. Press ENTER after typing the final digit of each number.
3. Type the first column from top to bottom; then move to the next column.
4. Keep your eyes on the copy.

1	444	455	466	544	566
2	555	644	656	456	654
3	666	445	466	554	556
4	664	665	456	654	454
5	464	546	564	655	456

B. THE , , AND KEYS

Use the J finger to control the 7, the K finger to control the 8, and the L finger to control the 9.

6	474	585	696	549	984
7	747	858	969	485	645
8	774	885	996	658	489
9	447	558	669	846	647
10	744	855	966	476	867

C. THE ![1], ![2], AND ![3] KEYS

Use the J finger to control the 1, the K finger to control the 2, and the L finger to control the 3.

11	414	525	636	215	326
12	141	225	336	634	435
13	144	552	663	324	145
14	441	255	636	263	346
15	144	252	363	431	265

D. THE ![0] KEY

Use the right thumb to control the 0.

16	404	901	580	407	802
17	505	101	690	508	506
18	606	202	410	609	700
19	707	303	520	140	800
20	808	470	630	250	900

E. THE ![.] KEY

Use the L finger to control the decimal (.) key.

21	6.6	7.6	1.2	6.5	9.8
22	3.2	4.4	7.7	5.5	8.8
23	2.2	6.6	9.3	1.1	1.0
24	3.1	8.4	7.1	9.3	3.4
25	4.5	8.3	9.9	6.5	3.8

Skillbuilding

F. NEW-KEY REVIEW

26	526	081	175	14.7	70.3	868	115
27	451	736	672	80.4	68.0	280	505
28	450	148	761	68.0	69.4	258	739
29	017	856	702	28.0	86.5	42	700
30	023	924	028	63.4	58.2	608	35
31	715	846	315	5.98	7.10	617	290
32	039	760	316	8.40	6.25	74	961
33	401	650	612	5.87	4.20	600	307
34	419	694	427	8.01	9.31	620	3
35	685	948	432	7.50	8.41	929	302

Enrichment • Supplementary Lesson

A. THE KEY

Use the Sem finger to control the plus (+) key. Press the plus key after each number except the last number in a column. Press ENTER after the last number to display the total.

1	310+	698+	579+	747+	706+
2	845+	252+	999+	833+	126+
3	133+	320+	841+	599+	403+
4	603	484	782	738	180

B. THE / KEY

Use the K finger to control the division (/) key. Press ENTER after the second number in each column to display the result.

5	858/728	912/771	814/238	542/236	956/895
6	595/104	527/970	739/129	771/292	590/485
7	121/494	181/376	984/533	814/820	836/237
8	696/998	293/432	160/189	485/181	922/172

C. THE − KEY

Use the Sem finger to control the minus (-) key. Press ENTER after the second number in each column to display the result.

9	826-477	929-229	332-519	378-112	53.4-31.2
10	569-873	350-847	571-334	878-766	82.6-26.6
11	970-856	528-428	402-986	745-830	55.8-80.2
12	250-152	190-346	439-109	526-923	66.4-41.1

D. THE * KEY

Use the L finger to control the multiplication (*) key. Press ENTER after the second number in each column to display the result.

13	406*363	733*835	923*419	645*618	21.8*18.6
14	214*331	554*843	492*103	135*889	58.8*70.7
15	199*927	572*604	756*375	276*942	84.4*77.1
16	885*286	778*358	601*793	192*672	19.3*99.0

E. NUMERIC KEYPAD REVIEW

Type the first column from top to bottom; then move to the next column. Press ENTER after the last number in each column to display the result.

17	933+	790/	338*	878-	512+	587+	764/
18	655-	835-	903+	444+	537*	25-	791-
19	175*	186*	579/	324/	890-	836*	762*
20	217	614	247	868	563	546	912

Basic Business Documents

Opportunities in Business and Administrative Careers

Occupations in the business and administrative services cluster focus on providing management and support services for various companies. The many positions found in this cluster include receptionist, bookkeeper, administrative professional or assistant, claim examiner, accountant, word processor, office manager, and chief executive officer. Managers and administrators are in charge of planning, organizing, and controlling businesses.

Management support workers gather and analyze data to help company executives make decisions. Administrative support workers perform a variety of tasks, such as recordkeeping, operating office equipment, managing their own projects and assignments, and developing high-level integrated software skills as well as Internet research skills. Ideally, everyone in business should be patient, detail-oriented, and cooperative. Excellent written and oral communication skills are definitely an asset as well.

Many companies have been revolutionized by advances in computer technology. As a result, keyboarding skill provides a definite advantage for those who work in business and administrative services. Now, more than ever, success in the business world is dependent upon adaptability and education.

Goals

Keyboarding

- Demonstrate improved speed and accuracy when operating the keyboard by touch.
- Type at least 36 words per minute on a 3-minute timed writing with no more than 4 errors.

Language Arts

- Demonstrate acceptable proofreading skills, including using proofreaders' marks correctly.
- Demonstrate acceptable language arts skills in punctuation and grammar.
- Demonstrate acceptable composing and spelling skills.

Word Processing

- Use appropriate word processing commands necessary to complete document processing activities successfully.

Document Processing

- Correctly format e-mail, correspondence, reports, and tables.

Objective Test

- Answer questions with acceptable accuracy on an objective test.

Word Processing and E-Mail

Orientation to Word Processing—A

Goals

- Demonstrate improved speed and accuracy while typing.
- Demonstrate acceptable language arts skills in comma usage and sentence structure.
- Correctly use the Word Manual and basic Word features.

A. WARMUP

alphabet

1 Jack's eloquence may prove hazardous for the six big shows.

concentration

2 deindustrialization superstitiousnesses comprehensibilities

easy

3 The new dogma may both disorient her and also let her down.

Skillbuilding

B. MAP+: ALPHABET

Follow the GDP software directions for this exercise to improve keystroking accuracy.

C. PROGRESSIVE PRACTICE: ALPHABET

Follow the GDP software directions for this exercise to improve keystroking speed.

Language Arts

Study the rules at the right.

D. COMMAS AND SENTENCES

Note: The callout signals in the left margin indicate which language arts rule from this lesson has been applied.

RULE
, direct address

Use commas before and after a name used in direct address.

Thank you, John, for responding to my e-mail so quickly.
Ladies and gentlemen, the program has been canceled.

RULE
fragment

Avoid sentence fragments.

Not: She had always wanted to be a financial manager. But had not had the needed education.
But: She had always wanted to be a financial manager but had not had the needed education.

Note: A fragment is a part of a sentence that is incorrectly punctuated as a complete sentence. In the first sentence above, "but had not had the needed education" is not a complete sentence because it does not contain a subject.

RULE
run-on

Avoid run-on sentences.

Not: Mohamed is a competent worker he has even passed the MCSE exam.
Not: Mohamed is a competent worker, he has even passed the MCSE exam.
But: Mohamed is a competent worker; he has even passed the MCSE exam.
Or: Mohamed is a competent worker. He has even passed the MCSE exam.

Note: A run-on sentence is two independent clauses that run together without any punctuation between them or with only a comma between them.

Edit each sentence to correct any errors.

4 You must be certain, Sean that every e-mail message is
5 concise. And also complete.

6 In addition, Sean, use a clear subject line the subject line
7 describes briefly the principal content of the e-mail
8 message.

9 You should use a direct style of writing, use short lines
10 and paragraphs.

11 The recipient of your e-mail message will be more likely to
12 read and respond to a short message. Than a long one.

13 Your reader will be grateful for any writing techniques.
14 That save time.

15 Another thing you should do Sean is to include an
16 appropriate closing, your reader should know immediately who
17 wrote the message.

Formatting

E. WORD PROCESSING: GETTING STARTED AND ORIENTATION TO WORD PROCESSING—A

GO TO
Word Manual

Study Getting Started and Lesson 21 in your Word Manual. Complete all of the shaded steps while at your computer.

Orientation to Word Processing — B

Goals

- Type at least 28wpm/3′/5e.
- Correctly use basic Word features.

A. WARMUP

alphabet	1	Jay took a big quiz and exam that forced a vast lower pain.
one hand	2	garage homily sea oil seated Honolulu ever jump eager plunk
easy	3	Nancy may go to the ancient chapel to sign her widow's vow.

Skillbuilding

Take a 1-minute timed writing on the boxed paragraph to establish your base speed. Then take a 1-minute timed writing on the following paragraph. As soon as you equal or exceed your base speed on this paragraph, move to the next, more difficult paragraph.

B. SUSTAINED PRACTICE: CAPITALS

4	The insurance industry will see some changes because	11
5	of the many natural disasters the United States has seen in	23
6	the last few years in places like California and Florida.	34

7	The major earthquakes in San Francisco, Northridge,	11
8	and Loma Prieta cost thousands of dollars. Faults like	22
9	the San Andreas are being watched carefully for activity.	33

10	Some tropical storms are spawned in the West Indies	11
11	and move from the Caribbean Sea into the Atlantic Ocean.	22
12	They could affect Georgia, Florida, Alabama, and Texas.	33

13	Some U.S. cities have VHF-FM radio weather stations.	11
14	NASA and NOAA are agencies that launch weather satellites	22
15	to predict the locations, times, and severity of storms.	34

1 | 2 | 3 | 4 | 5 | 6 | 7 | 8 | 9 | 10 | 11 | 12

Take two 3-minute timed writings.

Goal: At least 28wpm/3′/5e

C. 3-MINUTE TIMED WRITING

16	Once you learn to use a variety of software programs,	11
17	you will feel confident and comfortable as you are using a	23
18	computer. All you have to do is take that first step and	34
19	decide to strive for excellence.	41
20	Initially, you might have several questions as you	51
21	gaze up at a screen that is filled with icons. If you try	63
22	to learn to use just one or two commands each day, you may	75
23	soon find that using software is very exciting.	84

1 | 2 | 3 | 4 | 5 | 6 | 7 | 8 | 9 | 10 | 11 | 12

Formatting

D. WORD PROCESSING: ORIENTATION TO WORD PROCESSING — B

Study Lesson 22 in your Word Manual. Complete all of the shaded steps while at your computer.

Orientation to Word Processing — C

Goals

- Demonstrate improved speed and accuracy while typing.
- Demonstrate acceptable proofreading skills by comparing lines.
- Correctly use basic Word features.

A. WARMUP

alphabet

practice: *o* and *i*

easy

1 The lazy major was fixing Cupid's broken quiver and arrows.
2 oil Rio boil folio polio coin icon into Ohio olio silo void
3 Mr. Richfield is such a busy man he may not go via the bus.

Skillbuilding

B. MAP+: NUMBERS

Follow the GDP software directions for this exercise to improve keystroking accuracy.

PP

PRETEST » PRACTICE » POSTTEST

PRETEST

Take a 1-minute timed writing. Review your speed and errors.

C. PRETEST: Common Letter Combinations

4	He tried to explain the delay in a logical way. The	11
5	man finally agreed to insure the package and demanded to	22
6	know why the postal worker did not record the total amount.	34

    1 | 2 | 3 | 4 | 5 | 6 | 7 | 8 | 9 | 10 | 11 | 12

PRACTICE

Speed Emphasis:
If you made 2 or fewer errors on the Pretest, type each *individual* line 2 times.

Accuracy Emphasis:
If you made 3 or more errors, type each *group* of lines (as though it were a paragraph) 2 times.

D. PRACTICE: Word Beginnings

7 re reuse react relay reply return reason record results red
8 in inset inept incur index indeed intend inning insured ink
9 de dents dealt death delay detest devote derive depicts den

E. PRACTICE: Word Endings

10 ly lowly dimly apply daily barely unruly deeply finally sly
11 ed cured tamed tried moved amused tasted billed creamed fed
12 al canal total equal local postal plural rental logical pal

POSTTEST

Repeat the Pretest timed writing and compare performance.

F. POSTTEST: Common Letter Combinations

G. PROOFREADING TECHNIQUES

Study the proofreading techniques at the right.

Proofreading and correcting errors are essential parts of document processing. To become an expert proofreader:

1. Use Word's spelling feature to check for spelling errors; then read the copy aloud to see if it makes sense.
2. Proofread for all kinds of errors, especially repeated, missing, or transposed words; grammar and punctuation; and numbers and names.
3. Check for formatting errors such as line spacing, tabs, margins, and use of bold.

H. PROOFREADING

Compare these lines with lines 4–7 on page 83. Edit the lines to correct any errors.

13 A bushal of corn was thrown under the elm trees by the boy.
14 A pair of cosy socks and a cup of soup can fix me right up.
15 Andy will use eight hand singals if he is able to see them.
16 Blanche may go with me to town to visit my son and his pal.

Formatting

I. WORD PROCESSING: ORIENTATION TO WORD PROCESSING—C

GO TO
Word Manual

Study Lesson 23 in your Word Manual. Complete all of the shaded steps while at your computer.

Keyboarding Connection

Using Search Engines

How can you most efficiently find information on the Internet? Use a search engine! A search engine guides you to the Internet's resources. It analyzes the information you request, navigates the Internet's many networks, and retrieves a list of relevant Web sites. Google is one of the most popular search engines; others are Yahoo, Ask.com, and Microsoft's Bing.com.

A search engine examines electronic databases, wire services, journals, article summaries, articles, home pages, and user group lists. It can access material found in millions of Web sites. When you search on a specific key word, a search engine scans its large database, searches the content of Web pages, and then displays the information that most closely matches the words you're searching for.

Many large Web sites have a search function built in. This allows you to search only that site for relevant Web pages and information, like job postings on a company Web site or articles about a specific topic on a news Web site.

Your Turn: Try different search engines, and see which ones you like best. Choose three of your favorite search engines. Then conduct a search using the key words "touch typing." (Don't forget the quotation marks, but leave out the period.) Compare the results for each search engine.

Orientation to Word Processing — D

Goals

- Type at least 29wpm/3'/5e.
- Correctly use basic Word features.

A. WARMUP

alphabet   1 Xavier had picked several bright yellow jonquils for Mitzi.
frequent digraphs   2 in ink nine chin pin kind main sin mind tin skinny win inns
easy   3 A bushel of mangos and a box of grapes may be on the canoe.

Skillbuilding

B. PROGRESSIVE PRACTICE: NUMBERS

Follow the GDP software directions for this exercise to improve keystroking speed.

C. TECHNIQUE PRACTICE: SPACE BAR

Type each line 2 times, using your right thumb to strike the SPACE BAR in the center.

4 Ed and Jo can get to the spa if it is on the way to my car.
5 I hid a big car in my new lot, but I may not get it by two.
6 An elk and ape at the zoo do not eat any of the cod or gar.
7 I had a tan dog and a red cat on the big set for Jo to pet.

D. 3-MINUTE TIMED WRITING

Take two 3-minute timed writings.

Goal: At least 29wpm/3'/5e

8   If you ever feel tired as you are typing, you should   11
9 take a rest. Question what you are doing that is causing   22
10 your muscles to be fatigued. You will realize that you   33
11 can change the fundamental source of your anxiety.   43
12   Take a deep breath and enjoy the relaxing feeling as   54
13 you exhale slowly. Check your posture to be sure that you   66
14 are sitting up straight with your back against the chair.   78
15 Stretch your neck and back for full relaxation.   87
      1 | 2 | 3 | 4 | 5 | 6 | 7 | 8 | 9 | 10 | 11 | 12

Formatting

E. WORD PROCESSING: ORIENTATION TO WORD PROCESSING—D

GO TO
Word Manual

Study Lesson 24 in your Word Manual. Complete all of the shaded steps while at your computer.

Strategies for Career Success

Preparing a Job Interview Portfolio

Don't go empty-handed to that job interview! Take a portfolio of items with you. Definitely include copies of your resume and your list of references, with at least three professional references. Your academic transcript is useful, especially if you are asked to complete a company application form. Appropriate work samples and copies of certificates and licenses are also helpful portfolio items.

The interview process provides you the opportunity to interview the organization. Include a list of questions you want to ask during the interview.

A comprehensive portfolio of materials will benefit you by giving you a measure of control during the interview process.

Your Turn: Start today to compile items for your interview portfolio. Include copies of your resume, your reference list, and copies of certificates and licenses. Begin developing a list of interview questions. Think about appropriate work samples to include in your portfolio.

E-Mail Messages

Goals

- Demonstrate improved speed and accuracy while typing.
- Demonstrate acceptable language arts skills in composing sentences.
- Correctly use Word's e-mail feature.
- Correctly format an e-mail message.

A. WARMUP

alphabet   1   Playing jazzy vibe chords quickly excited my wife's senses.

number/symbol   2   (ali41@cs.com) (10%) Guy & Lee 7/8 In! $5.40 *f.o.b. #26-39

easy   3   Did an auditor sign a form that may name Toby to the panel?

Skillbuilding

B. 12-SECOND SPEED SPRINTS

Take three 12-second timed writings on each line.

4   A bushel of corn was thrown under the elm tree by the boys.
5   A pair of cozy socks and a cup of soup may fix me right up.
6   Andy will use eight hand signals if he is able to see them.
7   Blanch may go with me to town to visit my son and his pals.
     ' ' ' ' 5 ' ' ' 10 ' ' ' 15 ' ' ' 20 ' ' ' 25 ' ' ' 30 ' ' ' 35 ' ' ' 40 ' ' ' 45 ' ' ' 50 ' ' ' 55 ' ' ' 60

C. PACED PRACTICE

Follow the GDP software directions for this exercise to improve keystroking speed and accuracy.

Language Arts

D. COMPOSING SENTENCES

Answer each question with a complete sentence.

8   What is your favorite class this term, and why?
9   What is your ideal job when you graduate?
10   If you could live in a foreign country, which one would it be, and why?
11   What are your two favorite Internet sites?
12   What qualities do you look for in a friend?

Formatting

E. BASIC PARTS OF AN E-MAIL MESSAGE

TO BOX. Contains the name or e-mail address of each recipient; each name and/or address is usually separated by a semicolon or comma.

SUBJECT BOX. Contains a descriptive name for the message; typed with upper- and lowercase letters.

GREETING. Friendly opening; followed by a colon.

BODY. Message; type with short lines and paragraphs in plain text.

SENDER'S NAME. Sender's first name or first and last name.

WRITER'S IDENTIFICATION. Writer's identity and contact information; also known as a "signature" in some e-mail software.

F. E-MAIL MESSAGES

Do not send any e-mail messages without consulting your instructor.

REFER TO Reference Manual

R-5C and R-5D: E-Mail Message in Microsoft Outlook/Internet Explorer and E-Mail Message in MSN Hotmail

To format an e-mail message:

1. Use the address book feature or type the e-mail address of each recipient in the *To, Cc,* or *Bcc* box. A semicolon or comma is usually automatically inserted to separate several names.
2. If you use the reply feature, include the original message only if it helps the reader remember the topic more easily.
3. Use a descriptive, concise subject line with upper- and lowercase letters.

   Example: Items for Meeting Agenda

4. Use the attachment feature if you need to attach a file or document.
5. Use a friendly greeting. Follow the greeting with a colon. Use the recipient's first name or a courtesy title and last name for a more businesslike greeting.

   Examples: Hi, Jim: or Jim: or Mr. Andrews:

   Note: A greeting is optional but will be used throughout this book.

6. Keep paragraphs short, and type them with normal capitalization and punctuation. Typing in all-caps is considered shouting.
7. Type paragraphs single-spaced, and do *not* indent paragraphs.
8. Press ENTER 2 times between paragraphs only—do *not* press ENTER when you see a line break in the text.
9. After the last paragraph, press ENTER 2 times.

The remaining steps will vary depending upon your e-mail program. If your e-mail program inserts a signature automatically, you do not have to take any further steps other than proofreading. Refer to your e-mail software Help feature for steps on inserting a signature. If your e-mail software does not include a signature feature (and for the purposes of formatting e-mail messages consistently in this textbook), follow these steps:

1. Type your first name only for a friendlier closing, or type both your first and last name for a more businesslike closing. Press ENTER 2 times.

   Example: Sandy or Sandy Hill

   Note: A closing name is optional but will be used throughout this book.

2. Type your e-mail address, press ENTER, and type your phone number as shown in this example.

   Example:
   Sandra R. Hill
   E-mail: srhill@server.com
   Phone: 661-555-1223

3. Spell-check, proofread, and preview your document for spelling and formatting errors.
4. Type all e-mail messages using standard e-mail format. In this book, you will type only the e-mail greeting, body, and closing for all e-mail messages.
5. Refer to the model document on page 84 for correct formatting.

G. WORD PROCESSING: E-MAIL A DOCUMENT AND GDP REFERENCE MANUAL

GO TO
Word Manual

Study Lesson 25 in your Word Manual. Complete all of the shaded steps while at your computer. Then format the documents that follow.

Document Processing

Correspondence
25-1
E-Mail Message

Press ENTER 2 times *only between paragraphs* when you see ↓2X. In Word, lines wrap automatically as you approach the right margin. Your line endings in Word will *not* match those in the book.

In Word, when you type an e-mail address and then a space, an e-mail hyperlink is inserted automatically.

Hi, Renee: ↓2X

E-mail is easier to read when the message and subject line are short and concise. The paragraphs should be broken up into small ones whenever possible. ↓2X

If you wish to send a social e-mail to a large number of recipients, consider typing their e-mail addresses in the Bcc box, which stands for "blind carbon copy," rather than in the To box. This practice helps reduce spam junk mail, and your friends will appreciate your courtesy.

To add a friendly feeling to your message, greet your recipient by name. Adding your name in the signature also adds a personal touch. Make it easy for your reader to contact you by including a signature line that includes your name, e-mail address, and phone number if desired.

Proofread carefully for errors in typing, spelling, and formatting. Remember, Renee, that once you click the Send button, you can't get it back. Write messages you would be proud to have the world read. It could happen. ↓2X

Edward ↓2X

Edward Garcia
E-mail: egarcia@quickmail.com
Phone: 701-555-4832

Correspondence 25-2
E-Mail Message

The ¶ symbol indicates a new, blocked paragraph. The | symbol indicates the end of a line. Press ENTER as many times as needed.

Hi, Kim:

¶ I now have e-mail access using my new phone. You can send me the photos you took at our annual meeting because I will be able to access them immediately.

¶ Thank you, Kim, for bringing your digital camera to the meeting so that we could all enjoy the photos you took.

John | John Sanchez | E-mail: jsanchez@brightway.net | Phone: 404-555-6823

Strategies for Career Success

Goodwill Messages

Would you like to strengthen your relationship with a customer, coworker, or boss? Send an unexpected goodwill message! Your expression of goodwill has a positive effect on business relationships.

Messages of congratulations or appreciation provide special opportunities to express goodwill. These messages can be quite brief. If your handwriting is good, send a handwritten note on a professional note card. Otherwise, send a letter or e-mail.

A note of congratulations might be "I just heard the news about your (award, promotion, etc.). My very best wishes." An appreciation note could be "Thank you for referring me to . . . Your confidence and trust are sincerely appreciated."

Your Turn: Send a goodwill message to someone to express congratulations or appreciation.

Correspondence

Business Letters

Goals

- Type at least 30wpm/3′/5e.
- Correctly format a business letter in block style with standard punctuation.

A. WARMUP

alphabet   1 Six of the women quietly gave back the prizes to the judge.
concentration 2 electrocardiography gastroenterologists interdenominational
easy   3 A bushel of corn was thrown to the turkeys by Mr. McKenzie.

Skillbuilding

B. SUSTAINED PRACTICE: PUNCTUATION

Take a 1-minute timed writing on the boxed paragraph to establish your base speed. Then take a 1-minute timed writing on the following paragraph. As soon as you equal or exceed your base speed on this paragraph, move to the next, more difficult paragraph.

```
 4        Anyone who is successful in business realizes that the    11
 5  needs of the customer must always come first. A satisfied       23
 6  consumer is one who will come back to buy again and again.      34

 7        Consumers must learn to lodge a complaint in a manner     11
 8  that is fair, effective, and efficient. Don't waste time        22
 9  talking to the wrong person. Go to the person in charge.        34

10        State your case clearly; be prepared with facts and       11
11  figures to back up any claim. Warranties, receipts, bills,      22
12  and checks are all very effective. Don't be intimidated.        34

13        If the company agrees to work with you, you're on the     11
14  right track. Be specific: "I'll expect a check Tuesday,"        22
15  or "I'll expect a replacement in the mail by Saturday."         33
        1 | 2 | 3 | 4 | 5 | 6 | 7 | 8 | 9 | 10 | 11 | 12
```

Goal: At least 30wpm/3'/5e

C. 3-MINUTE TIMED WRITING

16	Holding a good business meeting may require a great	11
17	deal of thought and planning. Your meeting must be well	22
18	organized, and an agenda must be prepared. It may be hard	33
19	to judge how long a meeting will take or how many people	45
20	will discuss important issues.	51
21	A good leader is required to execute an agenda. He or	62
22	she must know when to move on to the next topic or when to	74
23	continue debate on a topic. After a productive meeting, a	85
24	leader will be pleased.	90

1 | 2 | 3 | 4 | 5 | 6 | 7 | 8 | 9 | 10 | 11 | 12

Formatting

D. BASIC PARTS OF A BUSINESS LETTER

LETTERHEAD. Printed name, address, and telephone number (and/or fax number and e-mail address) of the company.

DATE LINE. Month, day, and year of the letter; type 2 inches from the top of the page.

INSIDE ADDRESS. Name and address of the party to whom the letter is written; begin 4 lines below the date.

SALUTATION. Opening greeting; type 2 lines below the inside address.

STANDARD PUNCTUATION. A colon after the salutation and a comma after the complimentary closing.

BODY. Text or message of the letter; begin 2 lines below the salutation.

COMPLIMENTARY CLOSING. Closing farewell; type 2 lines below the body.

SIGNATURE. Handwritten signature of the writer.

WRITER'S IDENTIFICATION. Name, or title, or both of the writer; begin 4 lines below the complimentary closing.

REFERENCE INITIALS. Initials of the typist; type 2 lines below the writer's identification.

E. BUSINESS LETTERS IN BLOCK STYLE

To format a business letter in block style:

1. Type all lines beginning at the left margin.
2. Press ENTER 5 times to begin the first line of the letter 2 inches from the top of the page.
3. Type the date, and press ENTER 4 times.
4. Type the inside address. Insert 1 space between the state and ZIP Code.
5. After the inside address, press ENTER 2 times, type the salutation, and type a colon after the salutation for standard punctuation.
6. Press ENTER 2 times after the salutation, and single-space the paragraphs in the body.
7. Press ENTER 2 times between paragraphs only—do *not* press ENTER when you see a line break in the text.
8. Do *not* indent paragraphs in a block-style letter.
9. Press ENTER 2 times after the last paragraph, type the complimentary closing, and type a comma after the complimentary closing for standard punctuation.
10. Press ENTER 4 times after the complimentary closing, and type the writer's identification.
11. Press ENTER 2 times after the writer's identification, and type your reference initials in lowercase letters without periods or spaces.
12. Spell-check, proofread, and preview your document for spelling and formatting errors.

REFER TO
Word Manual

Appendix B, Using GDP Features in Document Processing, Reference Initials

Document Processing

Correspondence
26-3

Business Letter in Block Style

Type the current year whenever you see "20--."

↓5X
January 27, 20-- ↓4X

Ms. Laura Green
Account Executive
TurboNet Express
Two Pine Avenue
Long Beach, CA 90802 ↓2X

Dear Ms. Green: ↓2X

When you type text followed by two hyphens (--), followed by more text and then a space, a formatted em dash (—) will automatically be inserted.

Our company is interested in hosting an educational seminar this spring—one that will focus on meeting the growing need for information industry professionals to keep abreast of emerging new technologies. This year we are specifically interested in information on high-speed Internet connections. ↓2X

I understand that TurboNet Express specializes in these seminars and that you also help businesses analyze their needs and choose an appropriate solution. I am in the process of contacting several companies similar to yours that might be interested in conducting these seminars. If you will contact me by Thursday or Friday, we can discuss this further.

(continued on next page)

I appreciate the fine service we have always received from you in the past, and I look forward to hearing from you very soon. ↓2X

Sincerely, ↓4X

Kathleen Franco
Information Technology Specialist ↓2X

urs

Type your own reference initials in lowercase (no periods or spaces) in black whenever you see urs.

Correspondence 26-4
Business Letter in Block Style

In steps 1 and 3 (and in all similar instances in future jobs) do *not* type the period at the end of text to be revised if that punctuation is not needed.

Correspondence 26-5
Business Letter in Block Style

Open the file for Correspondence 26-3, and make the following changes:

1. Change the date to February 8.
2. Delete the last sentence in the first paragraph, and add these sentences:

   Advances in technology are nothing short of astonishing! This year, we would like to focus on models and procedures to save power in the workplace.

3. Change the writer's identification to Joon Soo Han and the job title to Technology Engineer.

May 25, 20-- / Ms. Laura Green / Account Executive / TurboNet Express / Two Pine Avenue / Long Beach, CA 90802 / Dear Ms. Green:
¶ Thank you so much for hosting the educational seminar last Tuesday that focused on the topic of high-speed Internet connections. Our company and our employees are now well prepared to make a decision about the best type of Internet connection for their particular needs.
¶ Because this seminar was so successful, I have been authorized to contract with TurboNet Express for a continuing series of seminars on any topics related to emerging new technologies and trends as they apply to the needs of our company and our employees. I will call you on Monday so that we can arrange for a meeting to finalize some contractual issues.
¶ Once again, thank you for a very successful and productive seminar!
Sincerely, / Kathleen Franco / Information Technology Specialist / urs

Business Letters With Enclosure Notations

Goals

- Demonstrate improved speed and accuracy while typing.
- Demonstrate acceptable language arts skills in comma usage.
- Correctly format a business letter in block style with an enclosure notation.

A. WARMUP

alphabet	1	Please quickly pack my box with the five dozen modern jugs.
one hand	2	revert unhook act him access pumpkin gave lymph fever union
easy	3	Hancock may work in the coalfield when he is not busy here.

Skillbuilding

B. MAP+: ALPHABET

Follow the GDP software directions for this exercise to improve keystroking accuracy.

C. PROGRESSIVE PRACTICE: ALPHABET

Follow the GDP software directions for this exercise to improve keystroking speed.

Language Arts

Study the rules at the right.

RULE
, independent clause

The underline calls attention to a point in the sentence where a comma might mistakenly be inserted.

D. COMMAS AND SENTENCES

Use a comma between independent clauses joined by a coordinate conjunction (unless both clauses are short).

Ellen left her job with IBM, and she and her sister went to Paris.
But: Ellen left her job with IB<u>M</u> and went to Paris with her sister.
But: John drov<u>e</u> and I navigated.

Note: An independent clause is one that can stand alone as a complete sentence. The most common coordinate conjunctions are *and*, *but*, *or*, and *nor*.

Use a comma after an introductory expression (unless it is a short prepositional phrase).

Before we can make a decision, we must have all the facts.
But: In 200<u>8</u> our nation elected a new president.

Note: An introductory expression is a group of words that come before the subject and verb of the independent clause. Common prepositions are *to*, *in*, *on*, *of*, *at*, *by*, *for*, and *with*.

Edit each sentence to correct any errors.

4 If you agree I will let Mr. Hancock know.

5 On Friday we will meet to discuss the upcoming campaign.

6 Mr. Ray will lead the delegation and Ms. Guy will be the
7 interpreter.

8 Ella dictated and I typed.

9 Melvin accepted a job in Miami that starts in July and then
10 left for a two-week vacation.

11 Now that it is light outside we can begin moving the
12 furniture.

13 It was a well-deserved victory and it didn't come any too
14 soon.

Formatting

E. ENCLOSURE NOTATIONS

To indicate that an item is enclosed with a letter:

- Type the word *Enclosure* on the line below the reference initials to indicate that an item is enclosed with a letter.

- Type the word *Enclosures* if more than one item is being enclosed.

Example: urs
Enclosure

Document Processing

Correspondence 27-6
Business Letter in Block Style

, independent clause

October 10, 20-- | Ms. Julie Mays | Travelwise International | 7301 East Gold Dust Avenue | Scottsdale, AZ 85258 | Dear Ms. Mays:
¶ Our company has decided to hold its regional sales meeting in Santa Fe during the second week of January, and I need information on a suitable conference site.
¶ We will need a meeting room with the following items: 30 computer workstations with wireless capability and a wireless Internet connection, copy stands, mouse pads, and adjustable chairs; a high-performance LCD projector with a large screen; and a wireless microphone and podium. The hotel should have a fax machine and an on-site business center. We might also need a messenger service.

(continued on next page)

¶ A final decision on the conference site must be made within the next two weeks. If you have any information on a suitable location in Santa Fe, please send it immediately. I have enclosed a list of conference attendees and included their room preferences. Thank you for your help.

Sincerely yours, | Nick Limpett | Marketing Manager | urs | Enclosure

Correspondence 27-7
Business Letter in Block Style

1. Open the file for Correspondence 27-6.
2. Change the inside address to 5421 North Scottsdale Road and the ZIP Code to 85250.
3. Change the first sentence as follows:

   Our company has decided to hold its annual national sales meeting during the first week of February in Santa Fe, and I need information on a suitable conference site.

4. Change the writer's name to William McDougal.

Correspondence 27-8
Business Letter in Block Style

October 10, 20-- | Mr. Nick Limpett | Marketing Manager | Secure Investments Inc. | 398 East Wacker Drive | Chicago, IL 60601 | Dear Mr. Limpett:

¶ Are you searching for a suitable conference site for your next corporate meeting? If so, the Paradise Valley Resort in Scottsdale, Arizona, offers you every amenity imaginable.

¶ Our luxury resort accommodations and stunning Sonoran Desert views are minutes away from the largest mall in the Southwest and hundreds of shops, galleries, and Scottsdale eateries. We are conveniently located only 12 miles from Phoenix Sky Harbor International Airport. Paradise Valley Resort has 40,000 square feet of flexible meeting space, including stunning outdoor venues. Our in-house audiovisual staff will make sure that your event is flawless.

¶ I've enclosed several brochures for your convenience. Let me know if I can be of service in any way. Your success is

our success, and I hope to hear from you soon.

Sincerely yours, | Ms. Julie Mays | Corporate Event Specialist | urs | Enclosures

Envelopes and Labels

28

Goals

- Type at least 31wpm/3'/5e.
- Correctly use Word's envelope, view gridlines, and label features.
- Correctly format an envelope and label, and fold a letter.

A. WARMUP

alphabet

practice: *a* and *s*

easy

1 Jack amazed a few girls by dropping the antique onyx vases.
2 ask has say sales bases areas scans seams sodas visas tasks
3 My neighbors may bid on the islands if the profit is there.

Skillbuilding

B. PACED PRACTICE

Follow the GDP software directions for this exercise to improve keystroking speed and accuracy.

C. 3-MINUTE TIMED WRITING

Take two 3-minute timed writings.

Goal: At least 31wpm/3'/5e

4	Credit cards can make shopping very convenient, and	11
5	they frequently help you record and track your spending.	22
6	However, many card companies charge high fees for using	33
7	their credit cards.	37
8	You must realize that it may be better to pay in cash	48
9	and not use a credit card. Look at all your options. Some	60
10	card companies do not charge yearly fees. Some may give	71
11	you extended warranties on goods you buy with their credit	83
12	cards. Judge all the details; you may be surprised.	93

1 | 2 | 3 | 4 | 5 | 6 | 7 | 8 | 9 | 10 | 11 | 12

Formatting

D. ENVELOPES

Word's envelope feature simplifies your task of addressing a standard No. 10 envelope measuring 9½ by 4⅛ inches.

To format an envelope:

1. Use Word's envelope feature to create an envelope.
2. The inside address is automatically inserted in Word's delivery address box if you are adding an envelope to an existing letter. Or you can type the recipient's name and address in upper- and lowercase style in Word's delivery address box.
3. If a return address is not printed on the envelope, type the sender's name and address in upper- and lowercase style in Word's return address box.
4. Use Word's default placement and default font for the delivery address and the return address.
5. Print the envelope immediately after creating it, or add the envelope to the document, and print it later.

Trend Electronics
2206 31st Street
Minneapolis, MN 55407-1911

Mr. Charles R. Harrison
Reliable Software Inc.
5613 Brunswick Avenue
Minneapolis, MN 55406

Standard large envelope, No. 10, is 9½ x 4⅛ inches.

E. FOLDING LETTERS

To fold a letter for a No. 10 envelope:

1. Place the letter face up, and fold up the bottom third of the page.
2. Fold the top third of the page down to about 0.5 inch from the bottom edge of the page.
3. Insert the last crease into the envelope first with the flap facing up.

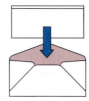

F. LABELS

Word's label feature simplifies the task of preparing various labels. You can use different label settings to print a full sheet of labels or to print a single label. You may want to use a mailing label as an alternative to printing an envelope.

To format a label:

1. Select the desired label, and note the label vendor and form number.
2. Use Word's label feature to create a single label or to create a full page of labels for the desired label form.
3. Use Word's default placement and default font for the labels.
4. After you prepare the labels, test the label position by printing your labels on a blank page before you print them on the actual label form. Make any necessary adjustments.

Ms. Irma Mayberry Garden Concepts Today 75-3982 Alii Drive Kailua-Kona, HI 96740	Ms. Irma Mayberry Garden Concepts Today 75-3982 Alii Drive Kailua-Kona, HI 96740	Ms. Irma Mayberry Garden Concepts Today 75-3982 Alii Drive Kailua-Kona, HI 96740
Ms. Irma Mayberry Garden Concepts Today 75-3982 Alii Drive Kailua-Kona, HI 96740	Ms. Irma Mayberry Garden Concepts Today 75-3982 Alii Drive Kailua-Kona, HI 96740	Ms. Irma Mayberry Garden Concepts Today 75-3982 Alii Drive Kailua-Kona, HI 96740
Ms. Irma Mayberry Garden Concepts Today 75-3982 Alii Drive Kailua-Kona, HI 96740	Ms. Irma Mayberry Garden Concepts Today 75-3982 Alii Drive Kailua-Kona, HI 96740	Ms. Irma Mayberry Garden Concepts Today 75-3982 Alii Drive Kailua-Kona, HI 96740
Ms. Irma Mayberry Garden Concepts Today 75-3982 Alii Drive Kailua-Kona, HI 96740	Ms. Irma Mayberry Garden Concepts Today 75-3982 Alii Drive Kailua-Kona, HI 96740	Ms. Irma Mayberry Garden Concepts Today 75-3982 Alii Drive Kailua-Kona, HI 96740
Ms. Irma Mayberry Garden Concepts Today 75-3982 Alii Drive Kailua-Kona, HI 96740	Ms. Irma Mayberry Garden Concepts Today 75-3982 Alii Drive Kailua-Kona, HI 96740	Ms. Irma Mayberry Garden Concepts Today 75-3982 Alii Drive Kailua-Kona, HI 96740
Ms. Irma Mayberry Garden Concepts Today 75-3982 Alii Drive Kailua-Kona, HI 96740	Ms. Irma Mayberry Garden Concepts Today 75-3982 Alii Drive Kailua-Kona, HI 96740	Ms. Irma Mayberry Garden Concepts Today 75-3982 Alii Drive Kailua-Kona, HI 96740
Ms. Irma Mayberry Garden Concepts Today 75-3982 Alii Drive Kailua-Kona, HI 96740	Ms. Irma Mayberry Garden Concepts Today 75-3982 Alii Drive Kailua-Kona, HI 96740	Ms. Irma Mayberry Garden Concepts Today 75-3982 Alii Drive Kailua-Kona, HI 96740
Ms. Irma Mayberry Garden Concepts Today 75-3982 Alii Drive Kailua-Kona, HI 96740	Ms. Irma Mayberry Garden Concepts Today 75-3982 Alii Drive Kailua-Kona, HI 96740	Ms. Irma Mayberry Garden Concepts Today 75-3982 Alii Drive Kailua-Kona, HI 96740
Ms. Irma Mayberry Garden Concepts Today 75-3982 Alii Drive Kailua-Kona, HI 96740	Ms. Irma Mayberry Garden Concepts Today 75-3982 Alii Drive Kailua-Kona, HI 96740	Ms. Irma Mayberry Garden Concepts Today 75-3982 Alii Drive Kailua-Kona, HI 96740
Ms. Irma Mayberry Garden Concepts Today	Ms. Irma Mayberry Garden Concepts Today	Ms. Irma Mayberry Garden Concepts Today

Full page of the same label, Avery standard, 5160, Address
(Note: Label form shown with "View Gridlines" active.)

G. WORD PROCESSING: ENVELOPES, VIEW GRIDLINES, AND LABELS

GO TO Word Manual

Study Lesson 28 in your Word Manual. Complete all of the shaded steps while at your computer. Then format the documents that follow.

Document Processing

Correspondence 28-9
Envelope

1. Prepare an envelope with the following mailing address:

   Mr. Brad Everett | Business Software Solutions | 1410 Monterey Road | San Jose, CA 95110

2. Insert the following return address:

   Marie Fletcher | ABV Systems Inc. | 7200 Cedar Street | Omaha, NE 68124

3. Add the envelope to a blank document.

Correspondence 28-10
Envelope

1. Open the file for Correspondence 27-8, and prepare an envelope for the letter.
2. Do not insert a return address.
3. Add the envelope to the letter.

Correspondence 28-11
Mailing Labels

1. Select an address label product about 1 inch deep, large enough to fit a 4-line address. Label choices will vary; however, Avery standard, 5160, Address is a good choice for laser and ink-jet printers.
2. Prepare address labels for the names and addresses that follow.
3. Type the addresses in order from left to right as you see them displayed next in the first row of labels.
4. Move to the second row of labels, and type them again from left to right.

Purchasing Department Abbott Laboratories 351 Abbott Park Chicago, IL 60064	Frank Zimmerly Cartridges, Etc. 1220 Charleston Road Oso Park, CA 90621	John Sanchez Adobe Systems 1585 Charleston Road Los Angeles, CA 90029
Mike Rashid Internet Services 901 Thompson Place Sunnyvale, CA 94088	Jennifer Reagan Aetna Life 151 Farmington Avenue Hartford, CT 06156	Bob Patterson Affiliated Publishing 135 Morrisey Blvd. Boston, MA 02107

Correspondence 28-12
Mailing Labels

1. Select an address label product about 1 inch deep, large enough to fit a 4-line address. Label choices will vary; however, Avery standard, 5160, Address is a good choice for laser and ink-jet printers.

2. Prepare a full page of the same label with the following address:

   Shipping and Receiving | E-Office Outlet | 1122 North Highland Street | Arlington, VA 22201

1. Open the file for Correspondence 27-6, and prepare an envelope for the letter.
2. Insert the following return address:

   Nick Limpett | Viatech
   Communications | 9835 Harvard
   Road, NE | Albuquerque, NM
   87111

3. Add the envelope to the letter.

Keyboarding Connection

Decoding the E-Mail Address

With most e-mail software, a header at the top of each e-mail message contains the sender's address. What is the meaning of the strange configuration of an e-mail address?

An e-mail address contains three parts: anyname@server.com. First is the identity of the e-mail user, whether a person's name or a general name for the recipient, such as helpdesk or customer service (before the @ symbol). Next is the name of the host computer or domain name the person uses (before the period). The third part is the zone, or domain, for the type of organization or institution or even the country indicator to which the host belongs (e.g., *.edu* = education; *.gov* = government; *.com* = company; or a country indicator such as *.de* for Germany, *.uk* for United Kingdom, *.fr* for France).

Be careful to include each part of an e-mail address, and check the spelling and punctuation completely. Even a small error will prevent your message from reaching the recipient. When creating an e-mail address for job searching, try to choose a user name close to your own and as professional as possible.

Your Turn: Have you ever sent an e-mail that did not reach its recipient because of an address error? What type of error did you make?

Memos and E-Mail
With Attachments

Goals

- Demonstrate improved speed and accuracy while typing.
- Demonstrate acceptable language arts skills in spelling.
- Correctly use Word's e-mail attachment feature.
- Correctly format a memo and an e-mail message with an attachment notation.

A. WARMUP

alphabet	1	Five jumbo oxen graze quietly with the nearby pack of dogs.
frequent digraphs	2	an and ant any ban can fan man pan ran tan van wan nana Ana
easy	3	Turn the handle to the right to dismantle the usual signal.

Skillbuilding

B. MAP+: SYMBOL

Follow the GDP software directions for this exercise to improve keystroking accuracy.

PPP

PRETEST » PRACTICE » POSTTEST

PRETEST

Take a 1-minute timed writing. Review your speed and errors.

C. PRETEST: Close Reaches

4	The growth in the volume of company assets is due to	11
5	the astute group of twenty older employees. Their answers	22
6	were undoubtedly the reason for the increase in net worth.	34

1 | 2 | 3 | 4 | 5 | 6 | 7 | 8 | 9 | 10 | 11 | 12

PRACTICE

Speed Emphasis:
If you made 2 or fewer errors on the Pretest, type each *individual* line 2 times.

Accuracy Emphasis:
If you made 3 or more errors, type each *group* of lines (as though it were a paragraph) 2 times.

D. PRACTICE: Adjacent Keys

7	as ashes cases class asset astute passes chased creased ask
8	we weave tweed towed weigh wealth twenty fewest answers wet
9	rt worth alert party smart artist sorted charts turtles art

E. PRACTICE: Consecutive Fingers

10	un undue bunch stung begun united punish outrun untie funny
11	gr grand agree angry grade growth egress hungry group graph
12	ol older solid tools spool volume evolve uphold olive scold

POSTTEST
Repeat the Pretest timed
writing and compare
performance.

F. POSTTEST: Close Reaches

Language Arts

Type these frequently
misspelled words,
paying special attention
to any spelling problems
in each word.

G. SPELLING

13 personnel information its procedures their committee system
14 receive employees which education services opportunity area
15 financial appropriate interest received production contract
16 important through necessary customer employee further there
17 property account approximately general control division our

Edit the sentences to
correct any misspellings.

18 All company personel will receive important information.

19 Are division has some control over there financial account.

20 There comitee has received approximately three contracts.

21 The employe and the customer have an oportunity to attend.

22 We have no farther interest in the property or it's owner.

23 When it is necessary, follow apropriate proceedures.

Strategies for Career Success

Preparing to Conduct a Meeting

Do you want to conduct a successful meeting? Meetings tend to fail because they last too long and attendees do not stay focused. First, determine the meeting's purpose (e.g., to make a decision or obtain/provide information).

Decide who needs to attend the meeting. Include those who can significantly contribute, as well as decision makers. Prepare an agenda, that is, a list of items to be discussed. Distribute it to attendees a few days before the meeting.

Choose where you will conduct the meeting, and schedule a room. Determine if you will be teleconferencing, videoconferencing, or needing audiovisual equipment. If appropriate, arrange for refreshments. Check the room temperature, acoustics, and lighting. Attention to these details will increase your chances for a successful outcome.

Your Turn: Think about a meeting you attended that was a failure. What could the meeting leader have done to better prepare for the meeting?

H. BASIC PARTS OF A MEMO

A memo is usually sent from one person to another in the same organization. E-mail in recent years has replaced memos as an efficient means of interoffice communication in many offices. However, memos are better suited for detailed messages of a more formal nature.

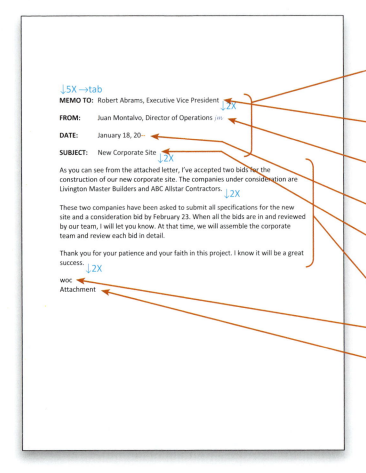

MEMO HEADINGS. Printed guide words typed in bold (including the colon); press TAB after the colon as needed to align the heading entries at the same point; begin 2 inches from the top of the page.

MEMO TO HEADING. Name of recipient; if a title is included, separate the name and title with a comma.

FROM HEADING. Name of writer; if a title is included, separate the name and title with a comma; followed by handwritten initials of sender.

DATE HEADING. Month, day, and year the memo was typed.

SUBJECT HEADING. Subject of the memo; if the subject wraps to a second line, press TAB at the start of the second line as needed to align the second line at the same point as the first line.

BODY. Text or message of the memo; type 2 lines below the subject heading.

REFERENCE INITIALS. Initials of the typist; type 2 lines below the body.

ATTACHMENT NOTATION. Indicates that something is attached; if used, type directly below the reference initials.

I. MEMOS

To format a memo on plain paper or on letterhead stationery:

1. Press ENTER 5 times to begin the first line of the memo 2 inches from the top of the page.
2. Type the headings (including the colons) in all-caps and bold: MEMO TO:, FROM:, DATE:, and SUBJECT:.
3. Press TAB as many times as needed to reach the point where each heading entry begins.
4. Press ENTER 2 times between each line of the heading and after the last line in the heading.
5. Type the body of the memo using blocked paragraphs, and press ENTER 2 times between paragraphs.
6. Press ENTER 2 times after the last paragraph in the body, and type your reference initials (not "urs") in lowercase letters without periods or spaces.
7. Spell-check, proofread, and preview your document for spelling and formatting errors.

J. MEMOS WITH ATTACHMENT NOTATIONS

To format a memo with an attachment, type the word *Attachment* (rather than *Enclosure*) on the line below the reference initials when material is physically attached (stapled or clipped) to a memo.

Example: urs
          Attachment

K. E-MAIL WITH ATTACHMENTS

Use the attachment feature in your e-mail software to attach one or more electronic files to an e-mail message.

To format an e-mail message with an attachment:

- Format the e-mail message as usual.
- No special formatting steps are needed when an attachment is sent. Do *not* type an attachment notation at the bottom of the e-mail message.
- Use the e-mail attachment feature to attach a file of some type to the message. A file attachment is automatically denoted by a special symbol (usually a paper clip).

L. WORD PROCESSING: E-MAIL—ATTACHMENT NOTATIONS

Study Lesson 29 in your Word Manual. Complete all of the shaded steps while at your computer. Then format the documents that follow.

Document Processing

Highlighted words are spelling words from the language arts activities; do *not* highlight them when you type.

↓5X →tab

MEMO TO: All Company Personnel ↓2X

FROM: Jerry Mitchell, Employee Relations Division *jm*

DATE: October 15, 20--

SUBJECT: Holiday Committee ↓2X

There has been a great deal of interest regarding the appropriate procedures for planning our upcoming holiday event next month. ↓2X

I have received requests from approximately 80 percent of our customers to organize some type of annual charitable event. This event will include all interested employees and customers and will provide an opportunity for everyone to contribute financially to local families in need.

It will be necessary to gather general information regarding the cost of renting a facility in our area, which will be ready next week. When I am through with that process and a contract has been signed, I will contact all interested personnel. If you are interested in participating in this important event, please return the attached sign-up sheet. ↓2X

urs
Attachment

MEMO TO: Amy Vigil, Human Resources | **FROM:** Dan Westphal | **DATE:** November 23, 20-- | **SUBJECT:** MedNet Benefit Plan

¶ Thank you for the brochure I received detailing the various options offered to employees through the MedNet plan. I need clarification on some of the important services included in the plan.

¶ Because both my wife and I are employees of Allied Aerospace Industries, do we have the choice of enrolling separately under different options? In our present plan, I know that this is appropriate.

¶ We have two dependents. Can we enroll each dependent under a different plan option, or is it necessary to choose either one option or the other for both? I know that in the past you have asked for evidence of their dependent status and dates of birth, which I have attached.

¶ If you need any further information, please let me know. Thank you very much for your help.

urs | Attachments

Hi, Doug:

¶ I now have ==appropriate== health insurance for my family. As a fellow ==employee==, you might be very ==interested== in obtaining ==further== details. I have attached a file I ==received== with a list of resources, ==procedures==, ==services==, and ==general== ==information== that I found useful.

¶ Researching these ==important== health insurance ==contracts== is ==necessary== so that you can make an informed choice for your own family. Feel free to contact me with any questions.

Elizabeth | Elizabeth Chavez | E-mail: echavez@freeweb.net | Phone: 661-555-3623

Correspondence Review

Goals

- Type at least 32wpm/3′/5e.
- Correctly use Word's italic and underline features.
- Correctly format a memo and an e-mail message with an attachment notation.
- Successfully complete a Progress and Proofreading Check with zero errors on the first scored attempt.

A. WARMUP

alphabet

number/symbol

easy

1 A dumpy kibitzer jingled coins as the exchequer overflowed.
2 eck@hotmail.com 92% Cho & Orr 9/13 (Shh!) $4.57 *2010 #86-3
3 When they visit downtown, the auditors fight for their bid.

Skillbuilding

B. 12-SECOND SPEED SPRINTS

Take three 12-second timed writings on each line.

4 The giant wiry dog put half of the bones down on the chair.
5 Leo may visit the island by the giant oaks on his tan bike.
6 Do not blame my firm for the low level of fuel in the tank.
7 Jake may try to fix the leaks in the pipes in the city gym.
   ' ' ' ' '5' ' ' '10' ' ' '15' ' ' '20' ' ' '25' ' ' '30' ' ' '35' ' ' '40' ' ' '45' ' ' '50' ' ' '55' ' ' '60

C. TECHNIQUE PRACTICE: TAB KEY

Press TAB 1 time between words where you see the → symbol. Type each line 2 times.

8 ale→ and→ Poe→ aha→ Ian→ ape→ ask→ Jew→ Lin→ Mel→ amp
9 Kai→ Meg→ Mag→ Ira→ adz→ Kim→ Liz→ Hal→ Ivy→ aid→ all
10 ark→ Jeb→ arc→ arm→ Una→ air→ Mel→ Lew→ aim→ Peg→ Nan
11 Uzi→ Leo→ Uri→ awe→ ail→ May→ axe→ Max→ Kim→ Nat→ Liv

Take two 3-minute timed writings.

Goal: At least 32wpm/3'/5e

Formatting

E. WORD PROCESSING: ITALIC AND UNDERLINE

GO TO
Word Manual

Study Lesson 30 in your Word Manual. Complete all of the shaded steps while at your computer. Then format the documents that follow.

Document Processing

Correspondence
30-17
Memo

Underline the text to be emphasized.

Italicize the book title.

MEMO TO: All Executive Assistants | **FROM:** Robbie Holt, Staff Development Coordinator | **DATE:** March 25, 20-- | **SUBJECT:** Standardizing Document Formats

¶ Last month we received our final shipment of new laser printers. The installation of these printers in your offices marked the final phaseout of all ink-jet printers.

¶ Because all of us can now use a variety of standardized fonts in our correspondence, please note the following change: <u>From now on, all titles in tables, correspondence, and reports should be set in Calibri 14</u>. This new formatting change will help us to standardize our communications.

¶ The latest edition of the book *Quick Reference for the Automated Office* has two pages of helpful information on laser printers. I have attached my comments. Please read these pages carefully, and we will discuss them at our next meeting.

urs | Attachment

Hi, Louise:

¶ The League of Women Voters is looking for volunteers to work at the various polling places during the upcoming elections. If you think you will be able to volunteer your time, please fill out and mail the attached schedule of availability. After I receive your schedule, I will contact you to confirm a location, time, and date.

¶ We are sending you the best-selling book *Great American Presidents* as a small token of our appreciation. Concerned citizens like you make it possible for the public to have a convenient place to vote. Thank you for your interest in this <u>very</u> worthy cause!

Paige | Paige Jones | E-mail: pjones@hotweb.net | Phone: 314-555-6972

Progress and Proofreading Check

Documents designated as Proofreading Checks serve as a check of your proofreading skill. Your goal is to have zero typographical errors when the GDP software first scores the document.

April 3, 20-- / Ms. Robbie Holt / Staff Development Coordinator / Health Care Incorporated / 1129 Market Street / Philadelphia, PA 19107 / Dear Ms. Holt:

¶ I understand that you were in charge of selecting some <u>fabulous</u> new laser printers for Health Care Incorporated in Philadelphia. I know you researched the needs of your branch and considered those needs in your choice. I certainly appreciate your effort.

¶ Several of us at Health Care Incorporated here in Los Angeles would be very interested in seeing the printers demonstrated as we are planning a major printer upgrade with training to follow as well. Would it be possible to schedule a demonstration soon? We are particularly interested in learning about any features that particularly influenced your printer choice.

¶ I have enclosed an article on laser printers from the latest issue of *Office Technology*. Please let me know your reaction to the article. If I can help you in any way to arrange the demonstration, I would be more than happy to do so.

Sincerely, / Jeffrey Keller / Staff Development Coordinator / urs / Enclosure

Italicize the magazine title.

Reports

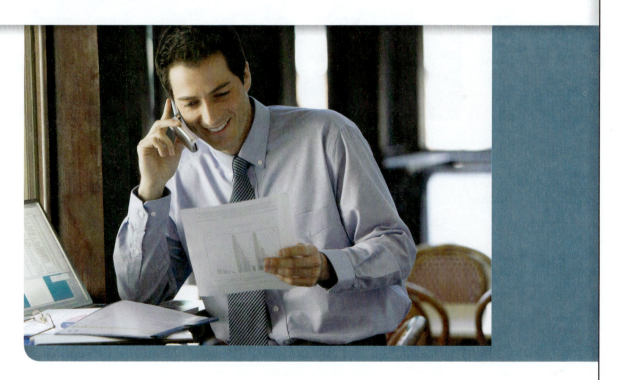

One-Page Business Reports

31

Goals

- Demonstrate improved speed and accuracy while typing.
- Demonstrate acceptable language arts skills in capitalization.
- Correctly use Word's alignment and font size features.
- Correctly format a business report with side headings.

A. WARMUP

alphabet   1   Jack's man found exactly a quarter in the woven zipper bag.

concentration   2   incomprehensibility counterinsurgencies distinguishableness

easy   3   The towns of Sydney and Burma are both due for a May visit.

Skillbuilding

B. MAP+: ALPHABET

Follow the GDP software directions for this exercise to improve keystroking accuracy.

C. PROGRESSIVE PRACTICE: ALPHABET

Follow the GDP software directions for this exercise to improve keystroking speed.

Language Arts

Study the rules at the right.

RULE
≡ sentence

RULE
≡ proper noun

RULE
≡ time

D. CAPITALIZATION

Capitalize the first word of a sentence.

Please prepare a summary of your activities.

Capitalize proper nouns and adjectives derived from proper nouns.

Judy Hendrix drove to Albuquerque in her new Pontiac convertible.

Note: A proper noun is the official name of a particular person, place, or thing.

Capitalize the names of the days of the week, months, holidays, and religious days (but do not capitalize the names of the seasons).

On Thursday, November 25, we will celebrate Thanksgiving, the most popular holiday in the fall.

Edit each sentence to correct any errors.

4 The american flag can be seen flying over the White House in
5 Washington, DC.

6 Our Country's flag is often seen flying over Government
7 buildings on holidays like July 4, independence day.

8 Memorial Day signals the end of spring and the start of
9 Summer.

10 Most Americans consider Labor day the beginning of the fall
11 season.

12 In december many people observe christmas and Hanukkah.

13 most government holidays are scheduled to fall on either a
14 Monday or a friday.

15 Sometimes the birthdays of Historical figures are also
16 celebrated.

Formatting

E. BASIC PARTS OF A BUSINESS REPORT

The two basic styles of reports are business and academic. An illustration for a business report with side headings, paragraph headings, and a list follows.

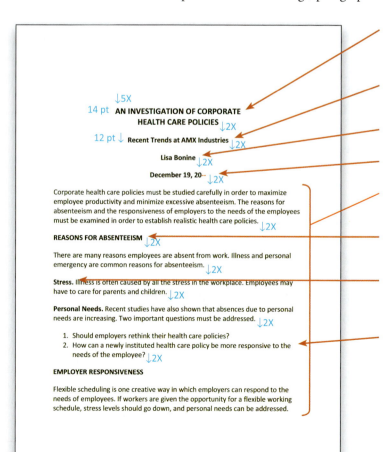

TITLE. Subject of the report; type 2 inches from the top of the page with a 14-point font size, in all-caps, in bold; center all title lines, and single-space 2-line titles.

SUBTITLE. Secondary or explanatory title; center, bold, and type 1 blank line below the title, in upper- and lowercase letters.

BYLINE. Name of the writer; center, bold, and type 1 blank line below the previous line.

DATE. Date of the report; center, bold, and type 1 blank line below the previous line.

BODY. Text of the report; type single-spaced, 1 blank line below the previous line at the left margin, with 1 blank line between paragraphs.

SIDE HEADING. Major subdivision of the report; type in all-caps and bold, 1 blank line below the previous line at the left margin.

PARAGRAPH HEADING. Minor subdivision of the report; type in bold (followed by a bold period) in upper- and lowercase letters, 1 blank line below the previous line, at the left margin.

LIST. Numbered or bulleted items; insert 1 blank line above and below the list, using Word's default list format; type single-spaced throughout.

F. BUSINESS REPORTS

To format a business report:

1. Use single spacing.
2. Press ENTER 5 times to begin the first line of the report 2 inches from the top of the page.
3. Change the font size to 14 point; and type the title in all-caps, centered, in bold. Single-space a 2-line title.
4. Press ENTER 2 times and change the font size to 12 point.
5. If the report includes a subtitle, byline, or date, type each item centered and in bold upper- and lowercase letters.
6. Press ENTER 2 times after each part of the heading block.
7. Press ENTER 2 times between all paragraphs.
8. Do not number the first page of a report, but insert a page number on all subsequent pages of a multipage report.
9. Spell-check, proofread, and preview your document for spelling and formatting errors.

G. BUSINESS REPORTS WITH SIDE HEADINGS

To format side headings in a business report:

1. Insert 1 blank line before and after side headings.
2. Type side headings in the default 12-point font at the left margin, in bold, and in all-caps.

H. WORD PROCESSING: ALIGNMENT AND FONT—SIZE

GO TO
Word Manual

Study Lesson 31 in your Word Manual. Complete all of the shaded steps while at your computer. Then format the documents that follow.

Document Processing

Report
31-1
Business Report

↓5X

14 pt **AN ANALYSIS OF BUSINESS CASUAL DRESS CODES** ↓2X

12 pt ↓ **Recent Trends in the Business World** ↓2X

≡ proper noun   **Louise McMabel** ↓2X

≡ time   **October 18, 20--** ↓2X

≡ sentence   Establishing corporate business casual dress codes requires both sensitivity and awareness of all the legal ramifications that such codes bring with them. Factors such as whether or not a job requires a uniform or requires certain attire for safety reasons can be extremely important in setting a dress code policy and in being able to enforce it. ↓2X

(continued on next page)

ESTABLISHING GUIDELINES ↓2X

≡ sentence

A policy manual should include all specifications regarding dress codes, including the more relaxed dress code known as business casual. If your company's policy manual does not precisely define what is considered "acceptable" business casual dress, you are likely to see a range of interpretations. Once expected dress code standards have been lowered due to vague guidelines, you will have a much more difficult time enforcing any guidelines later.

RESPONSIVENESS OF EMPLOYEES

≡ time

≡ proper noun

If employees are convinced that their image and dress directly affect the company's bottom line, they are more likely to be motivated to adhere to stricter dress code guidelines. If they know that a specified workday, such as a Friday, can be a day to relax their dress, they might consider it a reasonable trade-off to the stricter guidelines enforced during the other workdays. A professional image consultant from Dress for Success Inc. could conduct some workshops to educate employees regarding the importance of professional dress and how to dress professionally even when the standard is business casual.

POTENTIAL RESULTS

≡ time

If you decide to adopt a business casual dress code in the spring, note its effect on employee morale. You might find that teamwork increases and creativity rises. All these factors have the potential to increase productivity. Everyone wins!

Report 31-2
Business Report

Open the file for Report 31-1 and make the following changes:

1. Delete the subtitle, and change the byline to Renee Kare Oke.
2. Change the date to November 24.
3. Change the second side heading to EMPLOYEE RESPONSIVENESS.
4. Delete the last two sentences in the last paragraph at the end of the report.
5. Add the following sentences to the end of the last paragraph:

   Employees will feel empowered by the energy generated by a more casual work environment. When they arrive at work each Friday in casual attire, they will feel more relaxed and ready to work.

Multipage Business Reports

Goals

- Type at least 33wpm/3′/5e.
- Correctly use Word's page number, page break, and widow/ orphan control features.
- Correctly format a multipage business report with side and paragraph headings.

A. WARMUP

alphabet 1 By Jove, my quick study of lexicography won a bronze prize.
one hand 2 adverb hookup was ply target minimum beat knoll acted kinky
easy 3 The auditor from Dubuque had a problem with the amendments.

Skillbuilding

Take a 1-minute timed writing on the boxed paragraph to establish your base speed. Then take a 1-minute timed writing on the following paragraph. As soon as you equal or exceed your base speed on this paragraph, move to the next, more difficult paragraph.

B. SUSTAINED PRACTICE: ALTERNATE-HAND WORDS

4   When eight of them began a formal discussion on some   11
5 of the major issues, the need for a chair was very evident. 23
6 A chair would be sure to handle the usual work with ease.   34

7   The eight people in that group decided that the work   11
8 would be done only if they selected one person to be chair 23
9 of their group. They began to debate all the major issues. 34

10   One issue that needed to be settled right up front was 11
11 the question of how to handle proxy votes. It seemed for a 23
12 short time that a fight over this very issue would result. 35

13   The group worked diligently in attempting to solve the 11
14 issues that were being discussed. All of the concerns that 23
15 were brought to the group were reviewed in depth by them.   34

    1 | 2 | 3 | 4 | 5 | 6 | 7 | 8 | 9 | 10 | 11 | 12

Take two 3-minute timed writings.

Goal: At least 33wpm/3'/5e

C. 3-MINUTE TIMED WRITING

```
16        Be zealous in your efforts when you write business    10
17   letters. Your business writing must convey clearly what    22
18   it is you want people to read. All of your letters should  33
19   be formatted neatly in proper business letter format.      44
20        Before sending your letters, read them quickly just to 55
21   make sure that they explain clearly what you want to say.  67
22   Proofread the letters you write for correct grammar and    78
23   spelling. Use all of your writing skills to display the    89
24   best image. Your readers will welcome the effort.          99
```
```
     1 | 2 | 3 | 4 | 5 | 6 | 7 | 8 | 9 | 10 | 11 | 12
```

Formatting

D. MULTIPAGE BUSINESS REPORTS

To format a multipage business report:

1. Press ENTER 5 times to begin the first line of the report 2 inches from the top of the page.
2. Do not number the first page. Suppress the page number on the first page, and insert a page number in the top right-hand corner of the page header of all continuing pages.
3. Do not end any page with a single line, and do not begin any subsequent page with a single line.
4. Spell-check, proofread, and preview your document for spelling and formatting errors.
5. Refer to the illustration that follows to format the second page of a multipage business report.

2

Job candidates lie for any number of reasons. Many applicants have families to support and are willing to do anything to get the job.

CONCLUSION

It is clear that falsification is at hand more than ever, and it is equally clear that the value of ethics has been lost on some applicants. It is therefore up to the employer to figure out how best to test a potential employee's integrity.

PAGE NUMBER. Inserted on continuing pages only; typed inside the document header at the right margin.

BODY. Continues at the default top margin, 1 inch from the top of the page.

E. BUSINESS REPORTS WITH PARAGRAPH HEADINGS

To format paragraph headings in a business report:

1. Insert 1 blank line above the paragraph that includes a paragraph heading.
2. Type paragraph headings at the left margin, in bold, and in upper- and lowercase letters.
3. Follow the paragraph heading by a bold period and 1 space.

F. WORD PROCESSING: PAGE NUMBER, PAGE BREAK, AND WIDOW/ORPHAN CONTROL

GO TO
Word Manual

Study Lesson 32 in your Word Manual. Complete all of the shaded steps while at your computer. Then format the documents that follow.

Document Processing

**Report
32-3**
Business Report

> Remember to insert a page number on the second page and suppress it on the first page.

> Your page endings in Word will not match those in the book.

Italicize the words as shown.

ETHICAL ISSUES FACING EMPLOYERS AND JOB APPLICANTS
Mary Lincoln
February 12, 20--

¶Some job applicants "pad" their application with false information, such as phony salaries and nonexistent jobs. Even some well-known political figures have been guilty of listing a job on their resume during a period of time in which such a job never existed. When applicants are eager or even desperate to find a job, such ethical dilemmas will rise to the forefront.

FALSIFICATION

¶What is falsification? Certainly, adding information that is not true would seem to indicate a clear intent on the part of the applicant to falsify information. But how do you judge whether or not leaving out pertinent information or information that would cast you in a bad light qualifies as intentional falsification? These are gray areas that are not always easy to define.

¶**Honors and Grades.** Let's take a look at a more specific example. What if your grade point average at graduation had been just slightly higher to qualify you for a degree designation of *cum laude*, *magna cum laude*, or even *summa cum laude*? Clearly, it would be falsification to claim one of these designations when that designation was not earned. However, there is an ethical way to place yourself in the best light without falsifying information. If you earned an outstanding grade point average in the courses for your given major, it is certainly acceptable to state your correct grade point average and specify that the average reflects grades only for courses related to your declared college major or minor.

¶**School Activities.** Many applicants are willing to exaggerate or totally falsify their participation in school activities. In order to prove leadership ability, an applicant might be willing to say that he or she was president of a nonexistent club or perhaps organized some type of fictional fund-raising activity. Such deception is clearly falsification.

¶**Job Titles.** Another area rampant with deception is the list of previous job titles. In order to make a former job sound more impressive, a job contender might add a word or two to the title or perhaps rename the title altogether.

REASONS FOR LYING

Job candidates lie for any number of reasons. Some of them see getting a job as some sort of game in which the rules really don't matter. Others equate lying with cheating on an exam and rationalize the deception in some way. Many applicants have families to support and are willing to do anything to get the job.

(continued on next page)

CONCLUSION

It is clear that falsification is at hand more than ever, and it is equally clear that the value of ethics has been lost on some applicants. It is therefore up to the employer to figure out how best to test a potential employee's integrity, to investigate an applicant's history, and then to decide whether or not to hire this individual.

<table>
<tr><td>

Report
32-4
Business Report

</td></tr>
</table>

Open the file for Report 32-3 and make the following changes:

1. Change the byline to Ruth Carter.
2. Change the date to October 1.
3. Change the second side heading to REASONS FOR FALSIFICATION.
4. Add this paragraph to the end of the report:

The importance of ethical intentions in a future employee should never be underestimated. There is an old saying that honesty is the best policy. Honesty is expected and required in the workplace, and great dividends await those who make an exemplary work ethic a top priority.

Rough-Draft Business Reports With Lists

Goals

- Demonstrate improved speed and accuracy while typing.
- Correctly identify and apply basic proofreaders' marks.
- Correctly use Word's bullet and numbering features.
- Correctly format a rough-draft business report with lists.

A. WARMUP

alphabet	1	Jay began removing six dozen black quilts with petty flaws.
practice: *s* and *d*	2	sod sad deeds desks dosed dudes dusts sheds sides soda suds
easy	3	The men may be busy but they may go to the social with her.

Skillbuilding

B. MAP+: NUMBERS

Follow the GDP software directions for this exercise to improve keystroking accuracy.

PPP   PRETEST » PRACTICE » POSTTEST

PRETEST
Take a 1-minute timed writing.

C. PRETEST: Discrimination Practice

4	Steven saw the younger, unruly boy take flight as he	11
5	threw the coin at the jury. The brave judge stopped the	22
6	fight. He called out to the youth, who recoiled in fear.	33

     1 | 2 | 3 | 4 | 5 | 6 | 7 | 8 | 9 | 10 | 11 | 12

PRACTICE
Speed Emphasis:
If you made 2 or fewer errors on the Pretest, type each *individual* line 2 times.
Accuracy Emphasis:
If you made 3 or more errors, type each *group* of lines (as though it were a paragraph) 2 times.

D. PRACTICE: Left Hand

7	vbv verb bevy vibes bevel brave above verbal bovine behaves
8	wew west weep threw wedge weave fewer weight sewing dewdrop
9	fgf gulf gift fight fudge fugue flags flight golfer feigned

E. PRACTICE: Right Hand

10	uyu buys your usury unity youth buoys unruly untidy younger
11	oio coin lion oiled foils foist prior recoil iodine rejoice
12	jhj jury huge enjoy three judge habit adjust slight jasmine

F. POSTTEST: Discrimination Practice

Language Arts

Edit these sentences to correct any errors.

G. PROOFREADING

13 It doesnt matter how fast you can type or how well you now a
14 software program if you produce documents that are filled
15 with errors.

16 You must learn to watch for errors in spelling punctuation,
17 and formatting.

18 Look carefully between words and sentences.

19 Make sure that after a period at the end of a sentence, you
20 see one space.

21 Sometime it helps to look at the characters in the sentence
22 justabove the one you are proofreading to ensure accuracy.

Formatting

H. BULLETED AND NUMBERED LISTS

REFER TO
Reference
Manual

R-12D: Examples of Different Types of Lists

Numbers and/or bullets are used in documents to call attention to items in a list and to increase readability. If the sequence of the list items is important, use numbers rather than bullets.

To format bulleted and numbered lists in documents:

- Use the bullets or numbers feature to format the list using Word's default format.

- Use the same line spacing (single or double) between lines in the list as is used in the rest of the document.

I. BUSINESS REPORTS WITH LISTS

To format lists in a business report:

1. Press ENTER 2 times to insert 1 blank line above the list.
2. Between lines in the list, use the same spacing (single in a business report or double in academic reports) as is used in the rest of the document.

3. Insert 1 blank line below the list.
4. Spell-check, proofread, and preview your document for spelling and formatting errors.

J. BASIC PROOFREADERS' MARKS

Proofreaders' marks are used to indicate changes or corrections to be made in a rough-draft document that is being revised for final copy. Study the chart to learn what each proofreaders' mark means.

Proofreaders' Marks	Draft	Final copy
⌒ Omit space	data base	database
∨ or ∧ Insert	if hes going,	if he's not going,
☰ Capitalize	Maple street	Maple Street
℘ Delete	a final draft	a draft
# Insert space	allready to	all ready to
⎯ Change word	and if you	and when you
/ Use lowercase letter	our President	our president
∿ Transpose	they all see	they see all
SS Single-space	first line second line	first line second line
¶ New paragraph	. . . to use it. ¶ We can	. . . to use it. We can

K. WORD PROCESSING: BULLETS AND NUMBERING

GO TO Word Manual

Study Lesson 33 in your Word Manual. Complete all of the shaded steps while at your computer. Then format the documents that follow.

Document Processing

Report 33-5
Business Report

Lines are shown with extra spacing for the proofreaders' marks. Type the report with standard spacing.

EFFECTIVE WAYS TO
GET ACTIVE AS A FAMILY

By Mike Khouri

February 23, 20--

There is no doubt that parenting takes a great deal of time and more energy. Although it would seem that becoming active as a family group would expend even more energy and possibly create more stress the opposite is true. When the whole family participates in physical activities, children learn that being active is fun and makes everyone feel better.

(continued on next page)

GETTING STARTED

There are many ways in which you can get all family members up and participating in a newer, healthier lifestyle:

1. Make a list as a ~~f~~ amily of activities you would all like to do together, and post a schedule.

2. Make sure the list includes things everyone enjoys doing.

3. Plan a monthly activity ~~which~~ that involves walking out doors, such as a trip to the zoo or camping.

SETTING Family Rules

Once you have started this regimen, you will notice probably that the entire family has an increased energy level. However, you may still need a few family rules to keep every one on track:

- Set a limit on the number of television hours allowed.
- Set ~~limits~~ a limit on computer games and Internet use.
- Dont use food as a reward for participating in family activities.
- Make these activities a high priority in your daily and weekly routines.

If you practice these methods to create and maintain the energy levels for your ~~entire~~ family, you will find that these routines will become a ~~very~~ natural part of your daily life. Enjoy the change and experiment with new activities each week. You will be likely pleasantly surprised at the changes you see in the family unit.

Report 33-6
Business Report

Open the file for Report 33-5 and make the following changes:

1. Change the first side heading to HOW TO GET STARTED.
2. Change the second side heading to HOW TO SET FAMILY RULES.
3. Change the second numbered item to this: Make sure the list includes activities that are fun and upbeat.
4. Change the fourth bulleted item to this: Don't let things get in the way of family activity time.

Multipage Academic Reports With Lists

34

Goals

- Type at least 34wpm/3'/5e.
- Correctly use Word's line-spacing feature.
- Correctly format a multipage academic report with a list.

A. WARMUP

alphabet	1	Please pack my boxes with five dozen jugs of liquid veneer.
frequent digraphs	2	on bon con none noon don ion one son ton won onto moon font
easy	3	If she works downtown, Kay may make a visit to the old gym.

Skillbuilding

B. PROGRESSIVE PRACTICE: NUMBERS

Follow the GDP software directions for this exercise to improve keystroking speed.

C. TECHNIQUE PRACTICE: ENTER KEY

Type each line 2 times. Type each sentence on a separate line by pressing ENTER after each sentence.

4	Who? Go. So? Get it? Why not? Well? See to it. Why me? Eat!
5	Read it. Whew! Go slow. Where? Finished? Who, Tom? Type it.
6	Roll over. Wait. Sit. Beg. See him. What gives? Truly! Why?
7	Do it. Be there. Taxi? See me. All? Why him? We did. Don't!

D. 3-MINUTE TIMED WRITING

Take two 3-minute timed writings.

Goal: At least 34wpm/3'/5e

8	Companies that place major ads on the Internet use a	11
9	process called data mining. They look for patterns in the	22
10	quantities of data they get from those who visit Web sites.	34
11	Data mining tracks buying habits of customers and then	46
12	decides to send ads to them based on their current and past	58
13	buying patterns. Data mining can also be used to explain	69
14	buyer behavior and to look at trends. First, a survey is	80
15	filled out, and then the results are gathered and stored in	92
16	a file to be analyzed in detail at a later time.	102

| 1 | 2 | 3 | 4 | 5 | 6 | 7 | 8 | 9 | 10 | 11 | 12 |

Formatting

REFER TO
Reference
Manual

R-8A–B: Multipage
Business Report

E. BASIC PARTS OF AN ACADEMIC REPORT

The two basic styles of reports are business and academic. An illustration for a multipage academic report with side headings, paragraph headings, and a list follows.

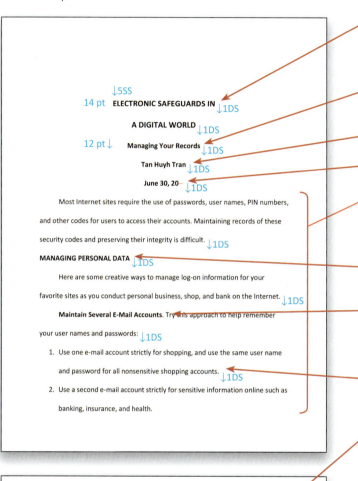

TITLE. Subject of the report; centered; typed 2 inches from the top of the page (single-space, press ENTER 5 times, and change to double spacing) in bold and all-caps, with a 14-point font size; 2-line titles are double-spaced.

SUBTITLE. Secondary or explanatory title; centered; typed 1 double space below the title, in bold, with upper- and lowercase letters.

BYLINE. Name of the writer; centered; typed 1 double space below the previous line, in bold.

DATE. Date of the report; centered; typed 1 double space below the previous line, in bold.

BODY. Text of the report, double-spaced; the first line of each paragraph is indented 0.5 inch, with 1 blank line between paragraphs. Subsequent pages continue at the default top margin, 1 inch from the top of the page.

SIDE HEADING. Major subdivision of the report; typed 1 double space below the previous line at the left margin, in bold and all-caps.

PARAGRAPH HEADING. Minor subdivision of the report; typed 1 double space below the previous line indented 0.5 inch from the left margin, in bold, with upper- and lowercase letters; followed by a period (also in bold).

LIST. Numbered or bulleted items in a report; typed using Word's default list indent, double-spaced, with 1 double space above and below the list.

PAGE NUMBER. Inserted on the continuing pages only inside the document header at the right margin.

F. ACADEMIC REPORTS

To format a multipage academic report with side headings and paragraph headings:

1. Press ENTER 5 times to begin the first line of the academic report 2 inches from the top of the page.
2. Change line spacing to double, and type the remainder of the report in double spacing.
3. Type the title in all-caps, centered, and in bold, and change the font size to 14 point. Double-space a 2-line title.
4. Press ENTER 1 time and change the font size to 12 point.
5. If the report includes a subtitle, byline, or date, type each item centered, in bold and upper- and lowercase letters.
6. Press ENTER 1 time after each line in the heading block.
7. Press ENTER 1 time between all paragraphs.
8. Type side headings at the left margin, in bold and all-caps.
9. Press TAB 1 time at the start of each paragraph and each paragraph heading to indent them 0.5 inch.
10. Type paragraph headings in bold and upper- and lowercase letters, and follow the paragraph heading with a bold period and 1 space.
11. Do not number the first page of a report, but insert a page number on all subsequent pages of a multipage report.
12. Do not end any page with a single line, and do not begin any subsequent page with a single line.
13. Spell-check, proofread, and preview your document for spelling and formatting errors.

G. ACADEMIC REPORTS WITH LISTS

R-12D: Examples of Different Types of Lists

To format lists in an academic report:

1. Press ENTER 1 time before beginning the list.
2. Apply either bullets or numbers, and type the list using Word's default format.
3. Between lines in the list, use the same spacing (double in academic reports) as is used in the rest of the document.
4. Press ENTER 1 time after completing the final entry in the list, and end the list.

H. WORD PROCESSING: LINE SPACING

Study Lesson 34 in your Word Manual. Complete all of the shaded steps while at your computer. Then format the documents that follow.

Document Processing

Report
34-7
Academic Report

↓5SS

14 pt **COMMUNICATION DYNAMICS WHEN** ↓1DS

SOCIALIZING AT WORK ↓1DS

12 pt↓ **Informal Social Support Systems** ↓1DS

Linda Padilla ↓1DS

October 30, 20-- ↓1DS

Longer work hours and increasing job demands are leading to social networking on the job. Mixing socially with coworkers requires a different tactic than socializing with friends and family. ↓1DS

(continued on next page)

BE YOURSELF ↓1DS

Conversation does not have to be trivial. You can take many approaches and may find that you are actually enjoying the process. ↓1DS

Talk About Personal Interests. Personal interests are usually great points to launch a conversation that is relaxed and interesting. Try this: ↓1DS

1. Talk about your favorite hobby. This is an easy way to help you relax since our hobbies bring up pleasant memories. ↓1DS

2. Food is always a safe topic that everyone enjoys. Chat about your favorite restaurant or your favorite exotic dish. ↓1DS

Ask Questions About Others. Obviously, you should avoid personal questions. Try not to ask anything you wouldn't want someone to ask you.

JUST LISTEN

Finally, don't be afraid to just listen. You don't have to talk all the time. Your coworkers will appreciate a supportive listener, and you might learn something in the process.

Report 34-8
Academic Report

Open the file for Report 34-7 and make the following changes:

1. Change the byline to Faith Tolerencia.
2. Add this paragraph at the end of the report:

Maintain good eye contact, avoid distractions, and stay active by asking mental questions. Let the other person know that you're listening by body language and meaningful responses. You might be surprised at the support you receive in return.

Keyboarding Connection

Business E-Mail Style Guide

Even though e-mail is relatively informal, you need to be succinct and clear. Greet your reader with a formal "Dear . . . ," or an informal "Hi . . . ," and so on. Put the most important part of your message first. Watch the length of your paragraphs; four to five lines per paragraph won't put off your reader.

Use asterisks, caps, dashes, and so forth, for emphasis. Avoid unfamiliar abbreviations, slang, or jargon. Not everyone who receives your business e-mail may know a particular catchword or phrase. Proofread your e-mail. Be concerned about grammar, punctuation, and word choice. Use your e-mail's spell checker.

End your business e-mail politely. Expressions of appreciation (e.g., "Thanks") or goodwill (e.g., "Best wishes") let your reader know you are finishing your message.

Your Turn: In Lesson 25 you learned how to format and compose e-mail messages. Create an e-mail message to send to a coworker, colleague, or friend. Review the e-mail for adherence to the guidelines listed above.

More Rough-Draft Reports

Goals

- Demonstrate improved speed and accuracy while typing.
- Demonstrate acceptable language arts skills in composing sentences.
- Identify and apply more proofreaders' marks.
- Correctly format a rough-draft, multipage academic report.
- Successfully complete a Progress and Proofreading Check with zero errors on the first scored attempt.

A. WARMUP

alphabet   1 The five boxing wizards jumped quickly into the next round.

number/symbol   2 jjoy@aol.com 66% (Ott & Poe) 5/8 Out! $2.16 *et al. #73-490

easy   3 Blanche may go with me to Yale to visit my son and his pal.

Skillbuilding

B. 12-SECOND SPEED SPRINTS

Take three 12-second timed writings on each line.

4 The man with the rifle may signal us to take the sign down.
5 The new city law may allow us to fish for cod on the docks.
6 The old chapel at the end of the big lake has an odd shape.
7 The old men may have a duel down by the lake at noon today.

`' ' ' '5' ' ' '10' ' ' '15' ' ' '20' ' ' '25' ' ' '30' ' ' '35' ' ' '40' ' ' '45' ' ' '50' ' ' '55' ' ' '60`

C. PACED PRACTICE

Follow the GDP software directions for this exercise to improve keystroking speed and accuracy.

Language Arts

D. COMPOSING SENTENCES

Answer each question with a complete sentence.

8 How much time do you spend each day reading and answering e-mail?

9 Which people do you correspond most often with in e-mail?

10 What kinds of errors do you find most often in e-mail?

11 Do you proofread your own e-mail messages before sending them?

12 What advice do you have for improving e-mail messages?

Formatting

REFER TO
Reference Manual

R-14C: Proofreaders' Marks

E. MORE PROOFREADERS' MARKS

Review the most frequently used proofreaders' marks introduced in Lesson 33. Then study the additional proofreaders' marks presented here.

Proofreaders' Marks		Draft	Final copy
ds	Double-space	ds first line / second line	first line / second line
. . . .	Don't delete	a ~~true~~ story	a true story
◯	Spell out	the only ①	the only one
⌐	Move right	Please send	Please send
¬	Move left	May 1	May 1
∼	Bold	Column Heading	**Column Heading**
ital	Italic	*ital* Time magazine	*Time* magazine
u/l	Underline	*u/l* Time magazine	Time magazine readers
⟋	Move as shown	readers will see	will see

A new paragraph may be formatted either by inserting a blank line before the paragraph in a single-spaced document or by indenting the first line 0.5 inch (⌐) in a double-spaced document.

F. WORD PROCESSING: CUT AND COPY; PASTE

GO TO Word Manual

Study Lesson 35 in your Word Manual. Complete all of the shaded steps while at your computer. Then format the documents that follow.

Document Processing

Report
35-9
Academic Report

ENDING PROCRASTINATION

Steven Rice

Every one at one time or another has put off some task, goal or important plan at work for any number of reasons. perhaps you think time is too short or the task isn't really that important. Either way, procrastination can lead to a stalled life and career.

EVALUATE YOUR SITUATION

Joyce Winfrey of Time Management Incorporated ~~has some very good advice that will help you to begin to move forward.~~ She says that you should ask yourself ② very basic questions about why you are procrastinating:

2. 1. Is there a valid reason for my procrastination?

1. 2. Am I procrastinating because the task at hand is not really what I want?

(continued on next page)

After you have asked yourself these questions, look deep within yourself. If you are looking for excuses, then asking these questions will be a waste of time. However, honest answers will clarify ~~your situation~~ *things*. Several techniques will help you get back on task.

PRACTICE NEW TECHNIQUES

Identifying and understanding the techniques ~~which~~ *that* follow is the first step. Once you know what to do, you can begin to practice these steps daily.

Take Baby Steps. Don't make any task bigger than it really is by looking at the whole thing at once. Break it down into baby steps that are manageable.

Dont Strive for Perfectionism. If you are waiting for the perfect solution or the perfect opportunity, you will *be* immobilized. Accept the fact that no one ~~and nothing~~ is perfect. Then accept your mistakes and move on.

Enjoy the Task. ~~Enjoy the task at hand and~~ find something in the task at hand that is positive and rewarding. Confront your fears with a plan of action.

Remind yourself of all these techniques daily. Post them *by* your telephone, your desk, or *in* your car. You will find that your personal life and career will gain momentum, and success will soon be yours.

TIPS ~~FOR HELPING YOU~~ *TO HELP*

PREPARE FOR YOUR EXAM

Betty Goldberg

June 8, 20--

¶ in school you have taken ~~some~~ *many* exams. Whether you are an excellent exam taker or a novice at the task, you *probably* have experienced a degree of stress related to your performance on an exam. There are some steps you can take to reduce the stress of taking an exam, and these suggestions will likely help you throughout your life.

PREPARING FOR THE EXAM

¶ Of course, it's always easier to take an exam from an instructor whom you have had in previous classes because you know what to expect.

(continued on next page)

¶ **Know What to Expect.** If you don't know what to expect, however, you need to prepare for all possibilities. Be sure that you review all pertinent materials for the exam—whether they come from classnotes, the textbook, field trips, or class room presentations.

¶ **Rely on Past Experience.** From past experience, you know whether the instructor likes to use objective or subjective questions, whether the instructor focuses on the textbook or on class notes, and the difficulty of the questions the instructor asks.

SURVIVING THE DAY BEFORE THE EXAM

¶ Be sure you know where and at what time the exam will be administered. Organize the materials you need to bring with you to the exam. You need a computer, pencils, pens, a calculators, CDs, or paper. Try to get a good nights sleep the night before the exam.

Taking the Exam

¶ Now that the day of the exam has arrived, try this to ensure that you perform well:

1. Arrive at the test sight early so that you are ready to take the exam when the instructor announces the beginning time. That means that you have to be sure to get up early enough to have a light breakfast before leaving for the exam.

2. Read the instructions provided very carefully on the exam to be sure you answer the questions correctly.

3. Keep track of time so that you don't get stuck and spend too much of your time on any one part of the exam.

   a. Try to keep a positive attitude.

¶ Relax as best you can. A relaxed performance is much more productive than a

stressed performance.

UNIT 8

Tables

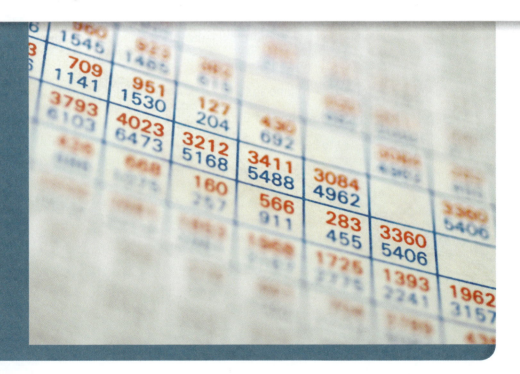

Boxed Tables

36

Goals

- Type at least 35wpm/3'/4e.
- Correctly use Word's table features to insert and resize a table.
- Correctly format a boxed table.

A. WARMUP

<table>
<tr><td>alphabet</td><td>1</td><td>Jack typed a requisition for long-sized white moving boxes.</td></tr>
<tr><td>concentration</td><td>2</td><td>interchangeableness paleoanthropologist extraterritoriality</td></tr>
<tr><td>easy</td><td>3</td><td>Bob owns a pair of ancient bicycles and a giant ivory bowl.</td></tr>
</table>

Skillbuilding

B. SUSTAINED PRACTICE: ROUGH DRAFT

Take a 1-minute timed writing on the boxed paragraph to establish your base speed. Then take a 1-minute timed writing on the following paragraph. As soon as you equal or exceed your base speed on this paragraph, move to the next, more difficult paragraph.

4	The pattern of employment in our country is undergoing	11
5	some major changes. Companies are slowly paring down their	23
6	permanent staffs to just a core group of critical managers.	35

7	This trend promotes what is called an acordion affect	11
8	in the workforce: The ability to expand and contract as the	23
9	time and balance sheets dictate. This provides flexibility.	35

10	All of these changes would make it tought for all unions	11
11	to stay a float. They donot possess satisfactory procedures	23
12	for organizing employes. Unions are trying to adapt faster.	35

13	Such services as elder or child care, counseling, debt	11
14	managment, and even health care maybe of great asistance	23
15	to employees, but employers may find it difficult to offer them.	35

1 | 2 | 3 | 4 | 5 | 6 | 7 | 8 | 9 | 10 | 11 | 12

Take two 3-minute timed writings.

Goal: At least 35wpm/3'/4e

C. 3-MINUTE TIMED WRITING

```
16        Technology that tracks eye movements is used by Web        11
17   designers to judge how people interact with Web pages. It      22
18   must find out which zone of the page is viewed first, which    34
19   feature is viewed most often, and how quickly a page comes     46
20   to the screen.                                                 49
21        Eye movements are tracked by use of hardware and data     60
22   analysis software. A camera is employed to find out the eye    72
23   movements of people who watch a screen. Pupil dilations and    84
24   scanning patterns of the eyes are measured to document the     96
25   amount of mental strain that has been exerted.                105
        1 | 2 | 3 | 4 | 5 | 6 | 7 | 8 | 9 | 10 | 11 | 12
```

Formatting

D. BASIC PARTS OF A TABLE

Tables have vertical columns (identified by a letter, such as Column A) and horizontal rows (identified by a number, such as Row 1). A table cell (identified by the column letter and row number, such as Cell A1) is created where a column and a row intersect. An illustration for a boxed table follows.

center page ↓
center horizontally

14 pt **LUXURY CRUISES ON ALASKAN YACHT CHARTERS**				
12 pt ↓ **New Cruise Rates** ↓1X				
Duration	**Restricted Rate** ↓1X	**Agent Rate**	**Difference**	**Savings**
8 hours	$ 350	$ 325	$ 25	7.1%
3 days	925	855	70	7.6%
5 days	1,500	1,375	125	8.3%
7 days	2,100	1,900	200	9.5%
10 days	3,000	2,700	300	10.0%
14 days	4,200	3,750	450	10.7%
21 days	6,300	5,500	800	12.7%

Row 1
Row 2
↓ Row 3
Column A   Column B →

2-line title
align bottom ↓
2-line column heading
2 spaces for each digit
3 spaces: 2 for each digit; 1 for each comma

TITLE. Merge cells in Row 1; center and type the title with a 14-point font, in all-caps and bold; if a subtitle is not used, insert 1 blank line after the title; single-space a 2-line title.

SUBTITLE. Center and type the subtitle on the line below the title, in upper- and lowercase bold letters; press ENTER 1 time to insert a blank line below the subtitle.

COLUMN HEADINGS. Center all column headings; press ENTER 1 time to split a 2-line column heading; bottom-align all column headings.

COLUMN ENTRIES. Left-align text column entries and right-align number column entries; capitalize only the first word and proper nouns; add spaces after a dollar sign to align with the widest column entry below (add 2 spaces for each digit and 1 space for each comma).

E. TABLES

You will learn to center tables horizontally and vertically in Lesson 38.

To format a table:

1. Use single spacing.
2. Insert a table with the desired number of columns and rows.
3. Format other parts of a table as indicated in the model document in Section D.
4. Capitalize only the first word and proper nouns in column entries.
5. Type all tables using standard table format.
6. Automatically adjust the column widths.
7. Spell-check, proofread, and preview your document for spelling and formatting errors.

F. WORD PROCESSING: TABLE—INSERT AND TABLE—AUTOFIT TO CONTENTS

GO TO Word Manual

Study Lesson 36 in your Word Manual. Complete all of the shaded steps while at your computer. Then format the documents that follow.

Document Processing

Table 36-1
Boxed Table

Brenda Riggs	President	Clausen Hall
Cameron Smith	Dean	Roosevelt Hall
Jamie Summers	Chairperson	Strathern Hall

Table 36-2
Boxed Table

Bonnie Frank, Executive Editor	Trenton, New Jersey
Robert Gales, Associate Editor	Lincoln, Nebraska
Omar Quinlan, Contributing Writer	Jefferson City, Missouri
Elena Plummer, Art Director	Santa Fe, New Mexico

Table 36-3
Boxed Table

1. Open the file for Table 36-2.
2. Change the name and title in Cell A1 to Corinne Easton, Film Editor.
3. Change the city and state in Cell B2 to Albany, New York.
4. Change the name in Cell A3 to Blanca Puscani.
5. Change the title in Cell A4 to Special Effects Animator.

Table 36-4
Boxed Table

Angel Barcos	Storyboard Artist	Academy of Fine Arts
Maggie Lester	Art Director	Art Institute of California
Chang Jin Lee	Special Effects Animator	Digital Media Technologies
Anita Bergman	Visual Effects Artist	Video Game Design School

Open Tables

Goals

- Demonstrate improved speed and accuracy while typing.
- Demonstrate acceptable language arts skills in using apostrophes.
- Correctly use Word's table features to merge cells and remove borders.
- Correctly format an open table with a table heading block.

A. WARMUP

alphabet   1   Def may just bring very exciting news to the plaza quickly.

one hand   2   street unholy sad you stated monopoly seat pink treat unpin

easy   3   Hal bought an authentic bible of the gospels in the chapel.

Skillbuilding

B. MAP+: ALPHABET

Follow the GDP software directions for this exercise to improve keystroking accuracy.

C. PROGRESSIVE PRACTICE: ALPHABET

Follow the GDP software directions for this exercise to improve keystroking speed.

Language Arts

Study the rules at the right.

RULE
' singular noun

RULE
' plural noun

RULE
' pronoun

D. APOSTROPHES

Use 's to form the possessive of singular nouns.

The hurricane's force caused major damage to North Carolina's coastline.

Use only an apostrophe to form the possessive of plural nouns that end in *s*.

The investors' goals were outlined in the stockholders' report.
But: The investors outlined their goals in the report to the stockholders.
But: The women's and children's clothing was on sale.

Use 's to form the possessive of indefinite pronouns (such as *someone's* or *anybody's*); do not use an apostrophe with personal pronouns (such as *hers, his, its, ours, theirs,* and *yours*).

She could select anybody's paper for a sample.
It's time to put the file back into its cabinet.

Edit each sentence to correct any errors.

4 The womans purse was stolen as she held her childs hand.

5 If the book is yours, please return it to the library now.

6 The girls decided to send both parents donations to the school.

7 The childs toy was forgotten by his mothers good friend.

8 The universities presidents submitted the joint statement.

9 The four secretaries salaries were raised just like yours.

10 One boys presents were forgotten when he left the party.

11 If these blue notebooks are not ours, they must be theirs.

12 The plant was designed to recycle its own waste products.

Formatting

E. TABLE HEADING BLOCK

The table heading block is typed in Row 1 and includes the title and subtitle (if any). To format a table heading block:

1. Merge the cells in Row 1.
2. Inside Row 1, center and type the title in all-caps and bold, with a 14-point font.
3. Single-space a 2-line title.
4. If a subtitle is *not* used, insert 1 blank line after the title.
5. Center and type the subtitle (if any) 1 line below the title in upper- and lowercase bold letters.
6. Insert 1 blank line after any subtitle.

F. WORD PROCESSING: TABLE—MERGE CELLS AND TABLE—BORDER

Study Lesson 37 in your Word Manual. Complete all of the shaded steps while at your computer. Then format the documents that follow.

GO TO
Word Manual

Table
37-5
Open Table

Open tables are shown with "View Gridlines" active. Remove borders on all open tables.

REFER TO
Word Manual

L. 28: View Gridlines

Document Processing

14 pt **CONTEMPORARY DESIGN'S NEWEST LOCATIONS** ↓1X	
12 pt ↓ The Glen Town Center	Tallahassee, Florida
Highland Park Square	Evergreen Park, Illinois
Myrtle Beach Mall	Myrtle Beach, South Carolina
Greenway Mall	Atlanta, Georgia

Table
37-6
Open Table

' singular noun

' plural noun

LOS ANGELES COUNTY'S PREREGISTRATION SCHEDULE ↓1X Regional Supervisors' Calendar ↓1X		
Artesia	Monday, February 14	11 a.m.
Stevenson Ranch	Monday, February 21	10 a.m.
San Gabriel	Monday, February 28	11 a.m.
Huntington Park	Monday, March 7	10 a.m.

Table
37-7
Open Table

' singular noun

' plural noun

MAR VISTA REALTY'S MILLION-DOLLAR AGENTS' LIST First-Quarter Data	
James Kealing	Santa Clarita
Carol Pajaro	Malibu
Patricia Morelli	Woodland Hills
Jan McKay	Northbridge
Daniel Aboud	San Luis Obispo

Strategies for Career Success

Turning Negative Messages Positive

Accentuate the positive. When communicating bad news (e.g., layoffs, product recalls, price increases, or personnel problems), find the positive.

People respond better to positive rather than negative language, and they are more likely to cooperate if treated fairly and with respect. Avoid insults, accusations, criticism, or words with negative connotations (e.g., *failed, delinquent,* or *bad*). You also should avoid humor, as it is often misinterpreted as callousness or disdain. Focus on what the reader can do rather than on what you won't or can't let the reader do. Instead of "You will not qualify unless . . . ," state, "You will qualify if you are . . ." An example of finding the positive is "Due to budget cuts, we will not be having a holiday party. Instead, we are planning to give everyone an afternoon off around the end of the year."

Manage your audience's response by providing an explanation to support your decision and examples of how they might benefit. Analyze your audience, and decide whether to give the negative news at the beginning, middle, or end of your message. Regardless of your approach, always maintain goodwill.

Your Turn: Review some of your written documents, and observe if they have a positive tone.

Open Tables With Column Headings

Goals

- Type at least 35wpm/3'/4e.
- Correctly use Word's features to align table information and center a table horizontally and vertically.
- Correctly format an open table with column headings.

A. WARMUP

alphabet

practice: *r* and *e*

easy

1 Just be very quick when fixing the zip codes for your mail.
2 red Rex eerie Erie elder emery enter erred every refer rear
3 Kay may visit the big island in May when she is down there.

Skillbuilding

B. PACED PRACTICE

Follow the GDP software directions for this exercise to improve keystroking speed and accuracy.

Take two 3-minute timed writings.

⭐ **Goal:** At least 35wpm/3'/4e

C. 3-MINUTE TIMED WRITING

4 Telecommuting is a word you may have heard before but	11
5 do not quite understand. Very simply, it means working at	23
6 home instead of driving in to work. Many people like the	34
7 convenience of working at home. They realize they can save	46
8 money on expenses like gas, food, or child care.	56
9 Most home office workers use a computer in their job.	67
10 When their work is done, they can just fax or e-mail it to	78
11 the office. If they must communicate with other workers,	90
12 they can use the phone, fax, or computer and never have to	102
13 leave their home.	105

    1 | 2 | 3 | 4 | 5 | 6 | 7 | 8 | 9 | 10 | 11 | 12

Formatting

D. COLUMN HEADINGS

Column headings describe the information contained in the column entries below them. To format column headings:

- Center all column headings.
- Type the column headings in upper- and lowercase letters and bold.

- If any column heading requires 2 lines, press ENTER 1 time to create the 2-line column heading; then bottom-align all column headings in that row.

center page ↓
center horizontally

TOP FIVE MANAGEMENT COMPANIES	
Capital Growth Funds ↓1X	
Metro Area ↓1X **Market**	align bottom ↓ **Business**
Atlanta, Georgia	Cedar Properties, Inc.
Charlotte, North Carolina	Kenco Realty Corporation
Norfolk, Virginia	The Westfall Group
New Orleans, Louisiana	Eden Pyramid Companies

Do not insert a blank line before a single-line column heading.

(Note: Table shown with "View Gridlines" active.)

E. WORD PROCESSING: TABLE—ALIGN BOTTOM, TABLE—CENTER HORIZONTALLY, AND TABLE—CENTER PAGE

GO TO
Word Manual

Study Lesson 38 in your Word Manual. Complete all of the shaded steps while at your computer. Then format the documents that follow.

Document Processing

Table 38-8
Open Table

Center all tables horizontally and vertically from now on.

center page ↓

14 pt **OFFICE SUPPLIES VENDOR LIST**	
12 pt ↓ **Pacific Print Works** ↓1X	
Product ↓1X **Category**	align bottom ↓ **Vendor**
Binders	Executive Offices Unlimited
Calendars	Savings to You Inc.
File folders	Office Products Today
Business forms	Atlantic-Pacific Systems

Table
38-9
Open Table

COMMITTEE ASSIGNMENTS	
Academic Committee Assignments	**Professor**
Institutional Integrity	Anne McCarthy
Educational Programs	Bill Zimmerman
Student Services	John Yeh
Financial Resources	Steve Williams

Table
38-10
Open Table

1. Open the file for Table 38-8.
2. Change the subtitle to `Office Supplies Max.`

3. Change the four product categories in Column A to these:

   `Envelopes`
   `Shredders`
   `Hole punches`
   `Sticky notes`

Table
38-11
Open Table

AVAILABILITY OF CABLESERVICES	
Type Of Service	**Available Currently**
Life line	Scottsdale
Basic	Phoenix
Expanded	Glendale
Expanded (per channel)	Camelback city

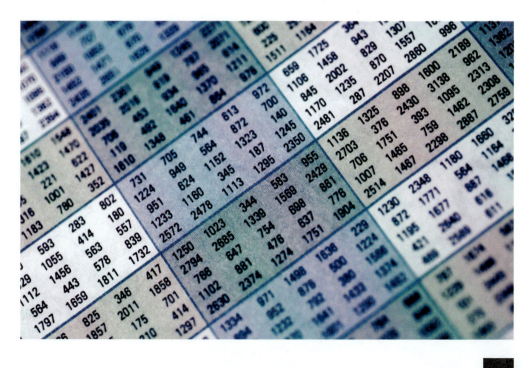

Ruled Tables With Number Columns

Goals

- Demonstrate improved speed and accuracy while typing.
- Demonstrate acceptable language arts skills in spelling.
- Correctly use Word's table features to align text and apply borders.
- Correctly format a ruled table with number columns.

A. WARMUP

alphabet	1	Six of the gunboats would be jeopardized by my quick moves.
frequent digraphs	2	en end den deny gene hen men lend menu pen ten oven yen Ben
easy	3	The city panel may work on an amendment to audit the firms.

Skillbuilding

B. MAP+: SYMBOL

Follow the GDP software directions for this exercise to improve keystroking accuracy.

PPP PRETEST » PRACTICE » POSTTEST

PRETEST
Take a 1-minute timed writing.

C. PRETEST: Horizontal Reaches

4	The chief thinks the alarm was a decoy for the armed	11
5	agent who coyly dashed away. She was dazed as she dodged	22
6	a blue sedan. He lured her to the edge of the high bluff.	34

          1 | 2 | 3 | 4 | 5 | 6 | 7 | 8 | 9 | 10 | 11 | 12

PRACTICE
Speed Emphasis:
If you made 2 or fewer errors on the Pretest, type each *individual* line 2 times.
Accuracy Emphasis:
If you made 3 or more errors, type each *group* of lines (as though it were a paragraph) 2 times.

D. PRACTICE: In Reaches

7	oy foyer loyal buoys enjoy decoy coyly royal cloy ploy toys
8	ar argue armed cared alarm cedar sugar radar area earn hear
9	lu lucid lunch lured bluff value blunt fluid luck lush blue

E. PRACTICE: Out Reaches

10	ge geese genes germs agent edges dodge hinge gear ages page
11	da daily dazed dance adapt sedan adage panda dash date soda
12	hi hints hiked hired chief think ethic aphid high ship chip

F. POSTTEST: Horizontal Reaches

Language Arts

G. SPELLING

Type these frequently misspelled words, paying special attention to any spelling problems in each word.

13 prior activities additional than faculty whether first with
14 subject material equipment receiving completed during basis
15 available please required decision established policy audit
16 section schedule installation insurance possible appreciate
17 benefits requirements business scheduled office immediately

Edit the sentences to correct any misspellings.

18 We requierd the office to schedule all prior activities.

19 The business scheduled the instalation of the equipment.

20 The decision established the basis of the insurance policy.

21 Please audit any additionl material available to faculty.

22 If possible, they would appreciate recieving them soon.

23 Section requirements to receive benefits were completed.

Formatting

H. RULED TABLES WITH NUMBER COLUMNS

REFER TO
Reference Manual

R-13B: Open Table
R-13C: Ruled Table

To format a ruled table with number columns:

1. Remove all table borders.
2. Apply borders to the top and bottom of Row 2 and to the bottom of the last row.
3. Center column headings, left-align text columns (or a mix of text and numbers), and right-align column entries with numbers that could be used in mathematical calculations.
4. Insert the dollar sign only before the amount in the first entry and before a total amount entry.

CLASS A SHARES
American World Growth and Income Fund

Investment	Offering Price	Dealer Commission
$ 205,000	2.5%	$ 4,100
500,000	2.0%	8,000
750,000	1.5%	9,000
1,000,000	0.5%	10,000

borders:
Row 2
last row—bottom

(Note: Table shown with "View Gridlines" active.)

3 spaces:
2 for each digit;
1 for each comma

2 spaces
for each digit

5. Align the dollar sign with the longest amount in the column, inserting spaces after the dollar sign as follows: allow 2 spaces for each digit and 1 space for each comma. In the first example, allow 2 spaces after the dollar sign. In the second, allow 3 spaces.

Examples:

$	5
	75
	15

$	375
	2,150
	49

6. If a table includes a total line, add a border above and below the total line. Use the word *Total* or *Totals* as appropriate, and add a percent or dollar sign if needed.

I. WORD PROCESSING: TABLE—ALIGN TEXT RIGHT AND TABLE—BORDERS, RULED

GO TO
Word Manual

Study Lesson 39 in your Word Manual. Complete all of the shaded steps while at your computer. Then format the documents that follow.

Document Processing

Table
39-12
Ruled Table

Highlighted words are spelling words from the language arts activities; do *not* highlight them when you type. This first ruled table is shown with "View Gridlines" active.

center page ↓
center horizontally

ACCOUNT SUMMARY
Vanguard Faculty Insurance Policy ↓1X

align bottom ↓ **Account Balance**	**Current Period**	**Year-to-Date Totals**
Fees	$ 4.25	$ 145.76
Highest available balance	98.16	5,326.48
Employer contributions	9.95	499.95
Completed transactions	25.43	39.76
Totals	$137.79	$6,011.95

Table
39-13
Ruled Table

HOLIDAY RESORT SUITES
Additional Rate Charges

Hotel	Rack Rate	Club Rate	3-Night Savings
Porter Ranch Inn	$ 92.00	$36.00	$168.00
Jamaican Inn	119.00	59.50	178.50
Casitas Suites	120.00	60.00	180.00
The Desert Inn Resort	135.00	75.50	178.50
First Street Courtyard	150.00	75.00	225.00

Table
39-14
Ruled Table

ESTABLISHED FUNDING RESOURCES

Fund	Current Year	Previous Year
Duncan Insurance	16.3%	2.0%
Strident Nova	9.3%	3.5%
First Value	10.7%	12.1%
Safeguard Policy	11.1%	9.7%
Vanguard Life	8.5%	10.1%

Keyboarding Connection

Searching the Web

Online search engines seek out Web pages based upon text the user types into the search box. The best results occur when users keep their search simple and specific. To search for a phrase, sentence, name, or title, put quotation marks around it; this instructs the search engine that you want results that have all those words together. For example, a search for **red bicycle** without quotation marks results in pages that may have *red* and *bicycle*, but maybe not both together. Using "red Schwinn bicycle" will produce pages that use that exact phrase.

Your Turn: From your Web browser, open a Web search engine site. Type various searches in the entry box of the search engine, and start the search. Compare the results you get from different search engines.

Formatting Review

40

Goals

- Type at least 36wpm/3′/4e.
- Correctly format an academic report, a business letter in block style, and a ruled table with a variety of features.
- Successfully complete a Progress and Proofreading Check with zero errors on the first scored attempt.

A. WARMUP

alphabet	1	Two joyful vixens squirted some milk upon the caged zebras.
number/symbol	2	edow@msn.com 38% Ely & May (6/9) Wow! $4.12 *ibid. #573-012
easy	3	The ten hens and turkeys in the cornfields may lay low now.

Skillbuilding

B. 12-SECOND SPEED SPRINTS

Take three 12-second timed writings on each line.

4 Bob owns a pair of old bikes and a new car he got from her.
5 Keith must work with a tutor when he has need of more help.
6 Nan may sign over the title to her car when she is in town.
7 The firm did not sign a form that may name me to the panel.
` ' ' ' '5' ' ' '10' ' ' '15' ' ' '20' ' ' '25' ' ' '30' ' ' '35' ' ' '40' ' ' '45' ' ' '50' ' ' '55' ' ' '60`

C. TECHNIQUE PRACTICE: SHIFT KEY

Type each line 2 times. After striking the capitalized letter, return the SHIFT KEY finger immediately to home-row position.

8 Andrew Bishop hid me from Cindy Dunn. Emma Ford owed money.
9 Gordon Harris and Irene Jenkins spied on Kelsey Lambertson.
10 Marie Nakamura asked Orlando Pena what Quentin Rice wanted.
11 Sid Tuy and Uri Vincent ate. Will Xiang and Yasir Zito won.

Goal: At least 36wpm/3'/4e

D. 3-MINUTE TIMED WRITING

```
12      Complaints by workers are often viewed as a negative   11
13 force in a workplace. In fact, the complaints should be    22
14 viewed as a chance to communicate with the employee and to 34
15 improve morale. To ignore the complaint does not make it go 46
16 away. If you just listen to complaints, you may help to     57
17 solve small problems before they turn into bigger ones.     68
18      Often workers expect a chance to be heard by a person  79
19 who is willing to listen to them quite openly. That person  91
20 must recognize that the employee has concerns that need     102
21 to be addressed at this time.                               108
      1  |  2  |  3  |  4  |  5  |  6  |  7  |  8  |  9  |  10  |  11  |  12
```

Document Processing

Report 40-11
Academic Report

RELATIONSHIPS AT WORK
Shannon Pacencia

Do you believe that as long as you get your work done at the end of the day, you have had a successful day on the job? If so, you are badly mistaken. Doing the work is only half the job. The other half is relating to and working with the people around you.

TAKE A TEAM APPROACH

Everything you do and every action you take affects those around you in a close working relationship. Operating as a team means thinking about others and taking actions that will help them reach their goals and achieve the goals of the company.

MAINTAIN A SPIRIT OF COOPERATION

When you work in a spirit of cooperation, those around you will reflect that spirit. Your job will be easier because you will minimize resistance.

VALIDATE THE OPINIONS OF OTHERS

You will find that this simple act of validation will go a long way in helping the spirit of your coworkers. Here are two simple ways to validate the opinions of others:

1.   Take time to listen to the issues and accomplishments of those around you.
2.   Reflect their opinions in your own words in a spirit of genuine interest.

There is a saying that states, "Your success is my success." Adopt this as your motto, and you will find a great deal of satisfaction at the end of each day.

1. Prepare an envelope for this letter; do not insert an inside address.

2. Add the envelope to the letter.

December 1, 20-- | Mrs. Janet Broers | 1291 ~~Bahama~~ *Obama* Court | Richmond KY 40475 |

Dear mrs. Broers:

¶ Thank you for choosing (Alliance Insurance) Of America. Open enrollment for your ~~medical~~ insurance plan is scheduled to begin the first day of January. I hope it was possible for you to review the materials you received last week. Selecting the right benefit plan for you and your family can be an over whelming task. To make ~~this~~ *your* decision a little easier, I have enclosed a brochure ~~with this letter~~ *that* summarizing the key features of each policy.

¶ (Please call me if I can help in any way.) You might want to browse through our website at www.iaa.com for further details.

Sincerely, | Denise Montoya | Customer Support | urs | enclosures

Table
40-15
Ruled Table

Progress and
Proofreading
Check

Documents designated
as Proofreading Checks
serve as a check of your
proofreading skill. Your
goal is to have zero ty-
pographical errors when
the GDP software first
scores the document.

PERSONAL ASSET ACCOUNTS
Albert Trevino

Account	Amount	Interest Rate
Interest Checking	$ 972.55	3.10%
Money Market	4,500.35	4.90%
Smart Saver	3,250.76	5.07%
Certificate of Deposit	550.00	7.41%

Outcomes Assessment on Part 2

Test 2

3-Minute Timed Writing

```
 1        From the first day of class, you have continuously     10
 2   worked to improve your typing skill. You have worked hard    22
 3   to increase your typing speed and accuracy. You have also    34
 4   learned to format letters, memos, reports, and tables. All   45
 5   of this work is quite an amazing accomplishment.             55
 6        In your lessons, you have worked on learning a wide     66
 7   range of word processing skills. You can expect to make      77
 8   even more progress if you will just practice your skills     88
 9   often. Learn as much as you can each day. Ask questions,    100
10   and then move toward a new goal each day.                   108
        1  |  2  |  3  |  4  |  5  |  6  |  7  |  8  |  9  |  10  |  11  |  12
```

Correspondence Test 2-21

Business Letter in Block Style

1. Add an envelope to the document.
2. Omit the return address.

January 10, 20-- | Ms. Christine Beltran | World wide Temp Professionals | 1200 Interstate Park Drive | Montgomery, AL 36109 | Dear Ms. Beltran:

¶ Each year many of the students in the computer applications department work on our campus and gain valuable experience on-the-job. This semester I have 3 students who have developed very exceptional skills. I have enclosed a list of their names in case you are interested in arranging any interviews. These students have all taken a variety of classes within our department and have worked in other disciplines with different supervisors. This exposure has given them valuable experience and insite into the demands of the workingworld. I know that you will be impressed with their backgrounds and experience.

¶ I will be calling you in the next few days so that we can discuss these students adn their qualifications in more detail.

sincerely, | Michelle Betts | Chair person | urs | Enclosure

PROPER TECHNIQUE AT THE KEYBOARD
Alex Harrington
April 13, 20--

Appropriate technique at the keyboard is essential for productivity as well as for health reasons. Two essential elements of keyboarding technique are proper placement of the computer monitor and the keyboard.

MONITOR

The computer monitor should be positioned in line with the keyboard, centered on the user. Ideally, the monitor should be slightly below eye level for the most comfortable viewing and should be tilted slightly away from you, forcing you to look down slightly.

In general, position the monitor as far away as possible while still being able to read the text clearly. To position the monitor appropriately, sit back in the chair and extend your arm horizontally; your middle finger should touch the middle of the screen. This way, you won't need to make excessive head movements to see the viewing area of the screen.

Monitors and Document Holders. To minimize head movement, place the document holder at the same height and distance as the monitor and at the same angle as the monitor, tilted slightly upward. Place the document holder next to the monitor opposite the mouse.

Monitors and Laptop Computers. Despite their convenience of use, laptop computers are not ergonomic because you cannot adjust the screen and keyboard independently for the most comfort. If you do a lot of typing on a laptop, consider purchasing an external monitor or an external keyboard to avoid straining yourself.

KEYBOARD

The keyboard should be in a straight line between your body and the monitor. There is no research showing that ergonomic (split) keyboards are superior to traditional keyboards; therefore, using an ergonomic keyboard design is an individual preference.

UNIVERSITY PHONE SERVICES
Current Rates

Category	One-Time Charge	Proposed Increase
Caller ID	$ 5	$ 1
Caller ID block	5	1
Analog line	35	5
Extension	26	10

Correspondence, Reports, and Employment Documents

Keyboarding in Education Careers

The education field has many career opportunities, including positions such as instructor, counselor, instructor assistant, administrator, media specialist, and curriculum specialist. Although two of three workers in educational services have professional and related occupations, the education field employs many administrative support, managerial, and service workers.

Instructor assistants provide support for classroom instructors in many ways, allowing instructors more time for lesson planning and actual teaching. Instructor assistants also grade assignments and tests, check homework, keep attendance records, and perform typing, data entry, and filing. Office administration staff perform similar functions for the heads of departments in colleges and universities and for the principals and education boards of elementary and secondary schools.

The use of computer technology in the educational setting is constantly growing. Proficiency with a computer, including keyboarding and formatting skills, is essential for success in the field. The use of the Internet in classrooms has expanded significantly, by helping instructors and students to communicate with each other, as well as to perform research for class assignments. Online learning is growing as well. Increasing numbers of higher education institutions use Internet-based technology to post lessons and coursework electronically, as well as to communicate with students. The *Gregg College Keyboarding & Document Processing* textbook and software are good examples of this development.

Goals

Keyboarding
- Type at least 40 words per minute on a 5-minute timed writing with no more than 5 errors.

Language Arts
- Demonstrate acceptable proofreading skills, including using proofreaders' marks.
- Demonstrate acceptable language arts skills in punctuation and grammar.
- Demonstrate acceptable language arts skills in composing and spelling.

Word Processing
- Use appropriate word processing commands to complete document processing activities successfully.

Document Processing
- Correctly format business and academic reports, business letters and personal-business letters, memos, e-mail, and resumes.

Objective Test
- Answer questions with acceptable accuracy on an objective test.

Correspondence

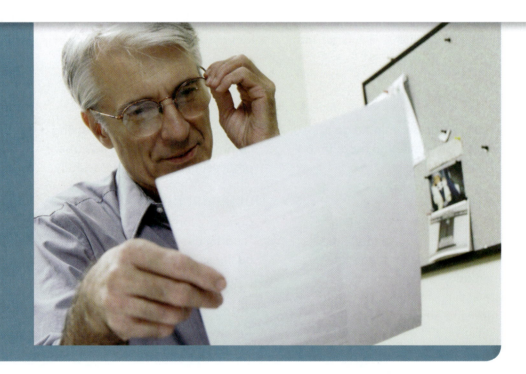

Personal Titles and Complimentary Closings in Letters

Goals

- Demonstrate improved speed and accuracy while typing by touch.
- Demonstrate acceptable language arts skills in using quotation marks and italics (or underline).
- Correctly format a personal title in correspondence.
- Correctly format a complimentary closing in correspondence.

A. WARMUP

alphabet   1   We have quickly spotted four women dozing in that jury box.

concentration   2   oversimplifications nonrepresentational professionalization

easy   3   The town may pay my neighbor for the work she did for them.

Skillbuilding

B. MAP+: ALPHABET

Follow the GDP software directions for this exercise to improve keystroking accuracy.

C. PROGRESSIVE PRACTICE: ALPHABET

Follow the GDP software directions for this exercise to improve keystroking speed.

Language Arts

Study the rules at the right.

RULE
" direct quotation

RULE
" title

RULE
title or title

RULE
, direct quotation

D. QUOTATION MARKS AND ITALICS (OR UNDERLINE)

Use quotation marks around a direct quotation.
> Harrison responded by saying, "Their decision does not affect us."
> But: Harrison responded by saying that their decision does not affect us.

Use quotation marks around the title of a newspaper or magazine article, chapter in a book, report, and similar terms.
> The most helpful article I found was "Multimedia for All."

Italicize (or underline) the titles of books, magazines, newspapers, and other complete published works.
> Grisham's *The Brethren* was reviewed in a recent *USA Today* article.

Use a comma before and after a direct quotation.
> James said, "I shall return," and then left.

Edit each sentence to correct any errors.

4 The newspaper ad in the March 1 "Tribune" was very
5 effective.

6 The Power of e-Commerce is an excellent chapter.

7 Maria answered the question by saying, "I agree."

8 Her title for the report was "The Internet in Action."

9 The magazine cover for "Newsweek" last month was excellent.

10 Karen interrupted by saying, That's exactly right!

11 The realtor replied "The first thing to consider is
12 location."

13 "The margin of error is very small" said Andy.

Formatting

E. PERSONAL TITLES IN LETTERS

> Standard punctuation refers to the use of a colon after the salutation and a comma after the complimentary closing.

Inside Addresses

Always use a courtesy title before a person's name in the inside address of a letter; for example, *Mr.*, *Mrs.*, or *Dr.*

Type a person's title on the same line with the name (separated by a comma), if the title is short, or on the line below. The title and business name may be typed on the same line (separated by a comma) if they are both short.

Personal Titles in Inside Addresses

Mr. James R. Yamamoto, Manager
National Security Systems

Mrs. Marilyn Broquette
Executive Director
Perimeter Hospital

Dr. Raymond Bishop
Manager, Velletti Oil Co.

Salutations

When possible, use a person's name in the salutation. The correct form for the salutation is the courtesy title and the last name. If you do not know the name of the other person, use a job title or *Ladies and Gentlemen*. A colon is used after the salutation in standard punctuation.

Dear Ms. Winston:

Dear Dr. Hamner:

Dear Mr. Sparanta:

Dear Sales Manager:

Ladies and Gentlemen:

F. COMPLIMENTARY CLOSINGS IN LETTERS

Every letter should end with a complimentary closing. Some frequently used complimentary closings are *Sincerely, Sincerely yours, Yours truly, Cordially,* and *Respectfully yours.*

In the closing lines, do not use a courtesy title before a man's name. If a woman wants to use her personal title, she may include it in parentheses in her handwritten signature or without parentheses in her typed signature (but not in both). A comma is used after the complimentary closing in standard punctuation.

Closing Lines

Sincerely yours,

Linda Humphries

Linda Humphries
Account Manager

Yours truly,

Juliet McCoy

Ms. Juliet McCoy
Marketing Director

Cordially,

Chris S. VanVliet

Chris S. VanVliet
Regional Supervisor

Document Processing

Correspondence 41-22

Business Letter in Block Style

title

" direct quotation

January 10, 20-- | Mrs. Gwen Hanover | 4034 Kennedy Lane | Mount Vernon, WA 98274-2340 | Dear Mrs. Hanover:

¶ You are one of several prospective buyers of a SunCity townhouse, and we thank you for the interest you have shown in our development project. The SunCity model received three national awards last month, and these awards were announced in the *SunCity Register* last week.

¶ I am enclosing a brochure that illustrates all six of our model townhouses. The specific square footage for each townhouse is included in this brochure, with details on room size, electrical outlets, and cable access points. Our builder said, "I will give a bonus for the first ten customers who purchase a townhouse," and he plans to follow through with his offer. The bonus is a free cable subscription for your first year of residency.

¶ Thank you, Mrs. Hanover, for the opportunity to work with you these past few days. If you have any questions, please let us know.

Sincerely, | Mrs. Kathryn Bennett | Sales Director | urs | Enclosure

Correspondence 41-23

Business Letter in Block Style

title

" direct quotation

May 20, 20-- | Mr. Winston A. Kahn | 1800 East Hollywood Avenue | Salt Lake City, UT 84108 | Dear Mr. Kahn:

¶ This past week we heard from many of our readers who enjoyed your rebuttal to our editorial in the *Utah Times* about the proposed airport site in Provo, Utah. Actually, you are 1 of over 30 listeners who indicated your desire for us to air your rebuttal.

¶ Of the more than 100 request letters for equal time, we selected yours because you touched on most of the relevant points of this topic. We especially liked your comment in which you said, "The airport site would be better situated in the heavily populated north side."

¶ We will contact you further about taping your rebuttal on June 4. Please read the enclosed disclaimer that we would like you to sign before airing the rebuttal.

Yours truly, | Sandra L. Green | General Manager | urs | Enclosure

Personal-Business Letters

Goals

- Type at least 36wpm/3'/3e.
- Correctly format a personal-business letter.

A. WARMUP

alphabet   1   Six crazy kings vowed to abolish my quite pitiful projects.

one hand   2   secret hominy dew hip beasts nonunion edge monk staff nylon

easy   3   The chairman may risk an amendment for the downtown island.

Skillbuilding

Take a 1-minute timed writing on the boxed paragraph to establish your base speed. Then take a 1-minute timed writing on the following paragraph. As soon as you equal or exceed your base speed on this paragraph, move to the next, more difficult paragraph.

B. SUSTAINED PRACTICE: SYLLABIC INTENSITY

4 Taking care of aging parents is not a new trend. This	11
5 issue has arisen more and more, since we are now living	22
6 longer. Companies are now trying to help out in many ways.	34

7   Help may come in many ways, ranging from financial aid   11
8   to sponsoring hospice or in-home respite care. Workers may   23
9   find it difficult to work and care for aging parents.   34

10   Why are employers so interested in elder care? Rising   11
11   interest is the result of a combination of several things.   23
12   The most notable is a marked increase in life expectancy.   34

13   Another trend is the increased participation of women,   11
14   the primary caregivers, in the workforce. Businesses are   23
15   recognizing that work and family life are intertwined.   33

1 | 2 | 3 | 4 | 5 | 6 | 7 | 8 | 9 | 10 | 11 | 12

Goal: At least 36wpm/3′/3e

C. 3-MINUTE TIMED WRITING

```
16        The size of their first paycheck after they finish       10
17   college seems quite high to a few young men and women. They   22
18   rent a place to live that is just too much to pay, or they    34
19   may buy a car with a huge monthly payment. For some, it       45
20   takes a while to learn that there are other items in the      57
21   monthly budget.                                               60
22        Some other budget items are food, student loans, car     71
23   insurance, rental insurance, credit card debts, health        82
24   insurance, utilities, and miscellaneous expenses. A good      93
25   goal is to put a regular amount from each paycheck into a     105
26   savings account.                                             108
```
    1 | 2 | 3 | 4 | 5 | 6 | 7 | 8 | 9 | 10 | 11 | 12

Formatting

D. PERSONAL-BUSINESS LETTERS

Personal-business letters are prepared by individuals to conduct their personal business. To format a personal-business letter:

1. Type the letter on plain paper or personal stationery, not letterhead.
2. Include the writer's return address in the letter directly below the writer's name in the closing lines.
3. Since the writer of the letter usually types the letter, do not use reference initials.
4. Spell-check, proofread, and preview your document for spelling and formatting errors.

Document Processing

Correspondence
42-24
Personal-Business Letter in Block Style

↓5X
October 1, 20-- ↓4X

Ms. Ruth Lee, Director
City Parks and Recreation Department
7034 Renwick Avenue
Syracuse, NY 13210-0475 ↓2X

Dear Ms. Lee: ↓2X

(continued on next page)

Thank you for the excellent manner in which your department accommodated our family last summer. About 120 Killians attended the reunion at Rosedale Park on August 21. Jeffrey Sparks said that Building 5 was an excellent facility for us to use for the reunion. ↓2X

As many of the Killian family pointed out to me, "We are not likely to find a facility as nice as Rosedale Park for holding our reunion." I would like to again request that Building 5 be reserved for our next year's family reunion on August 20. A confirmation of the date from your office will be appreciated. ↓2X

Sincerely, ↓4X

Jerry Killian
2410 Farnham Road
Syracuse, NY 13219

Correspondence
42-25
Personal-Business Letter in Block Style

Italicize (but do not underline) the title of the magazine.

July 13, 20-- / Mr. Alan R. Diaz, Administrator / Glencrest Nursing Home / 2807 Crossgate Circle / Lawrence, KS 66047 / Dear Mr. Diaz:

¶ Thanks to you and dozens of other people, the fall crafts sale at Glencrest was highly successful. I am very appreciative of the ways in which you helped. The highlights of the sale are going to be displayed in next Monday's issue of Glencrest Crafts.

¶ I particularly wish to thank you for transporting the display tables and chairs to Glencrest and back to the community center. Many people from the community center attended the sale and commented about how nice it was of you and your staff to support such an activity.

¶ Please accept my special thanks to you and your staff for supporting the many activities that benefit all Glencrest residents.

Sincerely, / Charles C. Brewster / 482 22d Street East / Lawrence, KS 66049

June 4, 20-- | Mr. Randall Mitchell | 5270 Rosecrans Avenue | Topeka, KS 67284 |

Dear Mr. Mitchell:

¶ Your presentation at the Sand Hills Country Club, "Steps for Succesful *s* Employment," was one of the most enjoyable our members have *ever* observed. I especially enjoyed the question-and-answer session at the conclusion of your wonderful presentation, and I received *many* favorable comments from other attendees as well.

¶ Our professor has suggested that we take the information you gave us and prepare a website that focuses on the *key* points 6 you mentioned in your speech. That way, many of our class mates can take advantage of your excellent advice when preparing for *their* 1st search job. We have also found *at least 20* several other sources to use on the world wide web that we plan to include *on* in our Web site that will be posted by the 10th of next month.

¶ This has been a very interesting assignment, thanks to the excelent *l* information you provided. The project has given *other* students an incentive to construct their own Web sites pertaining to job searches and interviewing techniques.

¶ Again, thank you for all your *excellent* ideas.

Sincerely, | James Fetter | 3421 Carlisle Avenue | Topeka, KS 67209

Strategies for Career Success

Nonverbal Communication

"It's not what he said, but how he said it." More than 90 percent of your spoken message contains nonverbal communication that expresses your feelings and desires. People respond to this nonverbal language.

Posture can convey your mood. For example, leaning toward a speaker indicates interest. Leaning backward suggests dislike or indifference. Your handshake, an important nonverbal communicator, should be firm but not overpowering.

Your head position provides many nonverbal signals. A lowered head usually expresses shyness or withdrawal. An upright head conveys confidence and interest. A tilted head signifies curiosity or suspicion. Nodding your head shows positive feeling, while left-right head shakes signify negative feeling. Your face strongly expresses your emotions. Narrow, squinting eyes signify caution, reflection, or uncertainty. Wide-open eyes convey interest and attention.

Your Turn: Turn off the sound on a television program. How much of the plot can you understand just from the nonverbal communication signals?

Memos and E-Mail With Lists

43

Goals

- Demonstrate improved speed and accuracy while typing by touch.
- Demonstrate acceptable proofreading skills by comparing lines of copy.
- Correctly format a list in correspondence.

A. WARMUP

alphabet

1 Joann packed my boxes with those five dozen jugs of liquor.

practice: *v* and *b*

2 verb Bev bevel bevy above livable vibe bovine brave visible

easy

3 She or I may pay for the Bible if we go to the busy chapel.

Skillbuilding

B. MAP+: NUMBERS

Follow the GDP software directions for this exercise to improve keystroking accuracy.

PPP

PRETEST » PRACTICE » POSTTEST

PRETEST
Take a 1-minute timed writing.

C. PRETEST: Vertical Reaches

4   Kim knew that her skills at the keyboard made her a   11
5 top rival for that job. About six persons had seen her race 23
6 home to see if the mail showed the company was aware of it. 34
          1 | 2 | 3 | 4 | 5 | 6 | 7 | 8 | 9 | 10 | 11 | 12

PRACTICE
Speed Emphasis:
    If you made 2 or fewer errors on the Pretest, type each *individual* line 2 times.
Accuracy Emphasis:
    If you made 3 or more errors, type each *group* of lines (as though it were a paragraph) 2 times.

D. PRACTICE: Up Reaches

7 se seven reset seams sedan loses eases serve used seed dose
8 ki skids kings kinks skill kitty kites kilts kind kids kick
9 rd board horde wards sword award beard third cord hard lard

E. PRACTICE: Down Reaches

10 ac races pacer backs ached acute laced facts each acre lace
11 kn knave knack knife knows knoll knots knelt knew knee knit
12 ab about abide label above abode sable abbey drab able cabs

F. POSTTEST: Vertical Reaches

Language Arts

G. PROOFREADING

Compare these lines with lines 4–7 on page 164. Edit the lines to correct any errors.

13 The eighty old books are to be thrown into the field today.
14 Alan may not take a part both of the toys out on the lanai.
15 Due to the big quake, our city may start to move all autos.
16 Glenn can take apart the old robot when he comes into town.

Formatting

H. CORRESPONDENCE WITH LISTS

Numbers or bullets may be used in correspondence to call attention to items in a list and to increase readability. If the sequence of the items is important, use numbers rather than bullets.

To format lists in correspondence:

1. Press ENTER 2 times to insert 1 blank line before the list.
2. Type the list using Word's default format.
3. Use single spacing between lines in the list.
4. Insert 1 blank line below the list.
5. Spell-check, proofread, and preview your document for spelling and formatting errors.

Document Processing

**Correspondence
43-27**
Memo

↓5X　　　　→tab

MEMO TO:　Members of the Convention Committee ↓2X

FROM:　Alfred A. Long, Convention Director

DATE:　September 8, 20--

SUBJECT:　Convention Locations ↓2X

As you know, this year's convention will meet in Kansas City, Missouri. It is the Executive Board's decision to rotate the convention site to each of the districts in our region. Our next three conventions will be held in the following locations: ↓2X

- Oklahoma City, Oklahoma
- Omaha, Nebraska
- Minneapolis, Minnesota ↓2X

(continued on next page)

In May the Board will travel to Oklahoma City to visit the location of our next convention site. When we return, we will draft our convention site proposal for you. ↓2X

urs

MEMO TO: Marian Dalton | **FROM:** Phyllis Schulte | **DATE:** April 9, 20-- | **SUBJECT:** Program Descriptions

¶ As you requested, I have contacted the speakers for our afternoon session discussions. All three speakers have sent me a brief description of their sessions, and they are listed in the order of presentation as follows:

1. Salon A. This session will discuss the economic growth of Pacific Rim nations.
2. Salon B. This session will present the impact of the World Wide Web on marketing strategies.
3. Salon C. This session will discuss the dynamics of econometrics.

¶ By next Monday I will send you an introduction for each speaker.

urs

Marian,

¶ As I indicated to you last week, I am sending you information on our three speakers' presentation titles for the Economic Seminar we have scheduled for October 20. Their presentation titles are as follows:

- Ms. Marcia Cantrell is vice president of economic forecasting for Business Trends Inc. She will be addressing the group in Salon A on the topic of "The Economic Growth of Pacific Rim Nations."
- Mr. Leonard Sanchez is marketing director for Superior Industries. He will be presenting in Salon B on the topic of "The Impact of the World Wide Web on Marketing Strategies."
- Dr. Adrian Guzman is CEO of Global Economic Research. His presentation will be held in Salon C. The title of his speech is "Dynamic Econometrics."

¶ I will send you each speaker's resume next week so that you can prepare suitable introductions for their sessions.

Phyllis Schulte | E-mail: pschulte@quickmail.com | Phone: 701-555-4832

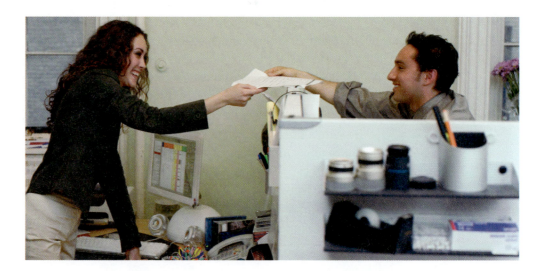

Letters With Indented Displays and Copy Notations and E-Mail With Copies

44

Goals

- Type at least 37wpm/3'/3e.
- Correctly format a letter with a copy notation and e-mail with copies.
- Correctly format correspondence with an indented display.

A. WARMUP

alphabet	1	Five bright vixens jumped while dozing fowl quacked loudly.
frequent digraphs	2	at ate bat cat eat tat fat hat mat oat pat rat sat vat beat
easy	3	It is a shame she works such chaotic anthems into her urns.

Skillbuilding

B. PROGRESSIVE PRACTICE: NUMBERS

Follow the GDP software directions for this exercise to improve keystroking speed.

C. TECHNIQUE PRACTICE: BACKSPACE KEY

Type each line 2 times, using your Sem finger to strike the BACKSPACE key.

The ← symbol means to backspace. For example, type *saw*, backspace, and type *y*, thus changing *saw* to *say*.

```
4  saw←y are←k mud←m aid←l her←n air←m hot←p box←y sot←y
5  keg←y spa←y ill←k mob←m tag←m tow←y ski←y age←o par←n
6  dad←m pat←y and←y rut←n rat←p zag←p cue←p dab←y big←n
7  via←m who←y flu←y gee←l cab←n bar←n was←y sue←m bog←o
```

D. 3-MINUTE TIMED WRITING

Take two 3-minute timed writings.

Goal: At least 37wpm/3'/3e

```
8        Each business should have its code of ethics. A code    11
9   contains rules of conduct and moral guidelines that serve     22
10  the company and its employees. Some general ethics that may   34
11  be recognized in the code are equal and fair treatment,       46
12  truth, and zeal on the job.                                   51
13        Companies may include a few rules in the code that      62
14  relate to their type of work. For example, if some laws       73
15  govern how they conduct business, an owner just might ask     85
16  employees to conduct all activities in a just and lawful      96
17  process. The code of business ethics should be equal for      107
18  all these workers.                                            111
       1  |  2  |  3  |  4  |  5  |  6  |  7  |  8  |  9  |  10  |  11  |  12
```

Formatting

E. LETTERS WITH COPY NOTATIONS

At times you may need to send a copy of your correspondence to people other than the addressee of the original document. A copy notation is included to indicate that someone else besides the addressee is receiving a copy.

To format a letter or memo with a copy notation:

1. Type the copy notation on the line below the reference initials or below the attachment or enclosure notation.
2. At the left margin, type a lowercase *c* followed by a colon.
3. Press the SPACE BAR 1 time, and type the name of the person receiving the copy.
4. If more than one person is receiving a copy, type the names on one line separated by a comma and space between each name.
5. Spell-check, proofread, and preview your document for spelling and formatting errors.

Sincerely, ↓4X

James R. Robertson
District Manager ↓2X

rts
Enclosure
c: T. Embers, J. McIntyre

F. E-MAIL WITH COPIES

Use the copy feature in your e-mail software when you wish to send the e-mail message to additional addressees.

To format an e-mail message with a copy:

- Format the e-mail message as usual.
- No special formatting steps are needed when a copy is sent. Therefore, do not type a copy notation at the bottom of the e-mail message.
- Type e-mail addresses for recipients as desired in the Cc box.

G. INDENTED DISPLAYS

To set off a quoted paragraph that has 4 or more lines of text or to emphasize a paragraph, format it as an indented display. To format a paragraph as an indented display:

- Insert 1 blank line before and after the indented display.
- Type the paragraph single-spaced and indented 0.5 inch from both the left and right margins (instead of enclosing it in quotation marks).
- Use the indent command in Word to format a displayed paragraph.
- Spell-check, proofread, and preview your document for spelling and formatting errors.

Some students work part-time and take classes over an extended period of years. Others obtain skills by attending career-specific schools. ↓2X

→indent 0.5" No matter what path is taken, all who seek advanced training face ←indent 0.5"
Indented   the problem of paying the ever-increasing costs of higher education.
display   Financial aid can be the answer. There are scholarships, loans, and
              grants that do not have to be repaid. ↓2X

It is important that you start your research early so that you have enough time to locate and meet application deadlines for a variety of awards. ↓2X

Sincerely, ↓4X

Charles R. Stone
Branch Manager ↓2X

mtr
Enclosure
Copy   c: Mrs. Coretta D. Rice, Dr. Thomas Moore
notation

H. WORD PROCESSING: INDENTATION AND E-MAIL—COPIES

GO TO Word Manual

Study Lesson 44 in your Word Manual. Complete all of the shaded steps while at your computer. Then format the documents that follow.

Document Processing

Correspondence 44-30

Business Letter in Block Style

Format this paragraph as an indented display.

May 11, 20-- | Mr. James Becker | 783 Wellcourt Lane | Mount Vernon, WA 98273-4156 | Dear Mr. Becker:

¶ Marvin Sirinek has informed me that you have a question pertaining to the maintenance proposal that was submitted by the directors and approved by management at the April board meeting. Specifically, your concern focused on the following segment from that proposal:

All maintenance proposals are subject to review within a reasonable timeframe, as initially defined in the RFP. Therefore, it is strongly recommended that no company representative sign a contract with the designated provider until the deadline to receive objections expires and all protests have been settled.

¶ To clarify any future misunderstandings with the interpretation of this paragraph, it should be recognized that all parties may object to any portion of the RFP for a period not to exceed 30 days from the date the RFP was officially signed by all parties. Sincerely, | Susan Booth | Director of Maintenance | urs | c: Marvin Sirinek

Correspondence 44-31

E-Mail Message

Sarah,

¶ Thank you for your article on "The Essentials for Computer Security." As you asked, I have reviewed the article and have the following suggestions for adding some additional points to those you mentioned:

1. Never leave your computer unattended.
2. Don't lock your computer in your car where it can be seen.
3. Consider investing in a cable lock system to secure your computer to your workstation.

¶ You have some excellent suggestions in your article. I am copying my assistant editor, Alan Kramer, so that he can provide any additional suggestions. Kevin | Kevin R. Stone | E-mail: kstone@quickmail.com | Phone: 701-555-8039

Letters in Modified-Block Style

Goals

- Demonstrate improved speed and accuracy when typing by touch.
- Demonstrate acceptable language arts skills in composing.
- Correctly format a letter in modified-block style.
- Successfully complete a Progress and Proofreading Check with zero errors on the first scored attempt.

A. WARMUP

alphabet

number/symbol

easy

```
1  A Jack in the Box quickly varied its menu with fudge pizza.
2  coy20@cox.net 70% Hsu & Van 5/7 Win! ($4.93) *op. cit #16-8
3  Andy will use eight hand signals if he is able to see them.
```

Skillbuilding

B. 12-SECOND SPEED SPRINTS

Take three 12-second timed writings on each line.

```
4  The eight old books are to be thrown into the fields today.
5  Alan may then take apart both of the toys out on the lanai.
6  Due to the big quake, the city may start to move all autos.
7  Glen may take apart the old robots when he comes into town.
   ' ' ' '5' ' ' '10' ' ' '15' ' ' '20' ' ' '25' ' ' '30' ' ' '35' ' ' '40' ' ' '45' ' ' '50' ' ' '55' ' ' '60
```

C. PACED PRACTICE

Follow the GDP software directions for this exercise to improve keystroking speed and accuracy.

Language Arts

D. COMPOSING SENTENCES

Answer each question with a complete sentence.

8 What are your best traits that you will bring to your job when you graduate?

9 Would you rather work for a large or a small company?

10 How much money do you expect to earn on your first job?

11 Would you like your first job to be in a small town or a large city?

12 What do you see yourself doing in ten years?

Formatting

E. MODIFIED-BLOCK STYLE LETTERS

Modified-block style is a commonly used format for business letters. The date, the complimentary closing, and the writer's identification line(s) begin at the horizontal centerpoint for each of these lines. **Note:** These lines are *not* centered horizontally.

1. Set a left tab at the centerpoint (at 3.25 inches).
2. Press ENTER 5 times to begin the letter 2 inches from the top of the page.
3. Press TAB 1 time to move to the centerpoint; then type the date of the letter.
4. Press ENTER 4 times; then type the inside address at the left margin.
5. Press ENTER 2 times; then type the salutation at the left margin, and press ENTER 2 times again.
6. Type the paragraphs blocked at the left margin; press ENTER 2 times after all paragraphs.
7. After typing the final paragraph, press ENTER 2 times; then press TAB 1 time to move to the centerpoint.
8. Type the complimentary closing; then press ENTER 4 times.
9. Press TAB 1 time to move to the centerpoint; then type the writer's identification. If the writer's identification is to be typed on 2 lines, press ENTER and TAB 1 time again for any additional line.
10. Press ENTER 2 times; then type the reference initials and remaining letter parts at the left margin.
11. Spell-check, proofread, and preview your document for spelling and formatting errors.

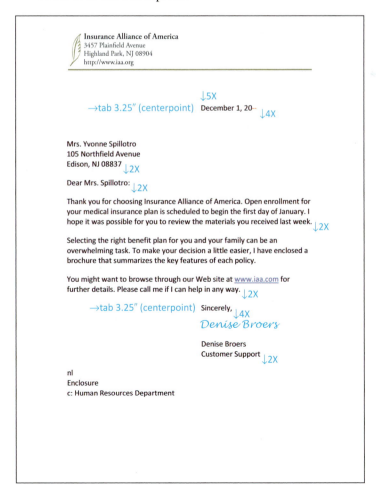

F. WORD PROCESSING: TAB SET—RULER TABS

GO TO
Word Manual

Study Lesson 45 in your Word Manual. Complete all of the shaded steps while at your computer. Then format the documents that follow.

Document Processing

Correspondence
45-32
Business Letter in Modified-Block Style

October 28, 20-- | Mr. and Mrs. Jacob Fang | 2308 Hannegan Road | Bellingham, WA 98226 | Dear Mr. and Mrs. Fang:

¶ We are pleased that you are interested in a Jennings home. Ollie Lucas, the agent who showed you the lot on Garfield Street, has referred your unanswered questions to me.

¶ Typically, 20 percent of the selling price is required as a down payment, but some of the lending agencies with which we work require a smaller down payment depending on your financial liquidity. Jennings Homes is not itself involved in home financing, but we work with several financial institutions in the Bellingham area. I encourage you to call on any of those included in the enclosed list to arrange for your financing needs.

¶ Yes, the Garfield lot can accommodate a full basement. If you prefer to add a basement to your new home, please let Mr. Lucas know of your intentions. We hope to hear from you soon so that we can start landscaping the lot to your satisfaction. Sincerely, | Gayle R. Sloan | Sales Director | urs | Enclosure | c: Loan Processing Dept.

Correspondence
45-33
Business Letter in Modified-Block Style

December 8, 20-- | Mr. Darryl Ward, Sales Manager | Bachmann's Nursery and Landscaping | 6823 Oneta Avenue | Youngstown, OH 44500-2175 | Dear Mr. Ward:

¶ As you requested on the telephone, I am providing the following list of events relating to the trees I purchased from your nursery:

1. On May 4, I purchased at your nursery in Salem four silver maples for the atrium outside our Salem office. We also purchased four Yoshino cherry trees at your branch in Canton the next day.

2. After about six months, one of the silver maples and one cherry tree had died. I phoned both the Salem and Canton branches the week of November 15, but no one returned my calls.

3. On November 20, I phoned your nursery in Salem in an attempt to have these trees replaced. Again, no one responded to my call.

(continued on next page)

¶ As these trees are under warranty for one year from the date of purchase, I expect that you will replace them at no charge. I look forward to hearing from you as to when the trees will be replaced.

Sincerely, / Roger Blalock / Grounds Manager / urs

December 21, 20-- | Mr. Roger Blalock | 4782 Saranac Avenue | Youngstown, OH 44505-6207 | Dear Mr. Blalock:

¶ As you requested in your December 8 letter, we will replace your trees without cost to you. The replacement trees will match the others you purchased in both size and color. I am enclosing a warranty for these new trees so that you can feel confident that we stand behind our product.

¶ We cannot predict the survival rate for any tree; however, for those that do not survive for a reasonable lifespan, we stand behind our warranty and replace those that expire during the first year they are planted.

¶ The communication breakdown that you experienced with our branch offices should not have occurred. We will take steps to ensure that this will not happen again. You can be confident that the appearance of your atrium will be restored. Thank you for shopping at Bachmann's.

Sincerely, | Mrs. Alice G. Schmidt | Co-owner | urs | Enclosure | c: Mr. Darryl Ward

Keyboarding Connection

Inedible Cookies

Is that cookie good for you? A cookie is a short text entry stored on your computer that identifies your preferences to the server of the Web site you are viewing.

Certain Web sites use cookies to customize pages for return visitors. Only the information you provide or the selections you make while visiting a Web site are stored in a cookie. You can control how your browser uses cookies.

Use the Help feature in your browser to find out how to control cookies. Try using the keywords "cookie" or "security" when you search the Help index. You will probably find some great tips on how to increase security when working on the Internet.

Your Turn: Access your browser's cookie policy defaults. Decide if you want to change them.

10

Reports

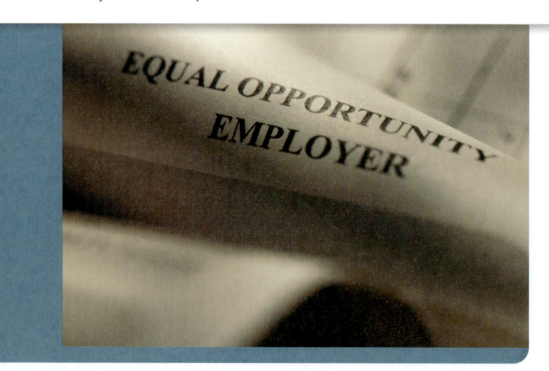

EQUAL OPPORTUNITY EMPLOYER

Left-Bound Business Reports With Indented Displays and Footnotes

Goals

- Type at least 37wpm/3'/3e.
- Correctly use Word's margin and footnote features.
- Correctly format a left-bound business report with a long quotation and footnotes.

A. WARMUP

alphabet   1   At the zoo a roving ox was quickly fed a tasty jumping bug.

concentration   2   straightforwardness uncommunicativeness departmentalization

easy   3   A pair of cozy socks or a cup of cocoa may fix me right up.

Skillbuilding

B. SUSTAINED PRACTICE: NUMBERS AND SYMBOLS

Take a 1-minute timed writing on the boxed paragraph to establish your base speed. Then take a 1-minute timed writing on the following paragraph. As soon as you equal or exceed your base speed on this paragraph, move to the next, more difficult paragraph.

4	The proposed road improvement program was approved by	10
5	the county commissioners at their last meeting. There were	23
6	about ten citizens who spoke on behalf of the project.	34

7   The plan calls for blacktopping a 14-mile stretch on   11
8   County Road 42356. This is the road that is commonly called   23
9   the "roller coaster" because of all the curves and hills.   34

10   There will be 116 miles blacktopped by J & J. Bros.   10
11   (commonly referred to as the Jeremy Brothers*). J & J's   22
12   office is at 1798 30th Avenue past the 22d Street bridge.   33

13   Minor road repair costs range from $10,784 to a high   11
14   of $163,450 (39% of the total program costs). The "county   22
15   inspector" is to hold the project costs to 105% of budget!   34

   1 | 2 | 3 | 4 | 5 | 6 | 7 | 8 | 9 | 10 | 11 | 12

Take two 3-minute timed writings.

Goal: At least 37wpm/3'/3e

C. 3-MINUTE TIMED WRITING

16	Now is a great time for you to look for a job. Most	11
17	employers look for people who have mastered a few office	22
18	skills. For example, if you have acquired good computer	33
19	skills and are capable of working with people around you	45
20	and are steadfast, you can find a good job. There are some	56
21	who will pay top dollar to find and keep good workers.	67
22	Your first impression on a prospective employer will	78
23	be a lasting one. Your resume should list your job skills,	90
24	your experience, and your personal information. Your zeal	102
25	when you interview for a job must come through.	111

1 | 2 | 3 | 4 | 5 | 6 | 7 | 8 | 9 | 10 | 11 | 12

Formatting

D. LEFT-BOUND REPORTS WITH FOOTNOTES

A left-bound report requires a wider left margin to allow for binding so that text is not hidden after the report is bound. To format a left-bound report, increase the left margin to 1.5 inches.

Footnote references indicate the sources of facts or ideas used in a report. Although footnotes may be formatted in various ways, they have many characteristics in common:

1. Footnote references are indicated in the text by superior figures.
2. Footnotes are numbered consecutively throughout a report.
3. Footnotes appear at the bottom of the page on which the references appear and are preceded by a divider line, which is automatically inserted when the footnote is created.
4. A footnote should include the name of the author, the title of the book (italicized) or article (in quotation marks), the publisher, the place of publication, the year of publication, and the page number(s).
5. If a footnote lists an online reference, it should also include the URL address and the date the source was accessed.
6. Spell-check, proofread, and preview your document for spelling and formatting errors.

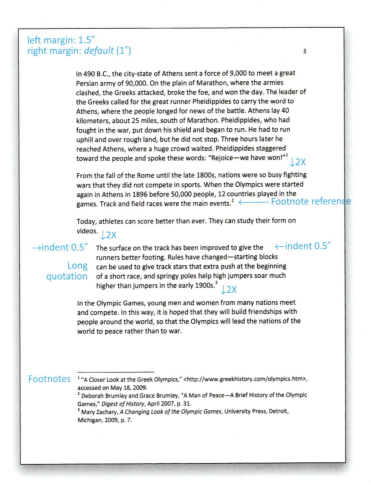

In 490 B.C., the city-state of Athens sent a force of 9,000 to meet a great Persian army of 90,000. On the plain of Marathon, where the armies clashed, the Greeks attacked, broke the foe, and won the day. The leader of the Greeks called for the great runner Pheidippides to carry the word to Athens, where the people longed for news of the battle. Athens lay 40 kilometers, about 25 miles, south of Marathon. Pheidippides, who had fought in the war, put down his shield and began to run. He had to run uphill and over rough land, but he did not stop. Three hours later he reached Athens, where a huge crowd waited. Pheidippides staggered toward the people and spoke these words: "Rejoice—we have won!"[1] ↓2X

From the fall of the Rome until the late 1800s, nations were so busy fighting wars that they did not compete in sports. When the Olympics were started again in Athens in 1896 before 50,000 people, 12 countries played in the games. Track and field races were the main events.[2] ← Footnote reference

Today, athletes can score better than ever. They can study their form on videos. ↓2X

→indent 0.5"   The surface on the track has been improved to give the   ←indent 0.5"
Long quotation   runners better footing. Rules have changed—starting blocks can be used to give track stars that extra push at the beginning of a short race, and springy poles help high jumpers soar much higher than jumpers in the early 1900s.[3] ↓2X

In the Olympic Games, young men and women from many nations meet and compete. In this way, it is hoped that they will build friendships with people around the world, so that the Olympics will lead the nations of the world to peace rather than to war.

Footnotes
_____
[1] "A Closer Look at the Greek Olympics," <http://www.greekhistory.com/olympics.htm>, accessed on May 18, 2009.
[2] Deborah Brumley and Grace Brumley, "A Man of Peace—A Brief History of the Olympic Games," *Digest of History*, April 2007, p. 31.
[3] Mary Zachary, *A Changing Look of the Olympic Games*, University Press, Detroit, Michigan, 2009, p. 7.

left margin: 1.5"
right margin: *default* (1")   3

E. WORD PROCESSING: MARGINS AND FOOTNOTES

GO TO Word Manual

Study Lesson 46 in your Word Manual. Complete all of the shaded steps while at your computer. Then format the documents that follow.

Document Processing

Report 46-13
Left-Bound Business Report

SHOPPING FOR A HOME

Antonio Valdez

¶ Buying a home is a process that many of us will go through in our life time. If we are like many other prospective buyers, we will experience this decision three or four major times in our working years. A home is often the largest purchase we will make, and it deserves therefore our careful attention. ~~We must be certain to look carefully at all the information available to us.~~

¶ "Many people think that the most important criteria on in shopping for a home is its site,"[1] ~~says James Carson~~. The site should be on land that is well drained and free ~~from~~ from flooding ~~that can cause extensive damage.~~ Check the ~~area~~ local city zoning plan to

(continued on next page)

determine if you have ~~choosen~~ selected a site that is free from flooding and highwater levels, ~~that can cause extensive damage~~. You should also check to see if the ground is stable. Ground that shifts can cause considerably severe cracks in foundations and walls.

¶ Cruise suggests that a ~~home~~ house survey be conducted in the early stages of your search:[2] Key problems are encroachments such as buildings, trees, or additions to the house that overlap the property line or may violate zoning regulations. The solution can be as simple as moving or removing trees or bushes ~~from the front or back of your house~~.

¶ A home purchase is a major under taking with a long list of items that must be investigated. To ensure that the building is structurally sound, many prospective buyers use the services of a building inspector. The walls, ceiling, and floors need (if you have a basement) proper insulation. "Both the depth and 'r' factor need to be checked for appropriate levels."[3] In addition, crossbraces should have been used between the beams supporting a floor.

¶ Carefully check the roof. Walk around the entire house so that you can view the roof lines from all angles. Are there any shingles missing, or is there water damage? Make note of any inconsistencies.

---

[1] David Sanders, "A New Home for the Millennium," *home planning magazine,* April 12, 2009, pp. 8-14.

[2] Karen Cruise, "Settlement Issues when Buying a New Home," *Home Finances,* 2010 July, p. 73.

[3] Raymond Stiles, "Home Construction Ideas," *The Do-It-Yourself Builder,* October 17, 2009, p. 22.

Report 46-14
Left-Bound Business Report

Open the file for Report 46-13 and make the following changes:

1. Delete the final paragraph in the report.
2. Add the following as the final paragraph in the report; insert the footnote as indicated.

In the footnote, format the book title in italics.

The roof should be checked to see if any shingles are missing. Finally, a thorough check should be made of the heating, cooling, and electrical systems in the home. "These features are as critical as any others to be examined."[4]

---

[4] Jennifer Corsi, Home Facilities Planning, University Press, Chicago, 2009, p. 184.

47

Reports in APA Style

Goals

- Demonstrate improved speed and accuracy while typing by touch.
- Demonstrate acceptable language arts skills in expressing numbers.
- Correctly use Word's header feature.
- Correctly format a report in APA style with author/year citations.

A. WARMUP

alphabet   1   His graceful bisque vases whizzed past in my taxi--no joke!

one hand   2   exceed kimono ads mop geared opinion cast onion weave plump

easy   3   Guthrie may clench his hand when they chant the old anthem.

Skillbuilding

B. MAP+: ALPHABET

Follow the GDP software directions for this exercise to improve keystroking accuracy.

C. PROGRESSIVE PRACTICE: ALPHABET

Follow the GDP software directions for this exercise to improve keystroking speed.

Language Arts

Study the rules at the right.

D. NUMBER EXPRESSION

RULE
 # general

In general, spell out numbers zero through ten, and use figures for numbers above ten.

     We rented two movies for tonight.

     The decision was reached after 27 precincts sent in their results.

RULE
 # figure

Use figures for

- **Dates. (Use *st, d,* or *th* only if the day comes *before* the month.)**

     The tax report is due on April 15 (not *April 15*th).

     We will drive to the camp on the 23d (or *23rd* or *23*rd) of May.

- **All numbers if two or more related numbers both above and below ten are used in the same sentence.**

     Mr. Carter sent in 7 receipts, and Ms. Cantrell sent in 22.

     But: The 13 accountants owned three computers each.

- **Measurements (time, money, distance, weight, and percent).**
  The $500 statue we delivered at 7 a.m. weighed 6 pounds.
- **Mixed numbers.**
  Our sales are up 9½ (or *9 1/2* or *9.5*) percent over last year.

Edit each sentence to correct any errors.

4 On the 3d of June, when she turns 60, 2 of her annuities will
5 have earned an average of 10 3/4 percent.

6 All seven investors were interested in buying 14 condos if
7 they were located within fifteen miles of one another.

8 The credit fee is fifteen dollars, and the interest is set
9 at 8 percent; escrow will close on March 23rd before five
10 p.m.

11 The parcel weighed two pounds.

12 She also mailed three large packages and twelve small
13 packages on June 4.

14 They paid 2.5 points on the loan amount.

Formatting

E. REPORTS IN APA STYLE

In addition to the traditional academic style, academic reports may also be formatted in APA (American Psychological Association) style. In the APA style, format the report as follows:

1. Use the default 1-inch margins, and 12-pt. Calibri throughout the report.
2. Double-space the entire report.
3. Insert a header for all pages; type a shortened title and insert an automatic page number that continues the page-numbering sequence from the previous page right-aligned inside the header.
   Note: APA style requires that page 1 be a title page and page 2 be an abstract. Thus, the first page of your APA report should be page number 3.
4. Type the title 1 inch from the top of the page centered using upper- and lowercase letters. Press ENTER 1 time and type the byline centered using upper- and lowercase letters. (Do not bold either the title or the byline.)
5. Indent all paragraphs 0.5 inch.
6. Type main headings centered, using upper- and lowercase letters. Press ENTER 1 time before and after the main heading.
7. Type subheadings at the left margin in italics using upper- and lowercase letters. Press ENTER 1 time before and after the subheading.
8. Spell-check, proofread, and preview your document for spelling and formatting errors.

top, bottom, and side margins: *default* (1")
double-space throughout

Computer History 3

Title — A Brief History of Computers

Byline — Joshua T. Reynolds

→ tab The first computer was probably the abacus, which was used about 5,000 years ago in Asia Minor. As we know them today, computers were first used just after the Second World War, around 1945. Since then, several computer enhancements have occurred. The following paragraphs summarize the major developments that occurred.

Main Heading — Early Computers

Computers were first run by vacuum tubes. The first computer was called the ENIAC, and it was used by the U.S. Census Bureau as well as by President Eisenhower's campaign to predict his presidential victory in 1952 (Burris, 2008). ← Citation

Subheading — *Enhancement of Speed* ← Italic

Transistors were used after vacuum tubes to run computers. These computers were known for their ability to accept instructions for a specific function that could be stored within the computer's memory. After that computer generation, integrated circuits replaced the transistors. As a result, computers became smaller, faster, and more powerful (Diaz & Moore, 2009).

The Intel chip was responsible for most of the changes taking place in computers in the last 30 years. Computers were becoming faster and faster; and

F. AUTHOR/YEAR CITATIONS

Any information based on other sources and used in a report must be documented or cited. The author/year method of citation includes the source information in parentheses at the appropriate point within the text. For more detailed information on APA citations, refer to the illustration in this book or consult the current APA style guide.

G. WORD PROCESSING: HEADERS

GO TO
Word Manual

Study Lesson 47 in your Word Manual. Complete all of the shaded steps while at your computer. Then format the documents that follow.

Document Processing

Global Warming 3

Report 47-15
Report in APA Style

A Brief History of Global Warming | April R. Baumgartner
¶ Earth's climate constantly changes, and many scientists believe that the temperature rises we see in this decade are a natural phenomenon that occurs every so many years. Around 25,000 years ago, it is believed that earth was covered by large areas of ice. And then, about 7,000 years ago, temperatures began to rise and the "Ice Age" came to an end.

general
general

Second Ice Age

general

¶ In the 14th century earth experienced the start of another Ice Age where much of the land mass was covered by glaciers, mostly in three areas: Alaska, Iceland, and the Scandinavian countries. By 1850, however, earth's temperatures had warmed to the point where the glaciers receded, uncovering millions of acres of fertile soil.

(continued on next page)

¶ Jean Baptiste Joseph Fourier, a French mathematician, was the first scientist to propose a theory of global warming. In 1824 he discovered that the earth's temperature was slowly rising. His theory was labeled the "greenhouse effect" because carbon dioxide traps heat in the earth's atmosphere.

¶ Fourier's theory was challenged by Milutin Milankovitch, who proposed that earth's changing temperatures were nothing more than a result of orbital changes of earth. But again in the 1950s, G. S. Callendar supported Fourier's greenhouse effect, and his work led others to increase their research efforts into the concept of global warming. Over 20 mathematical models have been used to analyze global temperatures, and these findings support a belief that global warming is directly related to human activity. It was at that time that scientists voiced their opinion that an increased level of carbon dioxide emissions would trigger an outbreak of global warming.

general

¶ The fear that carbon dioxide emisions were responsible for an increase in global temperatures prompted the international comunity to propose the creation of the kyoto protocol, an international agreement to fight global warming. Members of the this organization required countries to reduce their emission of green house gases.

Report
47-16
Report in APA Style

Open the file for Report 47-15 and make the following changes:

1. Place the insertion point at the end of the paragraph under the Second Ice Age heading, and press ENTER 1 time.
2. Type the subheading Global Warming Theories in italics at the left margin; then press ENTER 1 time.
3. Move the insertion point to the end of the document.
4. Press ENTER 1 time; then type Global Warming Today as a subheading; press ENTER 1 time.
5. Press TAB to indent the paragraph; then type the following text as the final paragraph in the report:

Scientists today disagree as to cause of global warming. Most support two theories: that the increased level of carbon dioxide emissions is responsible for global warming or that global warming is a natural phenomenon. All do agree, however, that global warming is an imminent problem that needs to be addressed in the future.

Reports in MLA Style

48

Goals

- Type at least 38wpm/3′/3e.
- Correctly format a report in MLA style.

A. WARMUP

alphabet   1   Meghan deftly picked valuable jewels, like onyx and quartz.

practice: *w* and *e*   2   web wet were where we elbow wed dew wide ewe wee wade endow

easy   3   Maud may signal her skepticism by her amendment to the bid.

Skillbuilding

B. PACED PRACTICE

Follow the GDP software directions for this exercise to improve keystroking speed and accuracy.

C. 3-MINUTE TIMED WRITING

Take two 3-minute timed writings.

Goal: At least 38wpm/3′/3e

```
 4        Some of us like to use the Internet for shopping. With  11
 5  just a simple click of the mouse, you can shop for almost     23
 6  any type of product. You can purchase books, cars, food,      34
 7  games, toys, zippers, boxes, and even golf clubs by using     46
 8  the computer to shop online.                                  52
 9        The advantages of using the Web to shop with such ease  63
10  are many. First, you can shop from any place that has some    75
11  access to the Internet. Second, you can compare all prices    86
12  with other places before you make any purchase. Third, you    98
13  can have your purchases shipped directly to you. All the      110
14  savings mount quickly.                                        114
```

   1 | 2 | 3 | 4 | 5 | 6 | 7 | 8 | 9 | 10 | 11 | 12

Formatting

D. REPORTS IN MLA STYLE

In addition to the traditional academic style and APA style, academic reports may also be formatted in MLA (Modern Language Association) style. If citations are used, usually the author's last name and page number are cited inside parentheses. For more detailed information on MLA style, refer to the illustrations in this book or consult the current MLA style guide.

In the MLA style, format the report as follows:

1. Use the default 1-inch margins, and 12-pt. Calibri throughout the report.
2. Double-space the entire report.
3. Insert a header for all pages; type the author's last name and the page number right-aligned inside the header.
4. Type each element of the heading information (your name, your instructor's name, the class name, and the date) on a separate line at the left margin.
5. Type the date using the day-month-year style (15 April 20--).
6. Center and type the title using upper- and lowercase letters. (Do not bold the title.)
7. Indent all paragraphs 0.5 inch.
8. Spell-check, proofread, and preview your document for spelling and formatting errors.

Document Processing

Report 48-17

Report in MLA Style

Remember to type the author's last name and page number right-aligned in the header.

Remember to double-space the entire report.

Michael Chu

Dr. Katherine Sanchez

Telecommunications 414

14 October 20--

Evaluating a Computer System

¶ Judging the effectiveness of a computer system has taken on a new dimension in the past few years, if for no other reason than the wide range of computer systems from which the user can select. It is, therefore, important that we investigate the criteria that should be considered in making this important decision.

¶ Probably the most obvious criterion to be considered when one purchases a computer system is speed. The value of a computer is directly related to its speed, and a computer's speed is typically measured in gigahertz (GHz). A gigahertz is one billion cycles per second, and the more gigahertz you have to work with, the faster your computer will run. However, computer manufacturers are starting to drop the gigahertz rating from computers because there are so many other factors that determine a computer's speed (Phillips 243).

¶ Another important consideration is memory. Software programs continue to expand and need more memory to run on today's computers. If a computer does not have sufficient memory, your computer will process slowly or not at all. When purchasing your new computer, do not settle for anything less than 8 to 12 GBytes of Dual or Tri-Channel memory.

¶ *Flexibility is also important because of the rapid turnover of hardware and software in the computer industry. The flexibility of a computer system is important for two reasons: to accommodate a variety of programs and to permit expandability. Hundreds and possibly thousands of software packages are available today to meet the needs of computer users. The computer you purchase must be able to accommodate this variety of software and be flexible enough to change with the increasing sophistication of software packages.*

Report 48-18

Report in MLA Style

Open the file for Report 48-17 and make the following changes:

1. Change the title of the report to Computer System Evaluation.
2. Delete the last sentence in the first paragraph of the report.
3. Place the insertion point at the end of the fourth paragraph; then add a new paragraph with the text that follows:

   Because of the substantial investment you make in a computer, you do not want to commit your resources to a computer that cannot be expanded to handle (1) newer, more powerful operating systems; (2) "memory-hungry" software packages; (3) network interfaces; and (4) additional users (Goebels and Hallock 129).

49

Report Citations

Goals

- Demonstrate improved speed and accuracy while typing by touch.
- Demonstrate acceptable language arts skills in spelling.
- Correctly use Word's hanging indent and AutoCorrect features.
- Correctly format a bibliography, a reference page in APA style, and a works-cited page in MLA style.

A. WARMUP

alphabet	1	The jinxed wizards plucked the ivy stem from the big quilt.
frequent digraphs	2	es ekes yes espy eves less desires ewes exes eyes fees mess
easy	3	Pamela may use a kayak and map to come to the old city dam.

Skillbuilding

B. MAP+: SYMBOL

Follow the GDP software directions for this exercise to improve keystroking accuracy.

PPP

PRETEST » PRACTICE » POSTTEST

PRETEST
Take a 1-minute timed writing.

C. PRETEST: Alternate- and One-Hand Words

4	The chair of the trade committee served notice that	11
5	the endowment grant exceeded the budget. A million dollars	22
6	was the exact amount. The greater part might be deferred.	34

1 | 2 | 3 | 4 | 5 | 6 | 7 | 8 | 9 | 10 | 11 | 12

PRACTICE
Speed Emphasis:
  If you made 2 or fewer errors on the Pretest, type each *individual* line 2 times.
Accuracy Emphasis:
  If you made 3 or more errors, type each *group* of lines (as though it were a paragraph) 2 times.

D. PRACTICE: Alternate-Hand Keys

7	amendment turndown visible suspend visual height signs maps
8	authentic clemency dormant figment island emblem usual snap
9	shamrocks blandish problem penalty profit thrown chair form

E. PRACTICE: One-Hand Words

10	pumpkin eastward plumply barrage poplin greater holly trade
11	manikin cassette opinion seaweed kimono created union exact
12	minimum attracts million reserve unhook scatter plump defer

POSTTEST
Repeat the Pretest timed
writing and compare
performance.

F. POSTTEST: Alternate- and One-Hand Words

Language Arts

Type these frequently
misspelled words, paying
special attention to any
spelling problems in each
word.

G. SPELLING

13 per other receipt present provided commission international
14 service position questions following industrial maintenance
15 well absence support proposal mortgage corporate management
16 upon balance approval experience facilities recommendations
17 paid because premium procedure addition directors currently

Edit the sentences to correct
any misspellings.

18 The international comission provided a list of proceedures.

19 That industrial maintainance proposal is curently in place.

20 The directers and management supported the recomendations.

21 Those present raised a question about a corporate morgage.

22 Six of the folowing persons have now given their aproval.

23 In edition, Kris has other experience at the facilitys.

Formatting

H. BIBLIOGRAPHIES

REFER TO
Reference
Manual

R-9B: Bibliography

A bibliography is an alphabetic listing of all sources of facts or ideas used or cited in a report. The bibliography is typed on a separate page at the end of a report. In general, titles of major works like books or magazine titles are italicized, and titles of minor works like articles from magazines are typed in quotation marks. For more detailed information on entries in a bibliography, refer to the illustrations in this book or consult a current style guide.

To format a bibliography:

1. Press ENTER 5 times to begin the first line 2 inches from the top of the page.
2. Center and type BIBLIOGRAPHY in all-caps, 14-pt. font, and bold; then press ENTER 2 times.
3. Apply a hanging indent and type the first line. Each entry will begin at the left margin, and the carryover lines will automatically be indented 0.5 inch by the hanging indent.
4. Single-space each entry in the bibliography, and press ENTER 2 times between each entry.

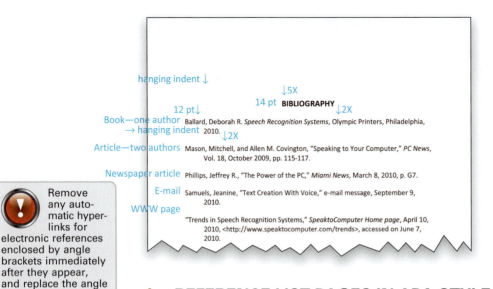

hanging indent ↓

↓5X

12 pt↓   14 pt **BIBLIOGRAPHY** ↓2X

Book—one author   Ballard, Deborah R. *Speech Recognition Systems*, Olympic Printers, Philadelphia,
→ hanging indent   2010. ↓2X

Article—two authors   Mason, Mitchell, and Allen M. Covington, "Speaking to Your Computer," *PC News*,
Vol. 18, October 2009, pp. 115-117.

Newspaper article   Phillips, Jeffrey R., "The Power of the PC," *Miami News*, March 8, 2010, p. G7.

E-mail   Samuels, Jeanine, "Text Creation With Voice," e-mail message, September 9,
2010.

WWW page

"Trends in Speech Recognition Systems," *SpeaktoComputer Home page*, April 10,
2010, <http://www.speaktocomputer.com/trends>, accessed on June 7,
2010.

> ⊘ Remove any automatic hyperlinks for electronic references enclosed by angle brackets immediately after they appear, and replace the angle brackets as needed.

➡ REFER TO
Reference Manual

R-10B: References in APA Style

I. REFERENCE LIST PAGES IN APA STYLE

A reference list is an alphabetic listing of all sources of facts or ideas used or cited in a report formatted in APA style. The reference list is typed on a separate page at the end of a report. For more detailed information on reference list entries, refer to the illustrations in this book or consult a current APA style guide.

To format an APA reference list page:

1. Use the default margins.
2. Double-space the entire page.
3. Insert a header, type a shortened title, and insert an automatic page number that continues the page-numbering sequence from the previous page right-aligned inside the header.

4. Center and type References at the top of the page in upper- and lowercase letters; then press ENTER 1 time.
5. Apply a hanging indent and type the first line. Each reference will begin at the left margin, and the carryover lines will automatically be indented 0.5 inch by the hanging indent.

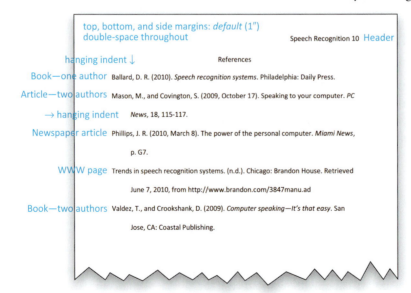

top, bottom, and side margins: *default* (1")
double-space throughout   Speech Recognition 10 Header

hanging indent ↓   References

Book—one author   Ballard, D. R. (2010). *Speech recognition systems*. Philadelphia: Daily Press.

Article—two authors   Mason, M., and Covington, S. (2009, October 17). Speaking to your computer. *PC*

→ hanging indent   *News*, 18, 115-117.

Newspaper article   Phillips, J. R. (2010, March 8). The power of the personal computer. *Miami News*,

p. G7.

WWW page   Trends in speech recognition systems. (n.d.). Chicago: Brandon House. Retrieved

June 7, 2010, from http://www.brandon.com/3847manu.ad

Book—two authors   Valdez, T., and Crookshank, D. (2009). *Computer speaking—It's that easy*. San

Jose, CA: Coastal Publishing.

J. WORKS-CITED PAGES IN MLA STYLE

REFER TO
Reference Manual

R-10D: Works Cited in MLA Style

A works-cited page is an alphabetic listing of all sources of facts or ideas used or cited in a report formatted in MLA style. This reference list is typed on a separate page at the end of a report. For more detailed information on reference list entries, refer to the illustrations in this book or consult a current MLA style guide.

To format a works-cited page:

1. Use the default margins.
2. Double-space the entire page.
3. Insert a header, type the author's last name, insert an automatic page number that continues the page-numbering sequence from the previous page right-aligned inside the header, and close the header.
4. Type Works Cited centered at the top of the page; then press ENTER 1 time.
5. Apply a hanging indent, and type the first line at the left margin; the carry-over lines will automatically be indented 0.5 inch by the hanging indent.

top, bottom, and side margins: *default* (1")
double-space throughout
hanging indent

Kramer 10 Header

Works Cited

Book—one author Ballard, Deborah R. *Speech Recognition Systems*. Philadelphia: Olympic Printers,

→ hanging indent 2010.

Article—two authors Mason, Mitchell, and Allen M. Covington. "Speaking to Your Computer." *PC News*

18 Oct. 2009: 115-117.

Newspaper article Phillips, Jeffrey R. "The Power of the PC." *Miami News* 8 March 2010: G7.

E-mail Samuels, Jeanine. "Text Creation with Voice." E-mail to the author. 18 Sept. 2010.

WWW page "Trends in Speech Recognition Systems." 10 Apr. 2010. 7 Sept. 2010

<http://www.speaktocomputer.com/trends/ad>.

K. WORD PROCESSING: INDENTATION—HANGING AND AUTOCORRECT—HYPERLINK

GO TO
Word Manual

Study Lesson 49 in your Word Manual. Complete all the shaded steps while at your computer. Then format the documents that follow.

Document Processing

Report
49-19
Bibliography

Italicize (but do not underline) the publication titles.

Highlighted words are spelling words from the language arts activities; do *not* highlight them when you type.

BIBLIOGRAPHY

Becker, Arnie, "Management Policies in Industrial Nations," *Modern Management*, Vol. 24, January 2010, pp. 22–24.

Champagne, Lester R., *CEO Questions and Recommendations*, Tennessee Valley Press, Nashville, 2009.

Driscoll, Andy, and Cynthia Rogge, "Procedures for Boards of Directors," *Daily Press*, San Francisco, 2009.

(continued on next page)

Hartwing Institute, Premium Mortgages, Lohr Press, Phoenix, 2008.

"Overdue Debts of our Nation," Corpamerica, June 18, 2010, <http://www.corporatedebt.com>, accessed on July 8, 2010.

Pearson, Jack E., "International Investment Guide Proposal," e-mail message, February 17, 2010.

An Economic Overview 12

Report 49-20
References in APA Style

References

Currin, C.D., & Terwilliger, Ernest, S. E. (2010). *A director's position on mortgage loans.* Burr Ridge, IL: Mcgraw-Hill/Irwin.

Dodsworth, W. R. (2009). Current guide to insurance premiums, *The Review Insurance,* XIX, 24-34.

Freeberg, S. A., Kingsford, M. A., & Soderbloom, Z. E. (2009). *The absence of experience in job interviews.* Minneapolis: The University Press.

Mueller, D. T., & Isaacson, R. D. (2010). *Questions about the present economic condition.* Retrieved June 11, 2010, from the world wide web: http://www.economicforecasts.com/june digest/forecasts.htm

Tindall, M. G. (2008). Adjusting the balance of additional indicators. *The Midwest Economic Forecaster,* 23.

Waldon, J. R. (2010). *american capitalism following the economic down turn.* Seattle: Puget Sound Press.

Worthington 18

Report 49-21
Works Cited in MLA Style

Works Cited

Anderson, Cody M. "Corporate Management Policies." E-mail to the author. 9 Nov. 2010.

Bartoletti, Lynda, et al. "E-commerce Support on the Internet." *Online Today.* Vol. 10. Aug. 2009: 123-124.

Conner, Shelby. *Recommendations for the New Online Resources.* Cheyenne: Mountain Press, 2010.

"Industrial Maintenance Facilities." *National Entrepreneur.* 18 Oct. 2009. 22 July 2010 <http://www.entrepreneurnews.com/facilities.htm>.

Lewis, Michael, and Walter R. Arnold. *Proposal for Approval of Online Purchases.* Miami: Keys Publishing House, 2010.

Tucker, James, and Arlene Hoffman. "International Commission on Internet Services." *Indianapolis Gazette,* 12 June 2009: B3.

Preliminary Report Pages

50

Goals

- Type at least 38/3'/3e.
- Correctly format a title page and a table of contents.
- Correctly use Word's tab set and dot leaders features.
- Successfully complete a Progress and Proofreading Check with zero errors on the first scored attempt.

A. WARMUP

alphabet 1 The judges quickly gave back six prizes to the famed women.
number/symbol 2 pnoe@att.net 270% Ivy & Day 3/8 Go! $17.59 *sic (#6423-145)
easy 3 The haughty widow with the auditory problem may ask for it.

Skillbuilding

B. 12-SECOND SPEED SPRINTS

Take three 12-second timed writings on each line.

4 Chris may clap his hands when they chant the songs at camp.
5 Hale saw a Bible of the gospel in the chapel near the lake.
6 Half of the maps may be for the land and half for the lake.
7 Ray may work in the field of coal when he is not busy here.
 ' ' ' '5' ' ' '10' ' ' '15' ' ' '20' ' ' '25' ' ' '30' ' ' '35' ' ' '40' ' ' '45' ' ' '50' ' ' '55' ' ' '60

C. TECHNIQUE PRACTICE: SPACE BAR

Type each line 2 times, using your right thumb to strike the SPACE BAR in the center.

8 My dad may ask me to dig up an old oak if it is in the way.
9 Ty can be at the bus by six if he can hop a cab on the way.
10 We may ask a tax pro to pay our tax for us if we owe a lot.
11 My new ad on the air may get a lot of men to buy a new car.

Take two 3-minute timed writings.

Goal: At least 38wpm/3'/3e

D. 3-MINUTE TIMED WRITING

```
12        The Web is a vast source of facts and data on many        10
13   topics. You can view many newspapers, zip through weather      22
14   reports, find a tax form and learn how to complete it, and     34
15   search for a job. You can find answers to health questions     46
16   and learn about world events almost as soon as they occur.     57
17        E-mail is another part of the Internet that people are    69
18   using more often. They use e-mail to keep in touch with        80
19   friends and family in a quick and efficient way that costs     92
20   very little. They can write down their thoughts and send       103
21   messages just as if they were writing a letter or memo.        114
```

1 | 2 | 3 | 4 | 5 | 6 | 7 | 8 | 9 | 10 | 11 | 12

Formatting

E. TITLE PAGE

Reports may have a title page, which includes information such as the report title, to whom the report is submitted, the writer's name and identification, and the date. To format a title page, follow these steps:

1. Center the page vertically and center all lines horizontally.
2. Center the title in all-caps and bold, using a 14-pt. font.
3. Press ENTER 2 times; then center the subtitle in upper- and lowercase and bold, using a 12-pt. font.
4. Press ENTER 12 times; then center the words Submitted to.
5. Press ENTER 2 times; then center the recipient's name and identification on separate lines, single-spaced.
6. Press ENTER 12 times; then center the words Prepared by.
7. Press ENTER 2 times; then center the writer's name and identification on separate lines, single-spaced.
8. Press ENTER 2 times; then center the date.

---

center page ↓

14 pt **USING TECHNOLOGY TO REACH STUDENTS
AT A DISTANCE** ↓2X

12X ↓ **Distance Learning Classrooms**
↓12X

Submitted to ↓2X

Alicia T. Gonzalez
Technology Coordinator
Media Systems, Inc. ↓12X

Prepared by ↓2X

Tracy Weller
Computer Specialist
Media Systems, Inc. ↓2X

October 21, 20--

F. TABLE OF CONTENTS

A table of contents is usually included in a long report. The table of contents identifies the major and minor sections of a report and includes page numbers preceded by dot leaders. Dot leaders are a series of periods that guide the reader's eye across the page to the page number typed at the right margin. To format a table of contents:

1. Press ENTER 5 times to begin the first line 2 inches from the top of the page.
2. Center and type CONTENTS in all-caps, 14-pt. font, and bold; then press ENTER 2 times.
3. Set a left tab at 0.5 inch; then set a right tab at 6.5 inches with dot leaders.
4. Change to 12-pt. font, and type the first main heading in all-caps.
5. Press TAB to insert dot leaders and to move to the right margin; then type the page number, and press ENTER 2 times.
6. Type the next main heading in a similar fashion. If the next item is a subheading, press TAB 1 time to indent the subheading 0.5 inch.
7. Type the subheading, and then press TAB to insert dot leaders and to move to the right margin; then type the page number.
8. Press ENTER 1 time to type the next subheading or 2 times to type a new main heading.
9. Continue in like fashion until the table of contents is complete.

↓5X

14 pt **CONTENTS** ↓2X

12 pt ↓ OUR COMPUTER SOCIETY .... → tab 6.5″ 2 ↓2X

HOW COMPUTERS WORK ....5 ↓2X

→ tab 0.5″ Input...5
Processing...7
Storage..8
Output..12 ↓2X

USING COMPUTER SOFTWARE 14

Word Processing...16
Spreadsheet 17
Database 19
Graphics 20

COMPUTERS AND YOUR CAREER..21

Management Information Systems..25
Careers in the Computer Industry...28
Careers in Business and Industry...32
Careers in Government...36

COMPUTERS AND YOUR FUTURE 38

BIBLIOGRAPHY 41

G. WORD PROCESSING: TAB SET—DOT LEADERS

GO TO Word Manual

Study Lesson 50 in your Word Manual. Complete all of the shaded steps while at your computer. Then format the documents that follow.

Document Processing

Report 50-22
Title Page

GLOBAL WARMING AND ITS IMPACT ON EARTH'S CLIMATE

Including a Discussion on Future Trends

Submitted to

Brandon T. Alexander
Technology Coordinator
Anthropogenic Division

Prepared by

Richelle R. Simmons
Science Coordinator
Anthropogenic Division

February 9, 20--

CONTENTS

THE POWER OF COMPUTERS

Some Predictions for the Internet and Artificial Intelligence

Submitted to

Jerry Santiago
Division Chief
Computer Dynamics Inc.

Prepared by

Marilyn R. Hasamara
Computer Consultant
Computer Dynamics Inc.

May 24, 20--

Progress and Proofreading Check

Documents designated as Proofreading Checks serve as a check of your proofreading skill. Your goal is to have zero typographical errors when the GDP software first scores the document.

THE POWER OF COMPUTERS
Some Predictions for the Internet and Artificial Intelligence
Marilyn R. Hasamara

¶ Much has been written about the impact of computers and how they will alter almost every activity in our lives for years to come. There is strong evidence that this prediction will soon become a reality. The purpose of this report is to summarize changes that we will likely see in the areas of Internet activity and artificial intelligence.

THE INTERNET REVOLUTION

¶ There is little doubt that connectivity to the Internet will continue to grow in this decade. The speed at which we access the Internet will also continue to grow. The transmission of information on the Internet today will be considered but a "snail's pace" when compared to what we can expect in just a few short years. Most

(continued on next page)

information will be transmitted at gigabit speeds and higher.[1] Computer security will also be enhanced exponentially, and the safety of transmitting sensitive data over the Internet will encourage many users to increase their use of online communications to conduct everyday business activities without fear of outside interference.

ARTIFICIAL INTELLIGENCE

¶ Artificial intelligence—generally known as AI—can be described as a computer's ability to assume an intelligence similar to that of the human brain. It enables a computer to reason and make decisions based on a preassigned set of facts or data.[2] But many experts predict that the computer's power will not stop there. They predict that computers will soon become much smarter than humans by a process in which "intelligent" computers create even more intelligent computers.

¶ It is also predicted that robots will displace humans from farms and factories; we will travel in cars, planes, and trains that are operated solely by computers; and traveling on the interstate highways will be as safe as watching television at home.

---

[1] Delores R. Polaski, "Tomorrow's Brainpower," *Internet for Tomorrow*, Vol. 8, February 2010, pp. 75-77.

[2] Timothy T. Reynolds, "Artificial Intelligence," *Journal of Computer Trends*, September 2009, pp. 23-24, 36.

Keyboarding Connection

Evaluating Internet Sources

Are you sure your Internet source has valid information? Because of the broad availability of the Internet and the lack of careful review stages like the ones built into print publishing, you must be cautious about the dependability of information you find on the Internet. Evaluate information on the Internet by the same standards you use to evaluate other sources of information.

The best way to ensure that information is valid is to get it from a reputable source. The Internet versions of established, reputable journals in medicine (for example, *Journal of the American Medical Association*), business (for example, *Harvard Business Review*), engineering, computer science, and so forth, warrant the same level of trust as the printed versions.

When you do not use established, reputable Web sites, use caution. Keep in mind that anyone can publish on the Internet. For many sources, there are no editorial review safeguards in place.

Your Turn: Search the Web for more assessment methods.

Employment Documents

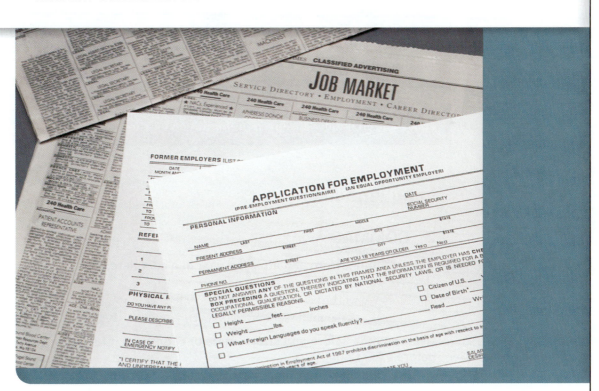

Resumes

51

Goals

- Demonstrate improved speed and accuracy while typing by touch.
- Demonstrate acceptable language arts skills in comma usage.
- Correctly format a resume.
- Correctly use Word's font and table column width features.

A. WARMUP

alphabet   1 Viewing those quizzical abstracts mixed up the hefty jocks.

concentration   2 interchangeableness incontrovertibility nonadministratively

easy   3 The men paid for their neighbor to make a robot for profit.

Skillbuilding

B. MAP+: ALPHABET

Follow the GDP software directions for this exercise to improve keystroking accuracy.

C. PROGRESSIVE PRACTICE: ALPHABET

Follow the GDP software directions for this exercise to improve keystroking speed.

Language Arts

Study the rules at
the right.

RULE
, date

RULE
, place

D. COMMAS

Use a comma before and after the year in a complete date.

We will arrive on June 2, 2009, for the conference.

But: We will arrive on June 2 for the conference.

But: Work should be submitted between November 2009 and December 2009.

Use a comma before and after a state or country that follows a city (but not before a ZIP Code).

Joan moved to Vancouver, British Columbia, in May.

Send the package to Douglasville, GA 30135, by Express Mail.

But: Send the package to Georgia by Express Mail.

Edit each sentence to correct any errors.

4 The warehouse building will be ready in September, 2008.

5 The attorney told a clerk to use June 30, 2009 as the date.

6 The books were sent to Los Angeles, CA, 90029 on July 13,
7 2009 and will arrive soon.

8 The move to Toledo, Ohio, was scheduled for November, 2008.

9 The meeting began on May 3 in Chicago at 9 a.m.

10 We shopped for souvenirs in Nogales, Sonora on Friday.

11 January 1, 2012 will be a special date for our company.

Formatting

E. BASIC PARTS OF A RESUME

When you apply for a job, you may be asked to submit a resume. The purpose of a resume is to convey your qualifications for the position you are seeking. A resume should include the following:

- Personal information (name, address, telephone number, and e-mail address).
- Your career objective (optional).
- A summary of your educational background and special training.
- Previous work experience.
- Any activities or personal achievements that relate to the position for which you are applying.

- References (optional). If an employer requests references, you should have at least three people who can tell a prospective employer what kind of worker you are.

Often, your resume creates the first impression you make on a prospective employer; be sure it is free of errors.

A resume can be formatted in various styles. Choose a style (or design one) that is attractive and that enables you to get all the needed information on one or two pages.

F. RESUME

To format a resume:

1. Press ENTER 5 times.
2. Insert an open table with 2 columns and 1 row for each section of the resume. **Note:** In the illustration on page 194, you would use 6 rows.
3. Merge the cells in Row 1.
4. Change to center alignment.
5. Type your name in all-caps in Cambria 14-pt. Bold in Row 1.
6. Change font size to 12 pt. and press ENTER 2 times.
7. Type your street address followed by a comma and 1 space; type your city followed by a comma and 1 space; then type your state followed by 1 space and your ZIP Code. Press ENTER 1 time.
8. Type Phone: followed by 1 space; then type your area code and phone number followed by a semicolon and 1 space.

9. Type e-mail: followed by 1 space and your e-mail address.
10. Press ENTER 1 time.
11. Apply a bottom border to Row 1.
12. Move to Row 2, Column A; then press ENTER 1 time.
13. Change font to Calibri Bold. Type the entry in Column A in all-caps; then press TAB to move to Column B.
14. Press ENTER 1 time, and type the information related to the Column A heading in Column B.
15. Press ENTER as needed in each section to insert 1 blank line between sections.
16. Type job titles and business names in italics.
17. Continue typing all entries until you are finished.
18. For any job descriptions, increase the left indent to 0.5 inch to reposition the information.
19. Decrease the width of Column A to accommodate the longest entry.

(Note: Table shown with "View Gridlines" active.)

G. WORD PROCESSING: FONT AND TABLE— CHANGE COLUMN WIDTH

Study Lesson 51 in your Word Manual. Complete all of the shaded steps while at your computer. Then format the documents that follow.

, place

MARTINA R. VALDEZ
4826 Foxworth Apartments, #201, Clio, MI 48420
Phone: 810-555-3424; e-mail: mvaldez@quickmail.net

OBJECTIVE   To pursue a career in graphic design.

, place

EDUCATION   Central Michigan Business College, Mt. Pleasant, Michigan
A.A. degree in graphic design

, date   Graduated: December 2009

, place   Clio High School, Clio, Michigan
, date   Graduated: June 2007

EXPERIENCE   *Office Assistant, Chambers Moving and Storage*

, place   Mt. Pleasant, Michigan
, date   June 2008 to December 2009
Composed and typed routine correspondence; filed customer
records; placed and answered telephone calls; prepared invoices;
updated online customer records.

Copy Editor, Clio Daily News

, place   Clio, Michigan
, date   June 2007 to June 2008
Assisted the news editor with designing and preparing copy for the
Clio Daily News; solicited subscriptions from local businesses; edited
copy for the New Business forum.

ACTIVITIES   Activities pursued while attending college:
- Newsletter Editor, 2009
- Member, Spanish Club, 2009
- President, Graphic Design Club, 2008-2009
- Member, Phi Beta Lambda, 2008-2009
- Vice President, Graphic Design Club, 2007

REFERENCES   Available upon request.

Open the file for Report 51-26, and make the following changes:

1. Change the name to `Connie R. Cameron`.
2. Change the address to `725 Dearborn Street, Lapeer, MI 48446`.
3. Change the phone number to `810-555-8956`.
4. Change the e-mail address to `ccameron@quickmail.net`.

5. Change the high school attended to `Lapeer Central High School, Lapeer, Michigan`.
6. Delete the third activity and replace it with the following: `Member, Intramural Tennis Team, 2009`.

Letters of Application

52

Goals

- Type at least 39wpm/5'/5e.
- Correctly format a letter of application.

A. WARMUP

alphabet	1	Sympathizing with those Quakers would fix their objectives.
one hand	2	stages phylum wet pop affect jumpily tact junky beard pinky
easy	3	The ancient emblem is the handiwork of the haughty prodigy.

Skillbuilding

Take a 1-minute timed writing on the boxed paragraph to establish your base speed. Then take a 1-minute timed writing on the following paragraph. As soon as you equal or exceed your base speed on this paragraph, move to the next, more difficult paragraph.

B. SUSTAINED PRACTICE: CAPITALS

4	There are several different approaches that one can	11
5	take when considering a major purchase. Some people make	22
6	the mistake of simply going to a store and making a choice.	34
7	When one couple decided to buy a chest-type freezer,	11
8	they looked at a consumer magazine in the library. The	22
9	Sears, Amana, and General Electric were shown as best buys.	34
10	That same issue of their magazine compared electric	11
11	ranges. Jonathan and Mary Anne found that the Maytag, Magic	23
12	Chef, Amana, and Gibson were determined to be best buys.	34
13	Best buys for full-size microwave ovens were the Sharp	11
14	Carousel, Panasonic, and GoldStar Multiwave. Good midsize	23
15	models were the Frigidaire, Panasonic, and Sears Kenmore.	34

1 | 2 | 3 | 4 | 5 | 6 | 7 | 8 | 9 | 10 | 11 | 12

Goal: At least 39wpm/5'/5e

C. 5-MINUTE TIMED WRITING

16	Have you completed your education when you graduate	11
17	from high school or finish your college work? Most people	22
18	look forward to reaching milestones, such as graduation or	34
19	completing a course. Have they learned everything they will	46
20	need to know to be successful in the real world? The answer	58
21	is not so simple.	62
22	Learning continues to occur long after you leave the	72
23	classroom. No matter what job or career you pursue, you	84
24	will learn something new every day. When you investigate	95
25	new ideas, ask questions, or find a different way to do a	107
26	job, you are continuing to learn. In the process, you gain	118
27	additional experience, develop new skills, and become a	130
28	better worker.	133
29	Getting along with your peers, for example, is not	143
30	something that you learn from studying books. You learn to	155
31	be a team player when you listen to your coworkers and	166
32	share your ideas with them. Do not hesitate to acquire new	178
33	skills or to initiate new ideas. Be zealous in your efforts	190
34	to continue your education.	195

1 | 2 | 3 | 4 | 5 | 6 | 7 | 8 | 9 | 10 | 11 | 12

Formatting

REFER TO
Reference Manual

R-12B:
Application Letter

D. LETTERS OF APPLICATION

A letter of application is a personal-business letter sent along with a resume to a prospective employer. Together, the letter and the resume serve to introduce a person to the organization.

The letter of application should be no longer than one page and should include (1) the job you are applying for and how you learned of the job, (2) the highlights of your enclosed resume, and (3) a request for an interview.

Document Processing

Correspondence
52-35
Personal-Business Letter in Modified-Block Style

March 8, 20-- | Ms. Violet Logan | Human Resource Director | proctor computer systems | 2489 Highland Ave. | Park City, UT 84060 | Dear Ms. Logan:

¶ Please consider me an applicant for the position of Data System Operator that was advertised in the February 25th edition of the Park City Press.

¶ In May I will graduate with an A.A. degree in office systems from Northern Utah College. My enclosed resume shows that I have completed courses in excel, Publisher, and Word. I also have considerable experience in working with web page

(continued on next page)

design. The skills I gained in using these software packages will be ~~helpful~~ extremely helpful to your ~~B~~ranch ~~O~~ffice in Provo.

¶ The position with your company is very ap~p~ealing to me. I would like an opportunity to interview with Proctor Computer Systems and can be reached at either 801-555-83~~3~~2 (cell) or 801-555-3872 (home).

¶ I look forward to hearing from you ~~soon~~.

Sincerely, | Marlene ~D.~ Hooper | 387 Amber Ave. | Lehi, UT 84043 | Enclosure

Correspondence
52-36
Personal-Business Letter in Block Style

May 17, 20-- | Mr. Daniel R. Gantz | Human Resources Director | Carrington Communications | 3024 Maple Lane | Commerce, TX 75428-2314 | Dear Mr. Gantz: ¶ Please consider me as an applicant for a position with Carrington Communications. As you can see on the enclosed resume, my strength is in communication arts. I have completed a number of courses in speech, English, and communication technology. My part-time employment with your company for the past three years convinced me that Carrington Communications is the place where I would like to work. ¶ I would like to arrange an interview with you for any possible openings this summer or fall. I can be reached at 903-555-7823. Feel free to leave a message on my answering machine if I am not home when you call. I look forward to the possibility of working for Carrington Communications. Sincerely, | Carmen S. Diamond | 489 Crescent Avenue | Greenville, TX 75401 | Enclosure

Correspondence
52-37
Personal-Business Letter in Modified-Block Style

Open the file for Correspondence 52-36, and make the following changes:

1. Use a modified-block style.
2. Change Mr. Gantz's title to `Director, Personnel Services.`
3. Delete the first sentence in the letter, and insert the following replacement: `I would like to apply for the Communications Specialist position advertised in the` `Commerce Journal on May 15.`
4. Add the following words at the end of the third sentence in the first paragraph: `that uniquely qualify me for an entry-level position.`
5. Change the telephone number to `903-555-3398.`

Interview Communications

Goals

- Demonstrate improved speed and accuracy while typing by touch.
- Demonstrate acceptable proofreading skills by editing lines of copy.
- Correctly format an academic report and a ruled table.

A. WARMUP

alphabet
substitution: *f* and *g*
easy

```
1  If fog makes Max shiver, quickly zip down and buy a jacket.
2  fig fang flag frog fang gift golf gulf goof gruff fogs flag
3  His civic goal for the city is for them to endow the chair.
```

Skillbuilding

B. MAP+: NUMBERS

Follow the GDP software directions for this exercise to improve keystroking accuracy.

PRETEST » PRACTICE » POSTTEST

PRETEST
Take a 1-minute timed writing.

C. PRETEST: Common Letter Combinations

```
4       They formed an action committee to force a motion for    11
5  a ruling on your contract case. This enabled them to comply   23
6  within the lawful time period and convey a common message.    35
        1 | 2 | 3 | 4 | 5 | 6 | 7 | 8 | 9 | 10 | 11 | 12
```

PRACTICE
Speed Emphasis:
   If you made 2 or fewer errors on the Pretest, type each *individual* line 2 times.
Accuracy Emphasis:
   If you made 3 or more errors, type each *group* of lines (as though it were a paragraph) 2 times.

D. PRACTICE: Word Beginnings

```
7  for forget formal format forces forums forked forest formed
8  per perils period perish permit person peruse perked pertly
9  com combat comedy coming commit common compel comply comets
```

E. PRACTICE: Word Endings

```
10  ing acting aiding boring buying ruling saving hiding dating
11  ble bubble dabble double enable feeble fumble tumble usable
12  ion action vision lesion nation bunion lotion motion legion
```

F. POSTTEST: Common Letter Combinations

Language Arts

G. PROOFREADING

Edit these sentences to correct any errors.

13 The Smith were please to learn from their insurance
14 agent that the covrage ona $50,000 life insurance policy
15 policy would be increased by $ 20,000 at no extra cost.

16 The continued to pay the same premum, not knowing that the
17 cash value of there original policy was being tappped each
18 month to pay an addition premium for hte new coverage.

Document Processing

**Report
53-28**
Academic Report

SUCCESSFUL INTERVIEWING TECHNIQUES

Raymond T. Argue

March 28, 20--

One of the chalenges that faces all prospective employees is thier performance during an interview. To be successful during an interview, there are *certain* steps you should take to ensure that you get the job.

DRESSING PROFESSIONALLY

You need to dress professionally for ~~your~~ *an* interview. How you dress says a lot about you, especially during a job interview. If you don't take care and dress professionaly, you may be telling the interviewer that this is the kind of attitude you'll display while on the job.[1]

DURING THE INTERVIEW

It's always a good idea to arrive a few minutes early for the interview. If you are late for an interview, you may be conveying to ~~the~~ *an* interviewer that you will bring this behavior with you to the job. When you are greeted by the interviewer, give a *same* *firm* handshake. When you enter the interview Room, don't sit down until the interviewer suggests that you do so. Be consious of your posture when you sit. The manner in which you maintain good posture can relay an appearance of confidence and attentiveness. Use grammar correct and speak in complete sentences. Project your voice so that the interviewer can hear your responses. Answer the questions you are *clearly* asked. Be brief and concise, and be careful not to ramble.

(continued on next page)

ENDING THE INTERVIEW

Near the end of the interview, the interviewer will likely ask you if you have any questions. Be prepared to ask questions, because your questions may relate to tell the interviewer that you are interested in working for this company. Do your research beforehand so that you are prepared to ask questions particular to the job for which you are applying and about the company itself.

End the interview on a positive note. Reaffirm your interest in working for the company and briefly restate how your visit to the company has enhanced your desire to be hired for the position for which you have applied. And lastly, don't forget to express a thank-you to all the people who interviewed you.[2]

Though many of the above suggestions are critical to successful interviewing, research shows that some interviewees continue to exhibit inappropriate behavior during the interview. See Table 1 below.

Table 1. INTERVIEW BEHAVIORS	
As observed by 100 interviewers	
Observed Behavior	**Percentage**
Poorly dressed for the interview	125
Incorrect grammar	12
Responses inaudible	9
Not prepared with questions	7

---

[1] James Sabin, "Effective Interviewing Techniques," *Interviewing Today,* August 9, 2010, p. 18.

[2] Roshena Karis, "Online Interviewing Techniques," *Your Interview,* February 22, 2010, <http://www.yourinterview.net/april>, accessed on April 8, 2010.

Table
53-17
Ruled Table

INTERVIEW SCHEDULE
Todd Giordelli
August 18, 20--

Scheduled Time	Location	Interviewer
7:30 a.m. to 9:00 a.m.	Cafeteria	Mr. Alan Spitzer, Communications Director
9:00 a.m. to 10:00 a.m.	Room B-212	Ms. Karen Eisner, Human Resources Director
10:00 a.m. to 11:30 a.m.	Room D-134	Ms. Maureen Schiller, Chief Marketing Officer
11:30 a.m. to 1:00 p.m.	Dining Room	Members of the Search Committee
1:00 p.m. to 1:30 p.m.	Building R	Tour of Building, David Carpenter
1:30 p.m. to 2:00 p.m.	Room C-220	Mr. Vince Moore, Executive Vice President
2:00 p.m. to 2:30 p.m.	Room C-226	Ms. Gayle Hartman, Senior Vice President
2:30 p.m. to 3:00 p.m.	Room C-230	Mr. Richard DeClark, CEO

Follow-Up Letters

Goals

- Type at least 39wpm/5′/5e.
- Correctly format a follow-up letter.

A. WARMUP

alphabet	1	Dave quickly spotted the four women dozing in the jury box.
frequent digraphs	2	ed edge wed Eddy bed eyed cede lied fed edited led axed red
easy	3	Disney World is a land of enchantment to the civic visitor.

Skillbuilding

B. PROGRESSIVE PRACTICE: NUMBERS

Follow the GDP software directions for this exercise to improve keystroking speed.

C. TECHNIQUE PRACTICE: TAB KEY

Press TAB 1 time between words. Type each line 2 times.

```
4  Kit→ Ida→ Joy→ ads→ Joe→ Jan→ Lev→ ago→ Ima→ are→ ace
5  Mom→ aft→ Job→ age→ Ham→ zip→ Obi→ Ott→ awl→ art→ Hsu
6  zoo→ Jon→ apt→ Pat→ ado→ zap→ Orr→ Ike→ Ned→ asp→ zag
7  ate→ Lou→ Mia→ Mac→ Jim→ zed→ add→ Pia→ Moe→ Lot→ Jay
```

Strategies for Career Success

Reducing Bias in Business Communication

Everything we do in business communication attempts to build goodwill. Bias-free language and visuals help maintain the goodwill we work so hard to create.

Bias-free language does not discriminate against people on the basis of gender, physical condition, race, age, or any other characteristic. Do not emphasize gender-specific words in your business vocabulary. Instead, incorporate gender-neutral words (for example, use *chair* instead of *chairman*) into your business communication.

Organizations that treat people fairly also should use language that treats people fairly. The law is increasingly intolerant of biased documents and hostile work environments. Practice nondiscriminatory behavior by focusing on individual merits, accomplishments, skills, and what you might share in common rather than illustrating differences. Treating every group with respect and understanding is essential to gaining loyalty and future business while cultivating harmonious relationships.

Your Turn: Review a document that you have recently written. Is the document bias-free?

Goal: At least 39wpm/5'/5e

D. 5-MINUTE TIMED WRITING

8	In the past, typing was a skill that was used only by	11
9	those who were secretaries, students, and office workers.	23
10	High school students who were in school and who had plans	34
11	for going on took a typing class so that they could type	46
12	their work with ease and skill. Often, students who wanted	57
13	to be hired to work in an office would make plans to take	69
14	advanced courses in typing.	75
15	As prices drop and as we have more and more advances	85
16	in technology of all types, people are recognizing that	97
17	they need typing skills. From the top executive to the	108
18	customer service agents, everyone needs to be able to use a	120
19	computer keyboard. Workers in almost any kind of business	131
20	use their keyboarding skills to perform their daily tasks.	143
21	Employers are looking for skilled workers who type	154
22	with consistent speed and accuracy. People who are able to	166
23	type documents accurately and enter data quickly are needed	178
24	for many types of careers. Keyboarding skills are important	190
25	for every manner of job.	195

1 | 2 | 3 | 4 | 5 | 6 | 7 | 8 | 9 | 10 | 11 | 12

Formatting

E. FOLLOW-UP LETTERS

As soon as possible after your interview (preferably the next day), you should send a follow-up letter to the person who conducted your interview. In the letter you should:

- Use a positive tone.
- Thank the person who conducted the interview.
- Mention some specific information you learned during the interview.
- Highlight your particular strengths.
- Restate your interest in working for that organization, and mention that you look forward to a favorable decision.

Document Processing

Correspondence 54-38
Personal-Business Letter in Block Style

May 25, 20-- / Mr. Daniel R. Gantz / Human Resources Director / Carrington Communications / 3024 Maple Lane / Commerce, TX 75428-2314 / Dear Mr. Gantz:

¶ It was a pleasure meeting with you yesterday and learning of the wonderful career opportunities at Carrington Communications. I enjoyed meeting everyone

(continued on next page)

in the Technology Division. Thank you for taking the time to share with me a brief history of the company and its move to the Commerce area.

¶ I believe my experience and job skills match very well with those you are seeking for a technology consultant, and this position is exactly what I had in mind when applying to Carrington Communications.

¶ I would appreciate hearing from you when you have made your hiring decision for this position. I am very much interested in joining the professional ranks at Carrington.

Sincerely yours, / Carmen S. Diamond / 489 Crescent Avenue / Greenville, TX 75401

Correspondence 54-39
Personal-Business Letter in Modified-Block Style

May 8, 20-- | Ms. Violet Logan | Human Resources director | Proctor Computer Systems | 2498 Highland Avenue | Park City, UT 84060 | Dear Ms. Logan:

¶ Thank you for the opportunity of interviewing yesterday with Proctor Computer Systems. Please extend my apreciation [p] to those in your Division [all of] who participated in the interview process.

¶ The interview gave me a good feeling about your [the] company. The positive information you shared with me about proctor convinced me that your Company is indeed where I'd like to work. I was very impressed with the pro gress you have made in the area of system enhancements and the positive outlook for future expansion in to the Park City market area.

¶ You may recall that I have had experience with the [all of] equipment you use at proctor. My strengths in computer software applications would blend well with your company profile.

¶ I look forward to hear [ing] from you soon regarding your immediate hiring decision.

Sincerely, | Marlene D. Hoper [o] | 387 Amber Avenue | Logon [Lehi], UT 84043

Correspondence 54-40
Personal-Business Letter in Modified-Block Style

Open the file for Correspondence 54-39 and make the following changes:

- Change the date of the letter to June 25, 20--
- Send the letter to Mr. Donald F. Hallada | Vice President of Human Resources | Technology Solutions, Inc. | Sulphur Springs, TX 75483

- Replace the first sentence with the following: Thank you for the opportunity to interview with Technology Solutions on June 24.
- Replace "Proctor" with Technology Solutions in the first, second, and third paragraphs.

Integrated Employment Project

Goals

- Demonstrate improved speed and accuracy while typing by touch.
- Demonstrate acceptable language arts skills in composing paragraphs.
- Correctly format an application letter, a resume, and a follow-up letter.
- Successfully complete a Progress and Proofreading Check with zero errors on the first scored attempt.

A. WARMUP

alphabet
number/symbol
easy

```
1 A campus TV quiz just asks why gold is buried at Fort Knox.
2 gilp@comcast.net (11%) Ng & Ma 4/5 No! $13.86 *Est. #20-972
3 Blair's penchant for a duck dish may make him go to a lake.
```

Skillbuilding

B. 12-SECOND SPEED SPRINTS

Take three 12-second timed writings on each line.

```
4 I am at my best when I am on a boat on an icy lake at home.
5 I will lend a hand to anyone if he or she signals for help.
6 We may take a number of maps to aid me when we visit there.
7 If they work in town, they may make a visit to the old gym.
   ' ' ' '5' ' ' '10' ' ' '15' ' ' '20' ' ' '25' ' ' '30' ' ' '35' ' ' '40' ' ' '45' ' ' '50' ' ' '55' ' ' '60
```

C. PACED PRACTICE

Follow the GDP software directions for this exercise to improve keystroking speed and accuracy.

Language Arts

D. COMPOSING PARAGRAPHS

Choose one of the phrases at the right; then compose a paragraph of three to four sentences on that topic.

8 My computer was working fine until it . . .
9 The Internet has helped me complete my class assignments by . . . .
10 The one thing I like best about e-mail is . . . .
11 I have several skills, but my best skill is . . . .

Document Processing

In the previous unit you learned how to prepare a resume, an application letter, and a follow-up letter—all of which are frequently used by job applicants. You will now use these skills in preparing the documents necessary to apply for the job described in the newspaper ad illustrated below.

DESKTOP PUBLISHER

InfoJobs' mission is to shape the future of desktop publishing. We have an immediate opening to work in a team environment with desktop publishers and technical editors.

This is an entry-level position within the Marketing Department in our Denver office. Applicant must have experience in using Word, Photoshop, and PageMaker. Good verbal and written communication skills are required. Should possess the ability to acquire new knowledge through formal and self-training. Associates degree or equivalent experience required.

InfoJobs offers an excellent medical and dental program for all employees.

If interested, send a letter of application and resume to:

Mr. Harrison Campbell
HRM Department
InfoJobs, Inc.
4590 Emerson Avenue
Denver, CO 80014

InfoJobs is an Equal Opportunity Employer.

Report
55-29
Resume

Prepare a resume for yourself as though you are applying for the job described in the ad above. Use actual data in the resume. Assume that you have just graduated from a postsecondary program. Include school-related activities, courses you have completed, and any part-time or full-time work experience you may have acquired. Make the resume as realistic as possible, and provide as much information as you can about your background.

Correspondence
55-41
Personal-Business Letter in Block Style

Prepare an application letter to apply for the position described in the ad. Date your letter April 15. Emphasize the skills you have acquired during your years in school and while working in any part-time or full-time positions. Use Correspondence 52-35 or 52-36 as guides for your letter.

Correspondence
55-42
Personal-Business Letter in Modified-Block Style

Assume that your interview was held on April 30 and that you would very much like to work for InfoJobs. It is now the day after your interview. Prepare a follow-up letter expressing your positive thoughts about working for InfoJobs. Use Correspondence 54-38 or 54-39 as guides for your letter.

JEFF METCALF

10454 Melody Drive, Denver, Co 80234
Phone: 303-555-2241; e-mail: jeffmet@allmail.net

OBJECTIVE To obtain a position as a desktop publisher in the Denver area.

EDUCATION Rocky Mountain Technical College, Colorado Springs, CO
A.A. Degree in Computer Systems
Graduated: December 2009

South City High School, Denver, Colorado
Graduated: May 2007

EXPERIENCE *Desk Clerk, Alpine Blue Resort*
Vail, Colorado
May 2006 to April 2007
Checked guests in and out, provided all information about rates and the kinds of services in the resort, assigned guests to rooms, and made guest reservations within computer reservation system.

Data records technician, Denver health center
Denver, Colorado
April 2007 to December 2009
Responsible for maintaining and updating a computerized system record for all hospital reports on patients. Updated medical histories and charts, and cross-indexed information for access in computer files.

ACTIVITIES Activities pursued while attending school:
- Colorado Data Technicians Association President, 2007 to 2008
- National Health care Employees Association, 2009 to present
- Dean's honor list, 2007 to 2009
- National Society, 2005 to 2007
- Class president, South High School, 2006 to 2007

REFERENCES Available upon request.

Italicize (but do not underline) the name of the newspaper.

June 19, 20-- | Mr. Wayne Durham | McDaniel Computer Communications | 348 Ellsworth Avenue | Denver, CO 80280 | Dear Mr. Durham:

¶ I am responding to your ad in the *Denver Post* for the position of desktop publisher.

¶ My degree in computer systems and my experience as a data records technician provide me with the computer background you are seeking. As you indicated in your ad, I would welcome the opportunity to complete the two-week formal training course you provide for this position.

¶ I gained valuable personal relations skills as an employee for Blue Alpine Resort, and my technical skills are well documented from 2007 to 2009 in my responsibilities as a data records technician for the Denver Health Center.

¶ I am very interested in working for Computer Enterprises and look forward to hearing from you regarding this position. If you would like to speak to me personally, you can reach me at 303-555-2214 or e-mail me at jeffmet@ allmail.net.

Sincerely, | Jeffrey Metcalf | 10454 Melody Drive | Denver, CO 80234

Progress and Proofreading Check

Documents designated as Proofreading Checks serve as a check of your proofreading skill. Your goal is to have zero typographical errors when the GDP software first scores the document.

~~May~~ June 30, 20-- | Mr. Wayne Durham | Mcdaniel Computer Communications | 348 Ellsworth Avenue | Denver, CO 80280 | Dear ~~Wayne~~ Mr. Durham:

¶ Thank you for taking the time to interview me about the desk top publishing position with McDaniel Computer communications. The information you shared with me has enhanced my interest in working for McDaniel.

¶ I was impressed with the responsibility*ies* you high lighted regarding this position, and your 2-week formal training course focuses precisely on the responsibilities I was seeking in a desktop publishing position.

¶ I hope to hear from you by *the end of* next week for a *positive* decision on my employment with McDaniel.

Sincerely, | Jeffrey Metcalf | 10454 Melody Dr. | Denver, CO 80243

Skillbuilding and In-Basket Review

In-Basket Review— Insurance

Goals

- Type at least 40wpm/5′/5e.
- Correctly format a business letter, a memo, and a boxed table.

A. WARMUP

alphabet	1	All questions asked by five watch experts amazed the judge.
concentration	2	antirevolutionaries disenfranchisements unconstitutionality
easy	3	All eight authentic antique autos may be lent to the firms.

Skillbuilding

B. SUSTAINED PRACTICE: PUNCTUATION

Take a 1-minute timed writing on the boxed paragraph to establish your base speed. Then take a 1-minute timed writing on the following paragraph. As soon as you equal or exceed your base speed on this paragraph, move to the next, more difficult paragraph.

4	The men in the warehouse were having a very difficult	11
5	time keeping track of that inventory. Things began to go	23
6	much more smoothly for them when they got the new computer.	34

7	Whenever something was shipped out, a computer entry	11
8	was made to show the changes. They always knew exactly what	22
9	merchandise was in stock; they also knew what to order.	34

10	Management was pleased with that improvement. "We	11
11	should have made the change years ago," said the supervisor	22
12	to the plant manager, who was in full agreement with him.	34

13	This is just one example (among many) of how the work	11
14	areas can be improved.* Workers' suggestions are listened	23
15	to by alert, expert managers. Their jobs are better, too!	33

| 1 | 2 | 3 | 4 | 5 | 6 | 7 | 8 | 9 | 10 | 11 | 12 |

Goal: At least 40wpm/5'/5e

C. 5-MINUTE TIMED WRITING

16	When you begin to think about a career, you should	10
17	assess your personal abilities and interests. Do you have	22
18	natural aptitudes in a certain area? Do you have special	33
19	interests or hobbies that you would like to develop into a	45
20	career? Do you enjoy working with other people, or do you	56
21	like to work on your own? Would you like to work in a large	68
22	office, or do you prefer to work outdoors? These questions	80
23	are important to consider when you think about your career.	92
24	Your quest to find the perfect career will be more	103
25	successful if you try to maximize the opportunities that	114
26	are available. For example, you might consider working with	126
27	an organization that offers you career counseling. A career	138
28	counselor is trained to help you determine your aptitudes	150
29	and interests.	153
30	You may contact some people who work in a career which	164
31	interests you and ask to shadow them on their jobs and ask	176
32	them questions. You might find a service online to help you	188
33	find an interesting career that can meet all of your goals.	200

1 | 2 | 3 | 4 | 5 | 6 | 7 | 8 | 9 | 10 | 11 | 12

Document Processing

Situation: Today is November 17. You are employed in the office of Advantage Insurance of Cedar Rapids, Iowa. Advantage handles auto, home, and life insurance coverage in Iowa and Minnesota. You work for Samuel R. Haney, vice president. Prepare the following letter for Mr. Haney.

Correspondence 56-45
Business Letter in Block Style

November 17, 20-- / Ms. Maribel Valez / District Manager / 568 Curtiss Avenue / Ames, IA 50010-3568 / Dear Ms. Valez:

¶ Several of our service representatives have indicated on our Web site chat room that new clients are becoming increasingly interested in the criteria to consider when evaluating their insurance carriers. Advantage has prided itself in years past on its reputable service record with its policyholders, and the service representatives have undoubtedly shared this record with prospective customers. However, we want to be certain that other characteristics about Advantage are also shared with these potential policyholders.

(continued on next page)

¶ *Please be sure that your representatives share the following service characteristics with potential customers:*

- *Our claims are handled quickly and with a minimum of "red tape."*
- *Our ratio of number of policies to number of complaints is the highest in the industry.*
- *No disciplinary actions have been taken against Advantage in the past 50 years.*

¶ *Please share this information with your service representatives, and inform them that updated information on our services is provided on our home page for their use or for their policyholders' use.*

Sincerely, / Samuel R. Haney / Vice President / urs

Correspondence 56-46 Memo

Mr. Haney has dictated the following memo for you to transcribe. As you can see, there are several rough-draft changes that you will have to make to the memo.

MEMO TO: Deanna Crews, training director

FROM: Samuel R. Haney, ~~Vice~~ President

DATE: November 18, 20--

SUBJECT: Training Seminar

¶ Our *new* agent training seminar will be held on Jan. 10, and we again plan to conduct 2 sessions each for auto and life insurance policies. You will be in charge of the ~~life~~ *auto* insurance seminars and Thomas Meeks will conduct the ~~life~~ insurance seminars.

¶ I expect that this year's auto insurance seminars will present our 6 basic coverage areas using the latest software presentation for the following topics:

alphabetize this list

- Collision
- Comprehensive
- Uninsured motorist
- Medical payments or personal injury protection
- Property damage liability
- Bodily injury liability

¶ We are the market leaders in *bodily* injury liability and property damage ~~liability~~ coverages. Therefore, you should plan to spend at least one-half of your presentation discussing our strengths in these coverages. In your presentation you *might like to* ~~should~~ include the fact that our coverages in these areas have more than surpassed those of our competitors for the past 5 years.

(continued on next page)

¶ Table 1 is attached to help you explain the *variety of* discounts offered for Iowa and Minnesota policyholders. | urs | Attachment

Table
56-18
Boxed Table

REFER TO
Reference Manual

R-13B: 2-line column heading
R-13C: Table number title

Prepare Table 56-18 as an attachment for the memo to Deanna Crews.

Table 1. DISCOUNT PROGRAMS (For Iowa and Minnesota)	
Discounts Available	**Discount Amount (%)**
Air bag	Up to 6.5
Antitheft device	Up to 10
Driver training course	Up to 2.5
Good driver	Up to 2
Good student	Up to 15
Multipolicy	Up to 5
Multivehicle	Up to 15
Professional driver's program	Up to 14

Keyboarding Connection

Avoiding E-Mail Flame Wars

Don't fan the flames! A flame is an offensive e-mail that expresses anger, criticism, or insults. If flames are transmitted to an e-mail list, they can produce a long list of flames and counterflames known as flame wars. Some e-mail lists have rules against this and will ban people who participate in or cause flame wars.

You may be tempted to join in, but this is a waste of everyone's time. Often the initial offense was merely a poorly worded e-mail that a reader interpreted as an insult. There are those who intentionally send inflammatory e-mail called flame bait. Resist the urge to send a cutting response, and consider whether the writer's intent was to provoke you.

If your reader misjudges something you wrote and becomes offended, just apologize. A timely apology can thwart a potential fire. Avoid miscommunication by watching how you word your e-mail.

Your Turn: Have you ever been insulted by an e-mail? What was your response?

In-Basket Review—Hospitality

57

Goals

- Demonstrate improved speed and accuracy while typing by touch.
- Demonstrate acceptable language arts skills in number expression and hyphenation.
- Correctly format an open table, a business letter, and a business report.

A. WARMUP

alphabet   1   Fred specialized in the job of making very quaint wax toys.

one hand   2   assets linkup bat kin tested phonily wave imply refer puppy

easy   3   He has on a tux and she has on a tan gown for their social.

Skillbuilding

B. MAP+: ALPHABET

Follow the GDP software directions for this exercise to improve keystroking accuracy.

C. PROGRESSIVE PRACTICE: ALPHABET

Follow the GDP software directions for this exercise to improve keystroking speed.

Language Arts

Study the rules at the right.

RULE
 # word

D. NUMBER EXPRESSION AND HYPHENATION

Spell out

- **A number used as the first word of a sentence.**

    Seventy-five people attended the conference in San Diego.
- **The shorter of two adjacent numbers.**

    We have ordered 3 two-pound cakes and one 5-pound cake for the reception.
- **The words million and billion in round numbers (do not use decimals with round numbers).**

    Not: A $5.00 ticket can win $28,000,000 in this month's lottery.

    But: A $5 ticket can win $28 million in this month's lottery.
- **Fractions.**

    Almost one-half of the audience responded to the question.

RULE
- number

Hyphenate compound numbers between twenty-one and ninety-nine and fractions that are expressed as words.

Twenty-nine recommendations were approved by at least three-fourths of the members.

Edit each sentence to correct any errors.

4 Seven investors were interested in buying 2 15-unit condos.

5 The purchase price for the buildings will be $3,000,000.00
6 each, which is 1/2 the total.

7 The computers were mailed in 5 40-pound boxes for 2/3 of the
8 price paid yesterday.

9 Our food chain sold hamburgers for $3.00 each last year.

10 I can sell nearly one-half of all the tickets at the gate on
11 November 13.

12 59 parking spaces are located within 1/2 mile of the city
13 center.

14 We must place our mailing pieces in 8 twenty-pound bags for
15 the mail clerk.

16 I don't believe more than 1/5 of the drivers have insurance.

Document Processing

Situation: Today is March 25, and you are employed in the office of Pacific Resorts in Oceanside, California. Your employer, the general manager, is Ms. Glenda Flowers. Ms. Flowers is attending a meeting in San Diego and has left the following documents for you to complete.

Table
57-19
Open Table

- number

PACIFIC RESORTS PROPERTIES
Beach Rental Units

Property	Rooms	Rental Rate In Season	Rental Rate Off Season
Buena Vista Landings	5	$4,750	$3,325
Cradle by the Sea	6	5,750	4,025
El Camino Lodge	4	3,500	2,450
Mission Bay Hideaway	5	4,500	3,150
Pacific House	6	5,800	4,050
Poinsettia Palace	4	3,375	2,350
Twenty-Two Pines Estates	5	4,250	2,975

March 25, 20-- / Mr. Shane O'Keefe / 723 Harrington Avenue / Madison, TN 37115 / Dear Mr. O'Keefe:

¶ We were pleased to hear of your interest in renting one of our prime beach units in Oceanside, California. I have enclosed a listing of all our current properties in the Oceanside area. We have 12 two-bedroom rentals, 16 three-bedroom rentals, and 9 four-bedroom rentals. Five of our three-bedroom units have already been rented for this season; one-half of the other 32 units are still available.

¶ Our Cradle by the Sea and Mission Bay Hideaway units have ocean views and garage facilities. The El Camino Lodge and Twenty-Two Pines Estates have a gorgeous mountain view and tennis courts. The Buena Vista Landings, Pacific House, and Poinsettia Palace have a private golf course. Our most popular units are El Camino Lodge and Poinsettia Palace, and they both rent for under $3,000.

¶ If you plan to rent one of our units, please be sure to notify us by e-mail or by calling our toll-free number at 1-800-555-3390.

Sincerely, / Glenda Flowers / General Manager / urs / Enclosure / c: Kimberly England, David Pollard

 # word
 # word
 # word
 # word
- number
 # word

Ms. Flowers has recently purchased a fishing resort on Lake Henshaw, California, and plans to open it on April 15. Type the following report and send it to the *Oceanside Press* so that it will appear in this Sunday's special *Travel and Tourism* section. Use a standard business format to prepare the report.

KAMP HENSHAW RESORT SCHEDULED TO OPEN | Pacific Resorts Properties | Oceanside, California

¶ Pacific Resorts is celebrating the grand opening of its newest resort property, Kamp Henshaw, located on the shores of Lake Henshaw in Santa Ysabel, California.

GENERAL INFORMATION

¶ The following information will give you an overview of our policies and accommodations:

¶ **Reservations.** The reservation desk will open on April 15 to reserve your cabin at our beautiful resort. You can reach reservations via the Internet by logging on to our Web site at http://www.henshawresort.com.

¶ **Accommodations.** Whether you're looking for deluxe accommodations or rustic surroundings, Kamp Henshaw has it all. You have a choice of rustic cabins nestled in the woods or large chalets overlooking Lake Henshaw. If you enjoy an evening of relaxation, each cabin includes a gazebo, out near the water's edge, that is screened in for a perfect evening of comfort.

(continued on next page)

¶ **Amenities.** Your lodging choice includes full kitchens for those who want to do their own cooking, or you can order a full meal through our catering service. Ten of our larger units have a game room with a large-screen television, DVD player, and computer workstation with Internet connection. We also have a library of DVD movies that you can rent. Outside the sliding glass door is a covered deck, equipped with a barbecue grill and hot tub.

LAKE HENSHAW

¶ Lake Henshaw is located on the southern slope of Palomar Mountain, 60 miles northeast of San Diego, California. Palomar Observatory is close by, and many tourists to the area take in a day to visit that location. Lake Henshaw encompasses approximately 1,100 acres of water and five miles of shoreline. It is widely known for its great crappie fishing and also has populations of catfish, bass, bluegill, and trout. The month of March is the wettest at Lake Henshaw, and June is the driest. Hiking is popular in the area, especially along the Gomez Trail. Twenty-five miles of hiking trails are open to the general public. Summertime temperatures are typically in the 80s, and nighttime temperatures drop down into the 60s. In the winter, temperatures typically run in the mid-50s during the day and in the 30s overnight.

PRICING INFORMATION

¶ We are offering a special introductory rate of $275 through December 1. This rate includes the following:

- Two-night stay for a family of four.
- Four admission tickets to the Palomar Observatory.
- Free rental of hiking gear for one 24-hour period.

¶ A full refund will be made on all hiking gear rented if there is inclement weather during the scheduled hike. If only a partial day of hiking is completed, one-half of the charges will be refunded.

In-Basket Review—Retail

Goals

- Type at least 40wpm/5′/5e.
- Correctly format an e-mail message, a memo, and a ruled table.

A. WARMUP

alphabet

substitution: *k* and *l*

easy

1　Maizie quickly paid Joan for the five new taxis she bought.
2　kill Karl luck kilo lake kale lick kilt leak kelp link like
3　The town may suspend its right to make an audit of the bid.

Skillbuilding

B. PACED PRACTICE

Follow the GDP software directions for this exercise to improve keystroking speed and accuracy.

Take two 5-minute timed writings. Review your speed and errors.

Goal: At least 40wpm/5′/5e

C. 5-MINUTE TIMED WRITING

4　　　Most workers will learn about their success on the job	11
5　at least once a year. The person in charge will be the one	23
6　to conduct these reviews. Even though the job review is	34
7　quite important, either party might not look forward to	45
8　such a meeting.	49
9　　　Frequently, an employee and a boss can view these	59
10　meetings as a time to discuss everything that the person	70
11　has done wrong in the last year. Such a negative approach	82
12　can add a lot of stress and tension between the employee	93
13　and management. In the long run, work performance suffers.	105
14　　　A good manager must learn a new way to conduct more	116
15　positive job reviews. Such a meeting might start by sizing	127
16　up what the employee has done to help improve things in the	139
17　past year. Positive comments may include coming to work on	151
18　time, working well with others, and being willing to pitch	163
19　in whenever needed.	167
20　　　Next, the areas for improvement are discussed. Then,	178
21　the employee should be given the chance to ask questions,	190
22　write a response to the appraisal, and get feedback.	200

　　1　|　2　|　3　|　4　|　5　|　6　|　7　|　8　|　9　|　10　|　11　|　12

Document Processing

Situation: Today is February 7. You are employed as an administrative assistant for Best Sports, a retailer for sports equipment and clothing in Albuquerque, New Mexico. Your employer is Mr. Raymond E. Abernathy, marketing director for Best Sports. Today, you are to prepare an e-mail message, a memo, and a table.

Correspondence 58-48
E-Mail Message

Hi, Brian:

¶ I talked to Lauren Emory earlier this morning, and she has agreed to host the district meeting in El Paso on April 9 and 10.

¶ In preparation for that meeting, would you please pull together the sales figures for last year and send them to Lauren so that she can include them in the sales presentation. For comparison purposes, here are figures for the year before last:

Quarter	District 1	District 2	District 3
First	$48,924	$72,230	$110,239
Second	45,220	76,137	115,330
Third	43,234	65,200	108,114
Fourth	47,899	73,249	113,233

Ray | Raymond E. Abernathy | E-mail: reabernathy@bestsports.net | Phone: 505-555-5690

Correspondence 58-49
Memo

MEMO TO: Lauren Emory | **FROM:** Raymond E. Abernathy, Marketing Director | **DATE:** February 7, 20-- | **SUBJECT:** District Meetings

¶ As you know, each year we rotate the location of our district meetings to one of our regional offices. This year our meeting will be held in El Paso. Would you please contact hotels in El Paso and select a suitable site for this year's meeting, which will be held on April 9 and 10.

¶ We decided at our last regional managers' meeting that this year's meeting would highlight our Internet sales campaign. Specifically, we want to focus on the following issues:

1. How can we improve our Web page design to attract a higher percentage of the market?
2. How can we improve our e-commerce procedures so that our order-processing routine is easier and faster for the average Web visitor?
3. What links can we add to our home page to encourage visitors to view a greater percentage of our product line?

¶ Please let me know when you have made arrangements for our meeting site. I look forward to meeting with all of you in April.

urs

Table 58-20
Ruled Table

MONTHLY BICYCLE SPECIALS
(BIKE)
Febuary 7, 20--

Model	Price	Special Features
Lemans	$590	17.5-inch frame; 27-speed drive train; adjustable seat
Serpentine	575	16-inch frame; light weight; 18-speed drivetrain
Triple Asd	450	17.5-inch frame; Carbon fork; linear-pull brakes
ATB Ultra	400	17-inch frame; Aluminum frame; 18-speed drive train

---

Strategies for Career Success

Formatting Your Resume

The format of your resume communicates important skills—neatness and the ability to organize. Make a good first impression by following these guidelines.

Watch the spacing on your resume. A crowded resume implies that you cannot summarize. Leave adequate white space between the section headings of your resume. Use different font sizes, boldface, and italics to separate and emphasize information, but avoid using too many different fonts or formatting your text too many different ways, as this can make your resume look busy or unprofessional. Font sizes should be between 10 and 14.

Print your resume on good-quality 8½″ × 11″ white or off-white bond paper (for example, 20-pound stock). Colored paper doesn't provide enough contrast when your resume is copied or faxed.

Proofread your resume for spelling errors and consistency of format. Ask a few friends to review it and provide feedback.

Your Turn: Print one copy of your resume on dark-colored paper and one copy on white paper. Photocopy each resume. Which provides the better contrast for readability?

In-Basket Review—Nonprofit

Goals

- Demonstrate improved speed and accuracy while typing by touch.
- Demonstrate acceptable language arts skills in spelling.
- Correctly format a business report and a boxed table.

A. WARMUP

alphabet | 1 | The four brawny guards just flocked up to quiz and vex him.

frequent digraphs | 2 | te tee ate byte tell tea termite ten Ute tent teed teen Ted

easy | 3 | The penalty for such an amendment may be too gory for them.

Skillbuilding

B. MAP+: SYMBOL

Follow the GDP software directions for this exercise to improve keystroking accuracy.

PPP

PRETEST » PRACTICE » POSTTEST

PRETEST
Take a 1-minute timed writing.

C. PRETEST: Close Reaches

```
4        Sally took the coins from the pocket of her blouse    10
5   and traded them for seventy different coins. Anyone could   22
6   see that Myrtle looked funny when extra coins were traded.  34
       1 | 2 | 3 | 4 | 5 | 6 | 7 | 8 | 9 | 10 | 11 | 12
```

PRACTICE
Speed Emphasis:
  If you made 2 or fewer errors on the Pretest, type each *individual* line 2 times.
Accuracy Emphasis:
  If you made 3 or more errors, type each *group* of lines (as though it were a paragraph) 2 times.

D. PRACTICE: Adjacent Keys

```
7   as asked asset based basis class least visas ease fast mass
8   we weary wedge weigh towel jewel fewer dwell wear weed week
9   rt birth dirty earth heart north alert worth dart port tort
```

E. PRACTICE: Consecutive Fingers

```
10  sw swamp swift swoop sweet swear swank swirl swap sway swim
11  gr grade grace angry agree group gross gripe grow gram grab
12  ol older olive solid extol spool fools stole bolt cold cool
```

F. POSTTEST: Close Reaches

POSTTEST
Repeat the Pretest timed writing and compare performance.

Language Arts

Type these frequently misspelled words, paying special attention to any spelling problems in each word.

G. SPELLING

13 development determine enclosed complete members recent site
14 permanent personal facility medical library however purpose
15 representative implementation electrical discussed eligible
16 organization performance minimum discuss expense areas next
17 professional arrangements separate changes reason field pay

Edit the sentences to correct any misspellings.

18 Members of the medicle and profesional group discussed it.

19 The development of the seperate cite will be completed.

20 A recent representive said the libary facility may be next.

21 A perpose of the electricle organization is to get changes.

22 However, the implimentation of changes will be permenant.

23 Arrangments for the enclosed eligable expenses are listed.

Document Processing

Situation: Today is November 15. You work for Quick Ride, a ride-share company located in Newton, Massachusetts. Your job responsibilities include preparing reports that summarize weekly commuter news, typing correspondence to advertise and promote Quick Ride's services, and communicating with area commuters who subscribe to Quick Ride's services. Today, you must (1) prepare a report that summarizes services offered by Quick Ride and (2) create a table that lists drivers scheduled for December.

Report 59-32
Business Report

QUICK RIDE

Newton's Premier Ride-Share

If you're tired of driving that one- to two-hour commute into Boston's busy metropolitan area, then let us take that burden off your shoulders. Quick Ride, the metro's premier ride-share company, is a very convenient, economical way to get to & from work. All you have to do is get on board!

Service AREAS

Quick Ride serves the cities of Newton, Needham, Welesley, Dedham, Dover, and Natick. Next month we will open routes to Boston, Wayland, Waltham, and Sudbury. In all, we have over 100 regular routes state wide, and service is expanding monthly. Easy access is guaranteed with all our routes. To view our entire service area, go to our Web Site, http://www.qr.com, and click the link to the Quick Ride regional service area map. The map gives all our routes, highlights specific pick up points, and

(continued on next page)

identifies our regional facilities service. The site also allows you to link directly with our reservations office to make or change a reservation or confirm your ride-share. Visit our site today and become a ride-share enthusiast.

COSTS OF COMMUTING

A recent article showed that commuting just 15 miles each way can cost a minimum of $1,200 per year; sharing the ride with someone else can cut your commuting expenses in half.[1] In addition to the cost of gas, you must also figure in other costs of transportation, such as maintenance on your vehicle, insurance premiums, depreciation, and finance charges.[2] You should also consider how you are helping the traffic congestion and air pollution problems by ride-sharing. And don't forget about being involved in an accident. Finally, you can reduce stress by ride-sharing because you can choose to leave the driving to someone else.

RESERVATIONS AND BENEFITS

If you want to make arrangements to reserve a seat on a Quick ride route, just call one of our professional service representatives at 1-800-555-Trip. Our representatives in the field have information on routes, schedules, ride availability, and other benefits. For example, we have an e-Ride available for you if there is an emergency that requires you to immediately get home. Here are some special benefits with Quick Ride:

- A free commute for every 500 commuting miles.
- Separate insurance and medical coverage.
- Flexible payment policies.
- 4 free taxi rides home per year in the event of illness or personal emergency.

¶ We believe you will find Quick Ride a convenient, reasonably priced alternative for your commute to Boston.

---

[1] Angela Snyder, "Environment Clean Up With Ride-Share," *Environmental Planning,* December 21, 2009, p. 18.

[2] Mel Ragsdale, *Cleaning Up America,* Bay Area publishing, Boston, 2010, p. 142.

Table
59-21
Boxed Table

QUICK RIDE DRIVERS
For December

From	To	Name	Telephone
Newton	Boston	M. Rainwater	617-555-8924
Newton	Cambridge	A. Castillo	508-555-8832
Dedham	Boston	M. Lopez	508-555-1223
Dedham	Medford	R. Chandler	774-555-3350
Dover	Boston	T. Blankenship	508-555-9012
Natick	Cambridge	R. Gaston	857-555-7702
Wellesley	Somerville	W. Moore	617-555-8855
Wellesley	Boston	A. Owens	508-555-7812
Needham	Lexington	R. Fairchild	508-555-1240
Needham	Boston	G. Saylor	774-555-3892

In-Basket Review— Manufacturing

60

Goals

- Type at least 40wpm/5′/5e.
- Correctly format a business letter, an open table, an e-mail message, and a memo.
- Successfully complete a Progress and Proofreading Check with zero errors on the first scored attempt.

A. WARMUP

alphabet	1	Two radio jocks helped fax my big quiz for driving lessons.
number/symbol	2	(mloy@usa.net) 45% Eng & Ray 4/7 Grr! $3.67 *p. 259 #28-013
easy	3	They may blame me for my penchant to laugh a lot in Peoria.

Skillbuilding

B. 12-SECOND SPEED SPRINTS

Take three 12-second timed writings on each line. The scale below the last line shows your wpm speed for a 12-second timed writing.

```
 4  He may go with us to the giant dock down by the handy lake.
 5  She is so good at her work and likes what she does as well.
 6  His civic goal for the city is for them to endow the chair.
 7  His body of work may charm the guests who visit the chapel.
    ' ' ' '5' ' ' '10' ' ' '15' ' ' '20' ' ' '25' ' ' '30' ' ' '35' ' ' '40' ' ' '45' ' ' '50' ' ' '55' ' ' '60
```

C. TECHNIQUE PRACTICE: ENTER KEY

Type each line 2 times. Type each sentence on a separate line by pressing ENTER after each sentence.

```
 8  Step on it. Stop now. We are. Get up. Enough? Be here. Why?
 9  See me. Who is he? So soon? Do it now. Who knew? We are up.
10  Busy? Find it? Go! Catch. Give. Begin. Who can go? Who did?
11  Why me? We can. Today. Really. Do not. See? When? Says who?
```

Take two 5-minute timed writings. Review your speed and errors.

 Goal: At least 40wpm/5'/5e

D. 5-MINUTE TIMED WRITING

12	Information technology is among the fastest-growing	11
13	job fields today and is also one of the fields to change	22
14	the quickest. The goal of many schools is to try to prepare	34
15	students to be specialists in a workplace that continues to	46
16	be challenging and will need to change quickly as advances	58
17	are made in technology.	63
18	Those who wish to work in a field that will not stand	74
19	still need to know all about the systems with which they	85
20	labor. Network administrators, for example, will often take	97
21	courses to certify that they have a sound knowledge of any	109
22	of the new hardware. They must also learn about specific	120
23	equipment and have an understanding of how new software	131
24	will function with hardware.	137
25	Those who wish to pass certification exams must have	148
26	the zeal, determination, and drive to complete all of the	160
27	requirements. They know that it will not be long before the	172
28	current systems will be upgraded or new software will be	183
29	released. They need to learn the latest systems and review	195
30	their certification again.	200

1 | 2 | 3 | 4 | 5 | 6 | 7 | 8 | 9 | 10 | 11 | 12

Document Processing

Situation: Today is August 31. You are an administrative assistant, and you work for Disk House Inc. in Boulder, Colorado. Your supervisor is Ms. Rhonda Mendoza, sales and marketing director. Ms. Mendoza has asked you to prepare the following documents for her while she is in a staff meeting this morning. The letter is to be prepared for her signature, the table will be enclosed with the letter, the e-mail is to be sent out ASAP, and she will initial the memo before sending it out this afternoon.

Correspondence
60-50
Business Letter in Block Style

August 31, 20-- | Ms. Sharon Chiro | 8731 Paseo de Peralta | Santa Fe, NM 87502-3214 | Dear Ms. Chiro:

¶ We were pleased to see that you have used our Web site at www.diskhouse.com to inquire about our online catalog. We specialize in computer drives of all types: CD-ROM, DVD, and hard drives. I have enclosed a listing of our most popular DVD writers that will appear online next week in our catalog. As a new customer, you are invited to visit our catalog and place your order at these special prices.

¶ Our online customers receive the same privileges as our hard-copy catalog shoppers. These online privileges include:

- No shipping charges.
- Toll-free customer support line.
- Discounts on purchases of ten or more items.
- Ninety-day warranties (parts and labor) on all purchases.

(continued on next page)

¶ We look forward to many years of doing business with you. Please e-mail me at rmendoza@diskhouse.com if you have any questions or would like additional information.

Sincerely, | Rhonda Mendoza | Sales and Marketing Director | urs | Enclosure | c: R. Hsu, S. Horton

Table 60-22
Open Table

DVD/BLU-RAY BURNERS
(Effective Dates September 3 to September 9)

Model No.	Part No.	Price	Specifications
5500 Blu-ray	64702-BR	$154.99	25 to 50 GB capacity
275 DVD	32102-DVD	75.50	8X Lightscribe
303 DVD	33420-DVD	82.50	16X notebook drive
6500 Blu-ray	74781-BR	178.00	6X Blu-ray ReWriter
7000 Blu-ray	81440-BR	185.75	100 GB capacity

Correspondence 60-51
E-Mail Message

Hi, Marlene:

¶ Your order for Internet service has been processed, and you can enjoy surfing the Web immediately. As a customer of Mountain Communications, a subsidiary of Disk House Inc., you will enjoy several benefits:

1. You will receive 24/7 customer service when using our service hotline at 1-800-555-3222.
2. You will be protected by M-Protect, Mountain's virus protection software.
3. You will receive 20 Mbytes of Web page space.
4. You will receive automated credit card billing.

¶ Thank you for joining Mountain Communications. Please e-mail us at support@mc.net if you have any questions, or call us on our service hotline.

Rhonda | Rhonda Mendoza | E-mail: rmendoza@diskhouse.com | Phone: 303-555-1345

MEMO TO: Martha R. Durham, Publications Department | **FROM:** Rhonda Mendoza, Sales and Marketing Director | **DATE:** August 31, 20-- | **SUBJECT:** Ad in the *Rocky Mountain Daily*

¶ Martha, please include the following criteria in our ad that will run in the *Rocky Mountain Daily* this Sunday:

1. Quarter-page ad.
2. Run-time: 10 days.
3. Location: Business Section and Classified Section.
4. Contact: Include telephone and fax numbers as well as e-mail address and home page URL.

¶ This is our first ad piece in the *Rocky Mountain Daily* since we ran that special promotion last March. Let's add some graphics to make this one an "eye-catcher."

urs

Strategies for Career Success

Writing a Job Application Letter

What's the goal of the letter that accompanies your resume? The goal is to get the interview. No two letters of application are alike.

In the opening paragraph, state your purpose (for example, the position applied for, or how you became aware of it).

In the middle section, sell yourself. Convince the reader that you are the best match for the job. If you respond to a job posting, match your qualifications to the job description. If you send an unsolicited letter, specify how the employer would benefit from your qualifications. Also, refer to your resume.

In the closing paragraph, show confidence in your abilities (for example, "I'm certain I can meet your needs for a . . .").Then state a specific time you will call to schedule an interview.

Your Turn: Obtain a job description for which you are qualified. List the job requirements, and then list your qualifications that match.

5-Minute Timed
Writing

1   People are often the most prized assets in a business. 11
2 Excellent firms know that having well-qualified workers is 23
3 an important step to ensure the success of the company. The 35
4 people in charge can play a huge part in how much success a 47
5 firm will have when they provide a workplace that is meant 58
6 to support teams of people who can work together to achieve 70
7 a common goal. 74
8   When people know they are being encouraged to work 84
9 toward achieving their own goals as well as the goals of 95
10 the company, they will respond by working to their highest 107
11 potential with ardor and zeal. 113
12   Managers need to show that they value the hard work 124
13 and long hours that employees put in to ensure the success 136
14 of the business. People thrive on compliments that show 147
15 their work is appreciated. They like to be rewarded in some 159
16 way when they have done an exceptional job. When those in 171
17 charge are successful in motivating the employees to work 182
18 to their full potential, their company will prosper. The 194
19 result is that each person wins. 200

    1 | 2 | 3 | 4 | 5 | 6 | 7 | 8 | 9 | 10 | 11 | 12

Correspondence Test
3-53
Business Letter in
Block Style

August 10, 20-- / Mr. Randy Strickland / Cambridge Properties / 832 Oldham Avenue / Knoxville, TN 37912-3841 / Dear Mr. Strickland:

¶ Let me introduce myself. I am committee chair of a group that monitors development projects in Knoxville, Tennessee. It was brought to my attention that your proposal to construct 100 three- and four-bedroom homes was approved by the city council last night. As a resident in a neighboring community, I wish to share with you the stipulations we would like you to incorporate in your development project:

- The new homes should have no fewer than 2,700 square feet of living space.
- All structures should have brick frontage.
- No external, unattached buildings should be constructed.

(continued on next page)

¶ Following these stipulations will ensure that your homes adhere to our community building codes.

Sincerely, / Dominique Walters / Committee Chair / urs /

c: D. McMillan, N. Snyder

Sarah,

¶ Our DTP certificate seminar will be held in Kansas City on March 14. Upon request of last year's participants, we want to be sure to include the topics scheduled in Table 1 below.

Table 1. SEMINAR SESSIONS

Session Topic	Scheduled Room	Scheduled Time
Web Page Design	Dakota	8:00 a.m. to 9:30 a.m.
Computer Graphics	Missouri	10:00 a.m. to 11:30 a.m.
Blu-Ray Technology	Gateway A	1:30 p.m. to 3:00 p.m.
Online Marketing Techniques	Gateway B	3:30 p.m. to 5:00 p.m.

¶ These were the four most popular topics at the regional meeting. Let's use a brochure design similar to the one we used at that meeting. I will send you a copy of the brochure tomorrow.

Chris | Chris Meadows | E-mail: cmeadows@commtech.com | Phone: 816-555-0782

AIR POLLUTION

¶ When we hear about pollution, we think of smog, traffic congestion, acid rain, and other pollutant-related terms. However, we also need to consider contaminants in the air we breathe and chemical pollutants around us. We need to be concerned about indoor air because it can affect the health, comfort, and productivity of workers.[1]

POLLUTANTS AND CONTAMINANTS

¶ Chemical pollutants include tobacco smoke and chemical spills. Particles include pollutants such as dust and dirt from drywall, carpets, and copying machines.[2] Biological contaminants can include bacteria, viruses, molds, pollen, and water spills. These contaminants cause allergic reactions that trigger asthma attacks for an estimated 17 million Americans.[3]

IMPROVING AIR QUALITY

¶ The three basic approaches to improving air quality include the use of filters to clean the air, the use of ventilation systems to remove the pollutants, and the use of air pressure to keep the pollutants "at bay." The method we use to improve air quality depends on how difficult it is to separate the impurities.

(continued on next page)

ADMINISTRATIVE RESPONSIBILITIES

¶ Office managers can help by reviewing records pertaining to air conditioning and ventilation systems. They can also help by providing training sessions for employees to learn about maintaining clean air. Finally, they can keep a record of reported health complaints related to polluted air and aid in resolving these complaints.

A TEAM EFFORT

¶ All workers can have a positive impact on improving the quality of the air they breathe. For example, simply making sure that air vents and grills are clean will help improve the quality of air. People who smoke should do so only in areas designated for smoking.

---

[1] Juan Montero, *Pollutants in America*, Southwest Press, El Paso, Texas, 2010.

[2] Julie Bergstrom, "Pollution in the Office," *Boston Globe*, June 17, 2009, p. B4.

[3] "Breathing Clean Air," April 8, 2010, <http://www.airamerica.com/dirty.htm>, accessed on May 13, 2010.

Strategies for Career Success

Interview Thank-You Letter

Expressing your appreciation is a very important follow-up step in your job search. Send a thank-you letter or e-mail within 24 hours after your interview.

In the opening paragraph, thank the interviewer for taking time to meet with you. Make a positive statement about the company or interview feature (for example, meeting potential coworkers).

In the middle paragraph, close the sale. Address any qualifications you neglected to mention. Turn around an interview weakness (for example, reconsider your statement that you wouldn't travel). Strengthen your relationship with the interviewer (for example, refer the interviewer to a good article on a topic in which he or she expressed interest).

In the closing paragraph, ask to be notified when the decision is made. A thank-you letter ensures that your last impression is a positive one.

Your Turn: After your next interview, send a thank-you letter to effectively close the sale.

Skillbuilding

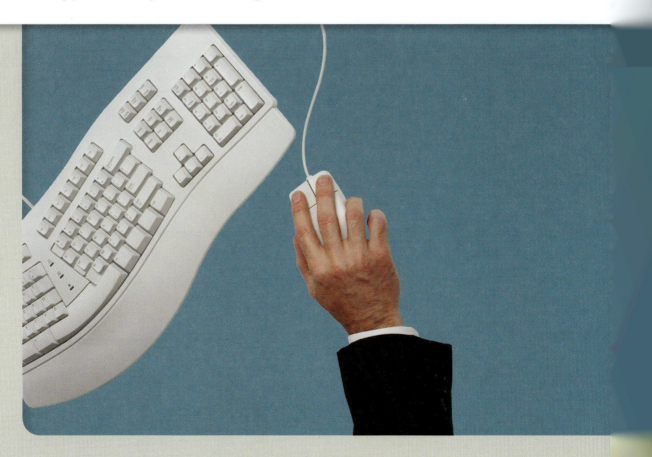

Skillbuilding

Progressive Practice: Alphabet

This skillbuilding routine contains a series of 30-second timed writings that range from 16 wpm to 104 wpm. The first time you use these timed writings, take a 1-minute timed writing with 3 or fewer errors on the Entry Timed Writing paragraph. Push moderately for speed.

Select a passage that is 1 to 2 wpm *higher* than your Entry Timed Writing speed. Then take up to six 30-second timed writings on the passage.

Your goal each time is to complete the passage within 30 seconds with no errors. When you have achieved your goal, move on to the next passage and repeat the procedure.

Entry Timed Writing

```
        Bev was very lucky when she found extra quality in the   11
home she was buying. She quietly told the builder that she       23
was extremely satisfied with the work done on her new home.      35
The builder said she can move into her new house next month.     47
       1  |  2  |  3  |  4  |  5  |  6  |  7  |  8  |  9  |  10  |  11  |  12
```

16 wpm

The author is the creator of a document.

18 wpm

Open means to access a previously saved file.

20 wpm

A byte represents one character to every computer.

22 wpm

Hard copy is usually text that is printed out on paper.

24 wpm

Soft copy is text that is displayed on your computer screen.

26 wpm

Memory is that part of your word processor that stores your data.

28 wpm

The menu is a list of choices used to guide a user through a function.

30 wpm

A sheet feeder is a device that will insert sheets of paper into a printer.

32 wpm

An icon is a small picture that illustrates a function or an object in software.

34 wpm

Active icons on your desktop represent the programs that can be run on your computer.

Skillbuilding

36 wpm	To execute means to perform an action specified by the user or also by a computer program.
38 wpm	Output is the result of a word processing operation. It can be either printed or magnetic form.
40 wpm	Format refers to the physical features which affect the appearance and arrangement of your document.
42 wpm	A font is a type style of a particular size or kind that includes letters, numbers, or punctuation marks.
44 wpm	Ergonomics is the science of adapting working conditions or equipment to meet the physical needs of employees.
46 wpm	Home position is the starting position of a document; it is typically the upper left corner of the display monitor.
48 wpm	The purpose of a virus checker is to find those programs that may cause your computer to stop working as you want it to.
50 wpm	An optical scanner is a device that can read text and enter it into a word processor without the need to type the data again.
52 wpm	Hardware refers to all the physical equipment you use while computing, such as the display screen, keyboard, printer, and scanner.
54 wpm	A peripheral device is any piece of equipment that will extend the capabilities of a computer system but is not required for operation.
56 wpm	A split screen displays two or more different images at the same time; it can, for example, display two different pages of a legal document.
58 wpm	To defrag the computer means that you are reorganizing the files so that related files will be located in the same general place on a hard drive.
60 wpm	With the click of a mouse, one can use a button bar or a toolbar for fast access to features that are frequently applied when using a Windows program.

Skillbuilding

62 wpm

Gadgets are typically controls which are placed on your desktop to allow you to have immediate access to frequently used information such as time and date.

64 wpm

Turnaround time is the length of time needed for a document to be keyboarded, edited, proofread, corrected if required, printed, and returned to the originator.

66 wpm

A local area network is a system that uses cable or another means to allow high-speed communication among many kinds of electronic equipment within particular areas.

68 wpm

To search and replace means to direct the word processor to locate a character, word, or group of words wherever it occurs in the document and replace it with newer text.

70 wpm

Indexing is the ability of a word processor to accumulate a list of words that appear in a document, including page numbers, and then print a revised list in alphabetic order.

72 wpm

When a program needs information from you, a dialog box will appear on the desktop. Once the dialog box appears, you must identify the option you desire and then choose the option.

74 wpm

A facsimile is an exact copy of a document, and it is also a process by which images, such as typed letters, graphs, and signatures, are scanned, transmitted, and then printed on paper.

76 wpm

Compatibility refers to when a computer is able to share information with other computers or also to communicate with different hardware. It could be accomplished by other methods.

78 wpm

Some operators like to personalize their desktops when they use Windows by making various changes. For example, they can change their screen colors or the pointer so that they will have more fun.

80 wpm

Wraparound is the ability of a word processor to move words from one line to another line and from one page to the next page as a result of inserting and deleting text or changing the size of margins.

82 wpm

It is possible when using Windows to evaluate the contents of different directories on the screen at the very same time. You can then choose to copy or move a particular file from one directory to another.

Skillbuilding

84 wpm

List processing is a capability of a word processor to keep lists of data that can be updated and sorted in alphabetic or numeric order. A list can also be added to any document that is stored in your computer.

86 wpm

A computer is a device that accepts data that are input and then processes those data to produce the output. A computer performs its work by using various stored programs that provide all the necessary instructions.

88 wpm

A word processor is more than a program that can process words. Word processors have many other capabilities such as merging documents; executing some mathematical equations; and inserting clip art, shapes, and pictures.

90 wpm

Help and support in Windows are available to assist you in finding answers to questions you may have about just how the computer functions. You can find help on topics like security, files, folders, printing, and maintenance.

92 wpm

When you want to look at the contents of two windows when using Windows, you might want to reduce the window size. Do this by pointing to a border or a corner of a window and dragging it until the window is the size that you want.

94 wpm

Scrolling means to display a very large quantity of text by rolling it horizontally or vertically past your display screen. As text disappears from the top section of your screen, new text will appear in the bottom area of your screen.

96 wpm

You have several options available to you when you print a document. For example, you can determine which printer to use, the pages you desire to print, the number of copies to be printed, the print quality desired, and the paper size used.

98 wpm

An ink-jet printer and a laser printer are popular printers used in a home office. Many users prefer an ink-jet printer because it is not as expensive to buy. But a laser printer provides a higher-quality print and is often the preferred choice.

Skillbuilding

100 wpm

E-mail, text messaging, cell phones, and chat rooms have enabled us to communicate quickly with people all around the globe. We can transmit a call or a message on the spur of the moment and receive a response to our call or message almost instantly.

102 wpm

Many different graphics software programs have been brought on the market in past years. These programs can be very powerful in helping with a business presentation. If there is a requirement to share data, using programs like these could be very helpful.

104 wpm

Voice mail is an essential service used by many people in the business world. This technology enables anyone placing a call to your phone to leave you a message if you cannot answer it at that time. This unique feature can help many workers be more productive.

Skillbuilding

Progressive Practice: Numbers

This skillbuilding routine contains a series of 30-second timed writings that range from 16 wpm to 80 wpm. The first time you use these timed writings, take a 1-minute timed writing with 3 or fewer errors on the Entry Timed Writing paragraph. Push moderately for speed.

Select a passage that is 1 to 2 wpm *higher* than your Entry Timed Writing speed. Then take up to six 30-second timed writings on the passage.

Your goal each time is to complete the passage within 30 seconds with no errors. When you have achieved your goal, move on to the next passage and repeat the procedure.

Entry Timed Writing

Their bags were filled with 10 sets of jars, 23 cookie 11
cutters, 4 baking pans, 6 coffee mugs, 25 plates, 9 dessert 23
plates, 7 soup bowls, 125 recipe cards, and 8 recipe boxes. 35
David delivered these 217 items to 20487 Mountain Boulevard. 47

1 | 2 | 3 | 4 | 5 | 6 | 7 | 8 | 9 | 10 | 11 | 12

16 wpm

There are 37 chairs in Rooms 24 and 156.

18 wpm

About 10 of the 39 boxes were torn on June 8.

20 wpm

Only 3 papers had errors on pages 28, 40, and 197.

22 wpm

My 46 letters were sent on May 10, June 3, and June 27.

24 wpm

The 79 freshmen, 86 juniors, and 54 seniors arrived at home.

26 wpm

The school needs 150 pens, 38 reams of paper, and 42 new folders.

28 wpm

Only 1 or 2 of the 305 new books had errors on pages 46, 178, and 192.

30 wpm

They met 10 of the 23 tennis players who received 4 awards from 5 trainers.

32 wpm

Those 8 vans carried 75 passengers on the first trip and 64 on the next 3 trips.

34 wpm

I saw 2 eagles on Route 86 and then 4 eagles on Route 53 at 9 a.m. on Monday, May 10.

Skillbuilding

36 wpm

The 17 firms produced 50 of the 62 records that received awards for 3 of the 4 categories.

38 wpm

The 12 trucks hauled 87 cows, 65 horses, and 49 pigs to the farm, which was 30 miles northeast.

40 wpm

She moved from 87 Bayview Drive to 659 Bay Street and then 3 blocks south to 4012 Gulbranson Avenue.

42 wpm

My 2 or 3 buyers ordered 5 dozen in sizes 6, 7, 8, and 9 after the 10 to 14 percent discounts were added.

44 wpm

There were 134 men and 121 women waiting in line at Gate 206 for the 58 to 79 tickets to the Cape Cod concert.

46 wpm

Steve had listed 5, 6, or 7 items on Purchase Order 243 when he saw that Purchase Requisition 89 contained 10 more.

48 wpm

Your items numbered 278 will sell for about 90 percent of the value of the 16 items that have code numbers shown as 435.

50 wpm

The managers stated that 98 of those 750 randomly selected new valves had about 264 defects, far exceeding the usual 31 norm.

52 wpm

Half of the 625 volunteers received over 90 percent of the charity pledges. Approximately 38 of the 147 agencies might enjoy this.

54 wpm

Merico hired 94 part-time workers to help the 378 full-time employees during the 62-day period when sales go up by 150 percent or more.

56 wpm

Kaye only hit 1 for 4 in the first 29 games after an 8-game streak in which she batted 3 for 4. She then hit at a .570 average for 16 games.

58 wpm

The mail carrier delivered 98 letters during the week to 734 Oak Street and also took 52 letters to 610 Faulkner Road as he returned on Route 58.

60 wpm

Pat said that about 1 in 5 of the 379 swimmers had a chance of being among the top 20. The best 6 of these 48 divers will receive special recognition.

Skillbuilding

62 wpm

It rained from 3 to 6 inches, and 18 of those 20 farmers were fearful that 4 to 7 inches more would flood about 95 acres along 3 miles of the new Route 79.

64 wpm

Those 17 sacks weighed 48 pounds, more than the 30 pounds that I had thought. All 24 believe the 92-pound bag is at least 15 or 16 pounds above its true weight.

66 wpm

They bought 7 of the 8 options for 54 of the 63 vehicles last month. They now have over 120 dump trucks for use in 9 of the 15 new regions in the big 20-county area.

68 wpm

Andy was 8 or 9 years old when they moved to 612 Glendale Street and away from the 700 block of Henry Lane, which is about 45 miles directly west of Boca Raton, FL 33434.

70 wpm

Doug had read 575 pages in the 760-page book by August 30; Darlene had read only 468 pages. Darlene has read 29 of those optional books since October 19, and Doug has read 18.

72 wpm

The school district has 985 elementary students, 507 middle school students, and 463 high school students. This total represents the greatest increase in total enrollment for us.

74 wpm

Attendance at last year's meeting was 10,835. Your goal for this year is to have 11,764 people. This might enable us to plan for an increase of 929 participants, a rise of 8.57 percent.

76 wpm

David's firm has 158 stores, located in 109 cities in the South. The company employs 3,540 males and 2,624 females, a total of 6,164 employees. About 4,750 of those employees work part-time.

78 wpm

Memberships were as follows: 98 members in the Drama Guild, 90 members in Zeta Tau, 82 members in Theta Phi, 75 in the Bowling Club, and 136 in the Ski Club. This meant that 481 joined the group.

80 wpm

The association had 684 members from the South, 830 members from the North, 1,023 members from the East, and 751 from the West. This total membership was 3,288; these numbers increased by 9.8 percent.

Skillbuilding

Paced Practice

The Paced Practice skillbuilding routine builds speed and accuracy in short, easy steps by using individualized goals and immediate feedback. You may use this program at any time after completing Lesson 9.

This section contains a series of 2-minute timed writings for speeds ranging from 16 wpm to 96 wpm. The first time you use these timed writings, take the 1-minute Entry Timed Writing with 2 or fewer uncorrected errors to establish your base speed.

Select a passage that is 2 wpm higher than your Entry Timed Writing speed. Then use this two-stage practice pattern to achieve each speed goal: (1) concentrate on speed and (2) work on accuracy.

Speed Goal. To determine your speed goal, take three 2-minute timed writings in total. Your goal each time is to complete the passage in 2 minutes without regard to errors. When you have achieved your speed goal, work on accuracy.

Accuracy Goal. To type accurately, you need to slow down—just a bit. Therefore, to reach your accuracy goal, drop back 2 wpm from the previous passage. Take consecutive timed writings on this passage until you can complete the passage in 2 minutes with no more than 2 errors.

For example, if you achieved a speed goal of 54 wpm, you should then work on an accuracy goal of 52 wpm. When you have achieved 52 wpm for accuracy, move up 4 wpm (for example, to the 56-wpm passage) and work for speed again.

Entry Timed Writing

If you can dream it, you can live it. Just follow your heart. There are many careers, which range from the mundane to the exotic to the sublime.

Start your career planning now by quizzing yourself about your talents, skills, and personal interests.

1 | 2 | 3 | 4 | 5 | 6 | 7 | 8 | 9 | 10 | 11 | 12

16 wpm

Your future is now, so you must seize every day.

After exploring your interests, quickly check the sixteen career clusters for a wide range of potential jobs.

18 wpm

When exploring various career options, think about what a job means for you.

Recognize that it can mean what you do just to earn money or what you find quite challenging overall.

20 wpm

If you acquire a job that you enjoy, then it means even more than simply earning an excellent wage.

It also means making a contribution, taking pride in your work, and utilizing all of your talents.

Skillbuilding

22 wpm

What is the difference between a job and a career? Think carefully. A job is work that you have to do for money.

A career is a sequence of related jobs that optimize your interests, experience, knowledge, and training.

24 wpm

Learn all about the world of work by looking at the sixteen career clusters. Most jobs are included in one of the clusters that have been organized by the government.

When exploring careers, list all the unique clusters that interest you.

26 wpm

Once you identify the career clusters that interest you, look at the jobs that are within each cluster.

Analyze exactly what skills and aptitudes are needed, what training is required, what the work setting is like, and what your chances for advancement are.

28 wpm

Use your career center and your school or a public library to research your career choice. Go on the Internet, and ask experts for their unique views of certain careers.

As you gather data about your job options, you might learn about new career options that are on the horizon.

30 wpm

You must gain insight into a career. You can become a volunteer, sign up for an internship, or even work in a part-time job in the field.

You will become more familiar with a specific job while you develop your skills. You will quickly gain prized experience, whether you choose that career or not.

Skillbuilding

32 wpm

No matter which path you choose, strive for a high level of pride in yourself and in your job. Your image is affected by what other people think of you as well as by what you think of yourself.

Next, analyze your level of confidence. If you have any self-doubts, strive to acquire more self-confidence and self-esteem.

34 wpm

Confidence is required for a positive attitude, and a positive attitude is required for success at work. While you may not control all that happens at work, recognize that you must control how you react to what happens.

Become more confident and cultivate positive thoughts, which will provide you with extra power in life and on the job.

36 wpm

Quite a few factors lead to success on the job. People who have analyzed these factors say that it is the personal traits one exhibits that determine who is promoted and who is not.

One of the best traits a person can have is the trait of being likable. That means that you are honest, loyal, courteous, thoughtful, pleasant, kind, considerate, and positive.

38 wpm

If you are likable, you will relate well with most people. If you have excellent social contact with others, it will humanize the workplace and make your work there more enjoyable. Think of all the hours you are required to spend with one another each day.

If you show that you are willing to collaborate with your coworkers, most likely you will also receive their cooperation.

Skillbuilding

40 wpm

Cooperation begins on the first day of your new job. When you work for a firm, you quickly become a part of that team. Meeting people and learning new skills can be quite exciting.

For some people, though, a new situation can trigger some anxiety. The best advice is to remain calm, do your job with zeal, learn the workplace policies, be flexible, avoid being too critical, and always be positive.

42 wpm

When you begin a new job, even if you have recently received your college degree, chances are you will start at the bottom of the organizational chart. Each of us has to start somewhere. Do not despair or become lazy.

With hard work, you should start your climb up the corporate ladder. If you are smart, you will quietly take on even the most tedious task, take everything in stride, and exercise any chance to learn.

44 wpm

If you think learning is restricted to an academic setting, think again. You have much to learn on the job, even if it is a position for which you have been trained.

As a new employee, you will not be expected to know everything. When necessary, do not hesitate to ask your employer questions. Learn all you can about your job and the company. Capitalize on the new information to enhance your job performance and to build toward success.

46 wpm

Begin every valuable workday by prioritizing all of your tasks. Decide which tasks must be done immediately and which can wait. List the most important items first; then determine the order in which each item must be done.

After you complete a task, then quickly cross it off your priority list. Maximize your time; that is, do not put off work you should do. If a job must be done, just do it. You will stay on top of your list when you utilize time wisely.

Skillbuilding

48 wpm

     Do not let the phone control your time. Learn how to manage all your phone calls. Phone calls can be extremely distracting from other duties, so be jealous of your quiet time. When making a phone call, organize the topics you want to discuss. Gather needed supplies such as pencils, papers, and files.

     Set a time limit and stick to the topic. Give concise answers, summarize the points discussed, and end your talk politely. Efficient phone usage will help you manage your time.

50 wpm

     As with everything, practice makes perfect, but along the way, we have all made some mistakes. Realize that the difference between successful people and those who are less successful is not that the successful people make fewer mistakes. It is just that they will never quit.

     Instead of letting mistakes bring you down, use your mistakes as opportunities to grow. If you make a mistake, be patient with yourself. You might be able to fix your mistake. Look for success to be just around the corner.

52 wpm

     Be patient as you learn how to take care of problems and accept criticism. Accepting criticism may be quite a test for you. Still, it is vital to many of us at work. Criticism that is given in a way to help you learn, expand, or grow is called constructive criticism.

     If you look at criticism as being helpful, it will be easier to deal with. You might be amazed to learn that some people welcome it since it teaches them the best way to succeed on the job. Try to improve how you accept helpful criticism from others.

Skillbuilding

54 wpm

People experience continuous growth during a career. Goal setting is a key tool to acquire for any job. Some people believe that goals provide the motivation we need to get to the place we want to be. Setting goals encourages greater achievements. The higher that we set our goals, the greater the effort we need to reach them.

Each time we reach a target or come closer to a goal, we should realize an increase in our confidence and in our performance, which leads to greater accomplishments. And the cycle continues to spiral for years.

56 wpm

One goal we must all strive for is punctuality. When employees are absent or just tardy, it costs the company money. If you are frequently tardy or absent, others have to do extra work to cover for you. If you are absent often, your peers may begin to resent you, which causes everyone stress in the department.

Being late and missing work might penalize your own relationship with your manager and have a negative effect on your career. To avoid such potential problems, develop a personal plan to ensure that you arrive every day on time and ready to work.

58 wpm

To hold a job is a chief part of being an adult. Some people start their work careers as teens. From the start, a range of work habits are developed that are as crucial to success as the actual job skills and knowledge that someone brings to his or her job.

What traits are expected of workers? What do employers look for when they rate their own workers? Vital personal traits would include being confident, helpful, positive, and loyal. If you are also kind, passionate, and organized, you may now have many of these qualities that employers value most of all in their staffs.

Skillbuilding

60 wpm

Being dependable is a required work trait. If a job must be done by a special time, the manager will be pleased to learn that his or her workers are going to meet that deadline. Those who are dependable learn to utilize their time to attain maximum results. Loyal workers can also be counted on, they have good attendance records, they are well prepared, and they get to work on time and ready to start.

If the firm wants to meet its goals, it must have a team of loyal and dependable workers. You, your peers, your supervisors, and your managers are all team members who work to reach their goals.

62 wpm

The ability to organize is an important quality for the worker who would like to display good work habits. The worker should have the ability to plan the work that needs to be done and then to be able to execute that plan in a timely manner.

An employer requires a competent worker to be well organized. If the office worker is efficient, he or she handles requests swiftly and deals with messages without delay. The organized worker does not allow his or her work to accumulate on the desk. Also, the organized worker will return all phone calls quickly and make lists of the jobs that still need to be done each day.

Skillbuilding

64 wpm

Efficiency is one work habit that is important. The efficient worker does each task quickly and starts work on the next task eagerly. He or she thinks about ways to save steps or time. For example, an efficient worker may plan just one trip to the copier with a number of copying jobs rather than take many trips to do each separate job.

Being efficient also means that you have all of the required supplies to finish each job. An efficient worker zips along on each project, uses his or her time wisely, and then stays focused on that one task. With careful and detailed planning, a worker who is efficient can finish tasks in less time.

66 wpm

Cooperation is another ideal work habit. It begins on the first day of the job and means that you quietly think of all team members when you make a decision. A person who cooperates is willing to do what is needed for the good of the whole group. For you to be a team player, you must take the extra steps to cooperate.

Cooperation may mean that you need to be a good sport if you are asked to do something you would rather not do. It may mean that you have to correct some mistakes made by another person in the office. When each employee has the interests of the company at heart and works well with other workers, then everyone is a good corporate citizen.

Skillbuilding

68 wpm

Enthusiasm is still another work trait that is eagerly sought after by employers. If you are enthusiastic, then you have lots of positive energy. This is reflected in your actions toward your work, coworkers, and employer. It has been noted that eagerness can be catching. If you show you are excited to try any project, then you may quickly not only achieve the highest praise but also will be considered for career advancement.

How much enthusiasm do you show at the workplace? Do you encourage people or complain to people? There should always be lots of good jobs for workers who are known to have a wealth of zeal and a positive approach to the jobs that they are assigned.

70 wpm

Acceptance is a work trait required of all of us. In the work world of today, each business includes both men and women of different religions, races, cultures, skills, and beliefs. You will interact with many types of people as customers, coworkers, and owners. Treat each one fairly, openly, and honestly.

All types of prejudice are hurtful, hateful, and, in short, unacceptable. Prejudice is not allowed at work. Each of us must learn to accept and even prize the many kinds of differences that are exhibited by all of us. Since so many diverse groups work side by side in the work world, it is vital that all workers maintain a high degree of shared insights. Embrace each of us for who we are.

Skillbuilding

72 wpm

It can be concluded that certain work habits or traits should play the major role in deciding the success of all workers. Most managers would be quick to agree on the high importance of these traits. It is most likely that these habits would be analyzed on performance appraisal forms. Promotions, pay increases, new duties, and your future with the company may be based on these yearly job assessments.

You should request regular job performance assessments even if your company does not conduct them. This feedback might then expand your job skills and career development by helping you grow. If you always look for ways to improve your work habits and skills, you will enjoy success in the world of work and beyond.

74 wpm

You can be sure that no matter where you work, you will use some form of technology. Almost every business depends on computers. Firms use such devices as voice mail, fax machines, cell phones, and personal digital assistants. These tools help us to do our work quickly and efficiently. They also take some of the drudgery out of our lives.

One result of the use of these tools is globalization, which means worldwide communication links between people. Our world has turned into one global village. We should expand our thinking beyond the office walls. We must become aware of what happens in other parts of the world. These events may directly affect you and your job. The more you know, the more valuable you will become to a company.

Skillbuilding

76 wpm

Each advance in technology has had an effect on all aspects of our lives. For example, the dawn of the age of the Internet has changed how people get and send data. It is the largest data network in the world. It is called the information superhighway since it is a vast network of big computers that can link people and resources around the world. It is an exciting medium to help you access current data and be more useful on the job and at home.

Without a doubt, we are all globally linked, and data technology services can support those links. The industry offers different job opportunities in dozens of fields. Keep in mind that keyboarding skills are required in this field as well as in most others. Touch-typing skills are just assumed in most jobs.

78 wpm

It is amazing to learn about the many jobs in which keyboarding skill is needed today. The use of a computer keyboard by executive chefs is a prime example. The chefs in large restaurants must prepare parts or all of the meals served while they direct the work of their staff of chefs, cooks, and others in and near the kitchens.

The computer has become a prime tool for a wide range of tasks, including tracking stocks of their food supplies. By seeing which items are favorites and which items are not requested, the chef can work out the food requirements, order food, and supervise the purchase of foods. Also, the computer has proved to be a very practical tool for such tasks as helping to plan budgets, prepare purchase orders for vendors, write menus, and print reports.

Skillbuilding

Advanced technology has opened the doors to a wide variety of amazing new products and services to sell. It seems that the more complex the products get, the higher the price of the products is and that the larger the sales commission is, the stiffer the competition is. To sell a technical product requires detailed product knowledge, good verbal skills, smooth sales rapport, and also expert typing skills.

Business favors those who have special training. For example, a pharmacy company may choose a person who has a strong knowledge of chemistry to sell its products. Sales is for those who enjoy using their command of persuasion to make the sales. The potential for good pay and commissions is quite high for the salesperson who is trained well. You should perhaps think about a job in sales.

As you travel about in your sales job or type a report at the office or create the Friday night pizza special for your new diner, you should always plan to put safety first. Accidents happen, but they do not have to happen regularly or to have such severe results. Accidents cost businesses billions of dollars each year in medical expenses, lost wages, and insurance claims.

Part of your job is to make certain that you are not one of the millions of people injured on the job each year. You may believe you work in a safe place, but accidents occur in all types of businesses. A few careless people cause most accidents, so ensure your safety on the job. Safety does not just happen. It is the result of the very careful awareness of those people who plan and put into action a safety program that benefits everyone.

Skillbuilding

84 wpm

In the world of today, you need more than the needed skills or the personal qualities to succeed on the job. Managers also expect all workers to have ethics. Ethics are the codes of conduct that tell a person or a group how to act. Workers who act ethically do not lie, cheat, or steal. They are honest and fair in all their dealings with others. In short, they are good citizens.

Workers who act ethically gain a good reputation for themselves and for their companies. They are known to be dependable. Unethical behavior can have a spiraling effect. A single act can do a lot of damage. Even if you have not held a job yet, you have had some experience with ethical problems. Life is full of a range of occasions to behave ethically. Do the right thing when faced with decisions. The ethics you follow will carry over into the workplace.

86 wpm

Now that you know what will be expected of you on the job, how do you make sure you will get the job in the first place? Almost everyone has at least once gone through the interview process for a job. For some, the interview is a traumatic event, but it does not have to be so stressful. Research is the key. Learn about the firm with whom you are seeking a job. Form a list of questions to ask. Interviews also provide you the chance to interview the organization.

Take a folder of items with you. Include copies of your data sheet with a list of three or more professional references, your academic transcript, and your certificates and licenses. Be sure to wear appropriate business attire. The outcome of the interview will be positive if you have enthusiasm for the job, match your skills to the needs of the company, ask relevant questions, and listen.

Skillbuilding

88 wpm

How can you be the strongest candidate for the job? Be sure that your skills in reading, writing, math, speaking, and listening are strong. These skills should enable you to listen well and communicate clearly, not only during the job interview but also at your place of work. This exchange of information between a sender and a receiver is known as communication.

It does not matter which career you choose; you will still spend most of your time using these basic skills to communicate with others. You should use the skills as tools to gain information, solve problems, and share ideas. You can also use these skills to help you meet the needs of your customers. Most of the new jobs in the next few years will be in industries that will require direct customer contact. Do not jeopardize your chances for success; make sure that you are able to communicate well with others.

90 wpm

Writing well can help you gain a competitive edge in your job search and throughout your career. Most of us have had occasion to write business letters whether to apply for a job, to comment on a product or service, or to place an order. Often it seems easy to sit back and let our thoughts flow freely. At other times, we seem to struggle to find the best words to use to express our thoughts in precisely the correct way. We all sometimes have these issues.

Writing skills can improve with practice. Use these principles to develop your writing skills. Try to use words that you would be comfortable using in person. Use words that are simple, direct, kind, and confident. When it is possible, use words that emphasize only the positive side. Remember to proofread your work. Well-organized thoughts and proper grammar, spelling, and punctuation will show your reader that you care about quality.

Skillbuilding

92 wpm

Listening is such a vital part of the communication process. It is the key for learning, getting along, and forming rapport. Do you think that you are an active or a passive listener? Listening should not be just a passive process. To listen actively means to analyze what is being said and to interpret what it means. Active listening makes you a more effective worker because you react to what you have heard as well as to what you have not heard.

Study these steps to expand your listening skills: Do not cut people off; let them finish their remarks before you speak. If what they said is unclear, write down your questions, and wait for the discussion to be finished until you ask them. Reduce personal and environmental noise so you can focus on the message. Keep an open mind. Remain attentive and maintain eye contact when possible. By using these skills, you can become even more confident and more effective.

94 wpm

Speaking is also a form of communication. In the world of work, speaking is an important way in which to share information. Regardless of whether you are speaking to an audience of one or one hundred, you will want to be sure that your listeners hear your message. Be clear about your purpose, your audience, and your subject. A purpose is the overall goal or reason for speaking. An audience is anyone who receives information. The subject is the main topic or key idea that you wish to analyze.

Research your subject. Use specific facts and examples to give you credibility. As you speak, be brief and direct. Progress logically from point to point. Speak slowly and pronounce clearly all your words. Is the quality of your voice friendly and pleasant or is it shrill and offensive? These factors influence how your message is received. A good idea is worthless if you cannot present it well, so take all the time you need to get ready.

Skillbuilding

96 wpm

Building a career is a process. You have looked at
all your interests, values, skills, talents, and feelings.
Your look into the world of work has begun, but the journey
does not stop here, for the present is the perfect place to
start thinking about the future. It is where you start to
take steps toward your goals. It is where you can really
make a difference.

As you set personal and career goals, remember the
importance of small steps. Each step toward a personal goal
or a career goal is a small victory. The feeling of success
encourages you to take other small steps. Each step builds
onto the next. Continue analyzing your personal world as
well as the world you share with others. Expect the best as
you go forward. Expect a happy life, loving relationships,
success in life, and fulfilling and satisfying work in a
job that you really love. Last but not least, expect that
you have something unique and special to offer the world,
because you do.

Skillbuilding

Supplementary Timed Writings

Supplementary Timed Writing 1

All problem solving, whether or not it is personal or academic, involves decision making. You make decisions in order to solve problems. On occasion, a problem occurs as a result of a decision you have made. For example, you may decide to smoke, but later in life, you might then face the problem of nicotine addiction. You may decide not to study math and science because you think that they are difficult. 11 23 35 46 58 70 82

Because of this choice, some career options may be closed to you. There is a consequence for each action. Do you see that events in your life do not just happen, but that they are the result of your choices and decisions? 93 108 116 127

How can you best prepare your mind to help you solve problems? A positive attitude is a great start. Indeed, your attitude will determine the way in which you may solve a problem or make a decision. Approach your studies, such as science and math courses, with a positive attitude. Try to think of academic problems as puzzles to be solved and not just as work to be avoided. 138 149 161 173 185 195 203

Critical thinking is a type of problem solving that allows you to decode, analyze, reason, assess, and process data. Since it is basic for all successful problem solving, you should try to explore, probe, question, and search for all the right answers. 213 224 235 248 253

A problem may not always be solved on the first try, so do not give up. Try, try again. To find a solution may take a real effort. Use your critical thinking skills to achieve success in a world that is highly competitive and demanding. 263 275 286 298 300

1 | 2 | 3 | 4 | 5 | 6 | 7 | 8 | 9 | 10 | 11 | 12

Skillbuilding

For many of us, the Internet is an important resource 11
in our private and public lives. The Internet provides us 23
with quick access to countless Web sites that may contain 34
news, products, games, and other types of data. The Web 45
pages on these sites can be designed, authored, and posted 57
by anyone from anywhere around the world, so you must use 69
critical thinking skills when reviewing these Web sites. 80

Just because something is said on the radio, printed 91
in the newspaper, or shown on television does not mean that 103
it is true. This applies to data found on the Internet as 115
well. Do not fall into the trap of believing that if it is 126
on the Net, it must be true. A wise user of the Internet 138
thinks critically about data found on the Net and evaluates 150
this material before he or she decides to use it. 160

When you assess a new Web site, think about who, what, 171
how, when, and where. Who refers to the author of the Web 183
site. The author may be a business firm, an organization, 194
or a person. What refers to the validity of the data. Can 206
this data be verified by a reputable source? 215

How refers to the viewpoint of the author. Are your 225
data presented without prejudice? When refers to the time 237
frame of your data. Do you have recent data? Where refers 249
to your data source. Are the data from a trusted source? 260

By answering these critical questions, you will learn 271
more about the accuracy and dependability of a Web site. 283
When you surf the Net next time, be quite cautious. Anyone 294
can publish on the Internet. 300

1 | 2 | 3 | 4 | 5 | 6 | 7 | 8 | 9 | 10 | 11 | 12

Skillbuilding

Most office workers perform a wide range of tasks in 11
their workday. These tasks may require them to handle phone 23
calls or forward personal messages, to send short e-mail 34
notes or compile complex office reports, or to write simple 46
letters or assemble detailed letters with tables, graphics, 58
and imported data. Office workers are thus a basic part of 70
the structure of the firm. 75

The office worker must use critical thinking in order 86
to carry out a wide array of daily tasks. Some of the tasks 98
are more urgent than other tasks and should be done first. 110
Some tasks take only a short time, while others take a lot 122
more time. Some tasks demand a quick response, while others 134
may be taken up as time permits or even postponed until the 146
future. Some of these tasks might require input from other 158
people. 159

Whether a job is simple or complex or big or small, 170
the office worker must decide what is to be done first by 182
setting the priority for each task. 189

When setting priorities, critical thinking skills are 200
essential. The office worker must assess each aspect of the 212
task. It is a good idea to identify the size of the task, 223
learn about its complexity, estimate the effort needed, 235
judge its importance, and set its deadline. 243

Once the office worker assesses a task that is to be 254
done within a certain span of time, then the priority for 266
completing all those tasks can be set. Critical thinking 277
skills, if applied well, can save the employer money, but 289
if they are applied poorly, they might cost an employer. 300

1 | 2 | 3 | 4 | 5 | 6 | 7 | 8 | 9 | 10 | 11 | 12

Skillbuilding

Each day business managers must make choices that keep 11
their firms running in a smooth, skillful, and gainful way. 23
Every decision needs to be quick and sure. 32

To make good decisions, all managers must use critical 43
thinking. They must gather all the needed facts so that 54
they can make sound, well-informed choices. Over time, they 66
can refine their skills. Then, when they face a similar 77
problem, they can use their knowledge to help them solve 89
new problems with ease and in less time. 97

What types of decisions do you think managers make 107
that involve critical thinking? Human resource managers 119
need to decide whom to hire, what to pay the new worker, 130
and where to place him or her. In addition, human resource 142
managers should be able to help resolve conflicts between 153
workers. 155

Office managers must purchase copy machines, software, 166
computers, and supplies. Top executives must make business 178
policies, appoint other managers, and assess the success of 190
the firm. Plant supervisors must set schedules, gauge work 202
quality, and assess workers. Sales managers must study all 214
of the new sales trends, as well as provide sales training. 226

Most managers use critical thinking to make wise and 237
well-thought-out decisions. They carefully check all the 248
facts, analyze these facts, and then make a final judgment 259
based upon these facts. They should also be able to clearly 271
discern fact from fiction. Through trial and error, most 283
managers learn their own ways to solve problems and find a 294
solution for their firms. 300

1 | 2 | 3 | 4 | 5 | 6 | 7 | 8 | 9 | 10 | 11 | 12

Skillbuilding

In most classes, teachers just want the students to analyze situations, draw conclusions, and solve problems. Each of these tasks requires students to use good thinking skills. How do students acquire these skills? What process do students follow to develop these skills?

During early years of life, children learn words and then combine these words into sentences. From there, they learn to declare ideas, share thoughts, and express their feelings. Students learn numbers and math concepts. They may learn to read musical notes, to keep rhythm, to sing songs, and to recognize popular and classical pieces of music. Students learn colors and shapes and start to draw.

During their early years, students learn the basic models of problem solving. One way for students to solve problems and apply thinking skills is to use the scientific approach. This approach requires a student to state the problem to be solved, collect the known facts about that problem, analyze the problem, and pose viable solutions. Throughout this process, teachers ask questions that force students to expand their thinking skills.

Teachers may want to ask questions such as these: Did you clearly state the problem? Did you get all the facts? Did you get the facts from the right place? Did you assume anything? Did you pose other possible answers? Did you keep an open mind to all solutions? Did you let your bias come into play? Did you take the time to listen to other people? Finally, does the solution make sense?

1 | 2 | 3 | 4 | 5 | 6 | 7 | 8 | 9 | 10 | 11 | 12

Skillbuilding

Supplementary Timed Writing 6

A major goal for all instructors in school is to teach 11
critical thinking skills to their class. This skill is the 23
process of deciding in a logical way what we should do or 35
believe, and it also involves an ability to compare and 46
contrast, solve problems, make decisions, analyze results, 58
and combine and use knowledge. Can you see that these are 69
important skills you can use all your life? 78

These skills help the student who later becomes a part 89
of the workforce. Whether someone is in a small business, 101
is in a corporate setting, or is self-employed, the world 112
of today is a competitive one, and skilled employees are 124
always in demand. 127

One part of gaining success in the workforce is having 139
the skill to deal with the mixed demands of the fast-paced 150
business world. A few of the required skills are insightful 162
decision making, creative problem solving, and productive 174
contact among diverse groups. 180

In school, we learn the basics of critical thinking. 191
This skill extends far beyond the borders of the classroom 203
and lasts a lifetime. We use critical thinking in all of 214
our daily lives. We constantly analyze and assess pursuits 226
such as music, movies, speech, fashion, magazine articles, 238
and television shows. 242

We all had experience using critical thinking skills 253
well before we even knew what they were. So you should keep 265
on learning and growing. The classroom can be the perfect 276
place for your exploration, so use that time to learn how 288
others solve problems. There are always new goals to reach. 300

1 | 2 | 3 | 4 | 5 | 6 | 7 | 8 | 9 | 10 | 11 | 12

Skillbuilding

One of the first steps you should take to unlock your 11
creativity is to realize that you have control over your 22
mind; your mind does not control you. Creativity is just 34
using a new or different way to solve a problem. 44

Many of our inventions have involved breakthroughs in 55
traditional ways of thinking, and the result has often been 67
amazing. For example, Einstein broke with the old ways and 78
tried obscure formulas that have changed all scientific 90
thought. Your attitude can form a mental block that may 101
keep you from exercising creativity. When you free up your 113
mind, the rest will follow. 118

Do your best to unleash your mind's innate creativity 129
by turning problems into puzzles. When you think of the 140
task as a puzzle, a challenge, or a game instead of as a 152
difficult problem, you will open up your mind and free your 164
creative side to operate. Creative ideas come when you are 176
enjoying yourself and are involved in unrelated tasks. 187

Old habits often restrict you from trying new ways of 198
solving problems. There is often more than one solution, so 210
strive to see each situation in a fresh, new light. How 221
many times have you told yourself that you must follow the 233
rules and perform tasks only in a certain way? 242

If you want to be creative, then look at situations in 253
a new light, break the pattern, explore new opportunities, 265
and challenge old rules. If you are facing a hard problem 277
and cannot find an answer, take a quick walk or relax for a 289
few minutes; you can then go back to the problem renewed. 300

1 | 2 | 3 | 4 | 5 | 6 | 7 | 8 | 9 | 10 | 11 | 12

Skillbuilding

Supplementary Timed Writing 8

Keyboarding is a very popular business course that	10
most students take. The major goals of a keyboarding course	22
are to develop touch control of the keyboard, to use proper	34
typing techniques, to build basic speed and accuracy, and	46
to receive considerable practice in applying those basic	57
skills to format letters, reports, tables, memos, and other	69
kinds of personal and business documents.	78
In the first part of a keyboarding course, you must	88
learn to stroke the keys by touch, using proven techniques.	100
You learn to strike the keys in a quick and accurate way.	112
After the keys are learned, you then focus your attention	123
on producing documents of many sizes and types.	133
When you first learn to keyboard, there may be certain	144
steps, guidelines, and exercises that should be followed.	156
There are rules to help you learn and in due time to master	168
the keyboard. To create each document requires that you	179
apply critical thinking. What format or layout should be	190
used? What font and font size would be best? Are all the	202
words spelled correctly? Does the document look neat on the	214
page? Are the figures accurate? Are the punctuation and	225
grammar correct?	228
Being creative also has a lot to do with risk taking	239
and courage. It takes courage to explore new ways to think	251
and to risk looking different and even to risk being wrong.	263
Your path to creativity is such a vital component of your	274
critical thinking skills. Allow your creative thoughts to	286
flow freely when you produce each keyboarding task. Enjoy	298
the journey.	300

1 | 2 | 3 | 4 | 5 | 6 | 7 | 8 | 9 | 10 | 11 | 12

Skillbuilding

More employees are injured using the computer keyboard 11
in the United States than using any other equipment in the 23
workplace. Therefore, you should find the most comfortable 35
and ergonomic position when you are keyboarding. 45

Your chair should be on rollers, be adjustable to fit 56
your individual height, and have substantial support for 67
your lower back. You should sit with your hips pushed as 78
far back in the chair as possible, and your thighs should 90
not touch the underside of the workstation. 99

Your monitor should be aligned with your keyboard and 110
centered opposite you. The display should be just slightly 122
below eye level and tilted away from you slightly. When you 134
sit back in the chair and hold your arm out horizontally, 145
your middle finger should touch the middle of the monitor. 157
That way you won't need to make excessive head movements to 169
see the viewing area of your screen. 176

A document holder should be positioned at the same 187
height and distance as the screen in order to minimize any 199
head movements and at the same angle as the screen. Place 210
the document holder to the side of the screen opposite the 222
mouse. Position the mouse at the identical height as the 233
keyboard, and you should move the mouse with your whole arm 245
and not just with your wrist. 251

There's no research to show that an ergonomic keyboard 263
is any more beneficial than the standard keyboard layout. 274
If your keyboard has pop-up legs, these should not be used 286
because a negative slope to the keyboard is by far the most 298
healthful. 300

1 | 2 | 3 | 4 | 5 | 6 | 7 | 8 | 9 | 10 | 11 | 12

Skillbuilding

One of the most important decisions we all have to 10
face is choosing a career. Your options can appear to be a 22
bit overwhelming at first. But you should not worry because 34
your critical thinking skills will help. 42

Start with a self-assessment. What are your interests? 54
Would you prefer to work inside or outdoors? Would you like 66
to work with numbers or with words? Are you an independent 77
type or would you rather work within a group? What are your 89
preferred courses? Think about each of these questions, and 101
then make a list of your interests, skills, aptitudes, and 113
values. What you learn about yourself might help you find 125
the career that is just right for you. 133

After you have explored your own interests, look at 143
the sixteen career clusters for a wide range of possible 155
jobs. Most jobs are included in one of these clusters that 166
have been organized by the government. During your search, 178
make a note of the clusters that interest you and look into 190
all the clusters. 194

Get as much information as you can by making use of 204
all available resources. Scan the employment section in the 216
major Sunday newspapers for job descriptions and salaries. 228
Search the Internet, which provides access to job listings 240
around the world. If you want to evaluate closely a certain 252
company, access its home page and look around. 261

Sign up for interviews with companies that visit your 272
campus. Talk with people in your field of interest to ask 284
questions and get advice. Taking the initiative in your job 296
search will pay off. 300

1 | 2 | 3 | 4 | 5 | 6 | 7 | 8 | 9 | 10 | 11 | 12

Index